DEAD RECKONING

A Josiah and Archibald story

by

Philip Whiteland

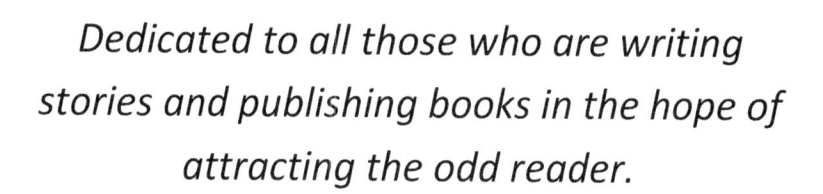

Dedicated to all those who are writing stories and publishing books in the hope of attracting the odd reader.

Dedicated also to the odd reader - you know who you are!

Dead Reckoning

Published by Philip Whiteland

Copyright © 2025 Philip and Hilary Whiteland

All Rights Reserved

This Print Edition published 2025

Also available in Kindle

All characters in this publication are fictitious and any resemblance to real persons, living or dead, is purely coincidental

Other fictional titles available from this author

A Dubious Undertaking and other stories*

Grave Expectations*

A Subsequent Engagement*

Bring Out Your Dead*

Waggy Dog Tales

Waggy Dog Tales 2

The Chronicles of a Young Lady (and her Maid)

* Josiah and Archibald stories

All of the above are available in both Print and Kindle editions.

Cover Design: Philip Whiteland *with the aid of MS Image Generator*

A Note from Archibald

Dear Mam.

I've been meaning to tell you about how it went in Spain with Mr. O. but, what with you dashing 'round doing stuff and me going to work, there just hasn't been time.

I don't really know where to start! It's a bit like them essays you had to do at school about 'What I Did On My Holidays'. I never knew what to put in them, either. I mean, nothing exciting ever happened, 'cept that time when we buried Nan on Rhyl beach and forgot about her and it was just as well that the local pub sent out a search party, when she didn't turn up at opening time, else we would never have found her.

You can't say nothing exciting happened with my trip to Spain, that's for certain.

I've got to say, from the off, it was good of Mr. O. to take me at all, 'cause he was supposed to be taking his fiancée, Samantha...you know, Ms. Knight...but I think he took pity on me 'cause of how I'd been dumped by *my* fiancée (yes, I know you didn't think she was good enough for me!)

Any road up, it should have been dead straight forward. We'd just got to go to Spain and pick up this dead toff's body so's we could bring it

Dead Reckoning

back here for burial. Nothing to it! Only, it all went wrong from the start 'cause our 'plane got diverted to Paris and we got kicked off on account of they thought we were terrorists! Bloody cheek! Then no other 'plane would touch us, so we had to go by coach to Alicante and that's no ruddy joke, I can tell you!

Turns out, the body wasn't in Alicante, after all, like what it should have been, and we had to go to this one-horse town called Santiago summatorother to get him. We bumped into this girl there, and she was a real looker, Mam. She offered to come with us, and the coffin, to help us and Mr. O. was all for it (I reckon he had a soft spot for her). Just as well she did, 'cause we had to go back by road again, which was a pain, and get the ferry.

Did I mention that we'd had some coppers following us? They'd been on the 'plane and then they turned up in that Santiago howsyourfather, an' all, which was a bit peculiar if you ask me.

Well, we got him back to Blighty, but instead of being an overnight thing it took us best part of a week! It didn't help that the ferry got caught in a storm and we couldn't dock until the next morning. So, we had a right rush to get the coffin back up here 'cause, in the meantime, his widow (who'd taken the right hump 'cause he'd snuffed it whilst he was...you know...*doing it* with someone what was massaging him) had scrapped the burial in the moreso...mauso...that stone box thingy and had put him down for a cheap and cheerful cremation.

Any road, when it came to the service, Mr. O.'s fiancée was doing it, on account of how she's a thingy, you know, one of them pretend vicars...celebrants, that's the one. The coffin's just about to go down the conveyor belt, type of thing, when the lid bursts open and the bloke

Philip Whiteland

what was supposed to be a toff is there with a gun on everybody. As luck would have it, the lid came back down and belted him on the nut and then them coppers what I told you about sprang into action and that was that.

Did I say I didn't think he looked much like a toff when we picked him up? Well, he didn't. He looked more like someone what had gone twelve rounds with that Furey bloke. Anyhow, he's only an escaped gangster, isn't he AND what really put the cat amongst the pigeons, his name's Frankie Knight and he's married to Mr. O.'s fiancée!

Well, you can imagine how things are back at work. Mr. O.'s got a face like fourpence, as you might say, and, 'cause of all the publicity about us having a gunfight at a posh funeral, business has gone right down the drain.

So, that's how it is, at the moment. I just keep hoping things'll get back to normal, or as normal as it ever gets at Oakshott & Underwood. We'll see, eh?

Your loving son,

Archibald.

Chapter One
Don't Leave Me This Way!

Josiah Oakshott was rummaging around in the stock room.

If he was going to be totally honest with himself, there was really no practical point to this exercise, other than providing a useful excuse for not returning to his office and facing the very clear indications that Oakshott and Underwood were, not to put too fine a point on it, in trouble. Apart from assessing these portents, he had done precious little, for the past few days, so rummaging seemed like a relatively harmless diversion.

A tuneless humming, apparently coming from the other end of the stock room, interrupted his increasingly dark train of thought. Unaware that there was anyone else in the vicinity, he went to investigate and was startled to discover Archibald Thurble, doing some rummaging of his own.

"Archibald!" He exclaimed, causing the object of his exclamation to visibly jump in the air, "what *are* you up to?"

"Not sure, to be honest, Mr. O." Archibald said, scratching his head, "I think it might be the chorus of something by Rick Astley, but I wouldn't swear to it!"

"No, Archibald, I meant, what are you *doing*!"

"Oh, right! Sorry, Mr. O., I was just looking for some handles" Archibald explained, flapping his arms to indicate his lack of success.

Dead Reckoning

"Give me strength! I didn't mean, what are you doing in the *stock room*" Josiah sighed wearily, "I meant, what are you doing *here,* at all! According to my wall-chart, you should still be on annual leave"

"Oh, right, yeah, sorry about that" Archibald looked a little bashful, "I thought, if it was all the same to you, I'd come back early"

"Well, it's fine with me, of course, Archibald, but you are entitled to take your full entitlement of leave, you know"

"Yeah, I know" Archibald nodded, "it was just that I got fed up and thought I might as well be here as anywhere"

"Not a ringing endorsement of your work ethic but, I suppose one can hardly complain" Josiah smiled a little, "I take it that Bilston did not hold your attention?"

"Well, it was alright" Archibald shrugged, "it was just like anywhere else, really, I suppose"

"I'll tell you what" Josiah said, "why don't you prepare the tea and biscuits, put an extra cup for yourself, and we'll discuss this back in my office? What do you say?"

"Oh yeah!" Archibald grinned, "just like old times, eh?"

"Indeed, Archibald"

A little while later, Josiah and Archibald sat at either side of Josiah's antique desk, in the somewhat dismal office. Archibald noted that the comfy sofa and coffee table, which Samantha Knight had introduced, as a modern touch to the furnishings, had now disappeared.

Josiah munched a biscuit, thoughtfully,

"I had rather wondered what you might find to do with yourself in Bilston, Archibald?"

"Not much to be honest" Archibald slurped his tea, "I found a little B&B what was quite nice. The landlady was lovely, she insisted on cooking me dinner an' all, which was good of her. It's just…there's not much to do in the day and there's a damn sight less at night"

"Ah!" Josiah nodded, "I did wonder if you might attempt to make contact with either of the Ryder sisters, with whom you were once linked?"

"Not really," Archibald responded, gloomily, "I went and had a look at where their chip shop was – that looked ok and it was right busy. Then I went and had a look at where Electra and Tiff&EE's place is going to be, but that was still being converted so there wasn't much to see there, to be fair"

"Did you not meet either of the young ladies?"

"No, I didn't" Archibald shook his head, vigorously, "I could see Flo serving at the chppy, but I didn't go in and there was no sign of Electra"

"I feared that you might have aspirations to rekindle your romance" Josiah looked at his employee with some concern.

"Nah, what's done is done, innit?" Archibald, shrugged, tugged a sleeve and looked thoughtful, "I didn't really go there for that. It was just…I couldn't think of anywhere else, to be honest and, seeing as how it was where everyone else seemed to be going, I thought…"

"Yes, I take your point" Josiah drew another biscuit from the collection on the plate before him and nibbled, appreciatively.

"How about you and Ms. Knight?" Archibald felt emboldened to ask, as Josiah had brought up the subject of his ex-fiancée.

"I think we can safely say that the curtain has been decidedly rung down on that particular episode, Archibald" Josiah said, firmly.

Dead Reckoning

"Oh!" Archibald replied, looked down and scuffed his shoes a couple of times.

There was a pregnant pause for a few seconds, only interrupted by the ticking of the long-case clock in the corner. Finally, Archibald broke the awkward silence:

"You've managed without me, then?" He ventured, with a grin.

"In all honesty, Archibald, we could probably manage without at least half of the workforce, as things stand at present" Josiah looked exceedingly glum.

"Problems, Mr. O.?"

"Problems, indeed, Archibald" Josiah sighed, "I'm afraid that, being a party to, what could easily have been, and in fact was described in the local press as, a 'shoot-out' at the Crematorium, does not act as a positive advertisement for our business" Josiah stirred his tea, moodily, "a number of commissions for funeral services, commissions that I would have anticipated would come to us, have instead been placed with our competitors. In short, we are losing business at an alarming rate"

"But...but...they can't blame you for all that malarkey, surely?" Archibald spluttered.

"They can, and they do, Archibald" Josiah nodded, "I fear that, if this goes on, I may have to take some radical steps in order to keep the business afloat"

"What...you don't mean like...*redundancies*?" Archibald whispered the last word.

"Well, I wouldn't like this to be common knowledge, and I trust I can count on your discretion?" Josiah raised an eyebrow.

"Oh, yeah, 'course" Archibald nodded, furiously.

"Well, yes, it may come to that" Josiah looked very grim indeed, "if business does not pick up, I may be forced to, as the current parlance has it, 'let some people go'"

"Makes it sound like you've got them locked up in chains!" Archibald observed.

"Yes, it's not a phrase I'm particularly taken with" Josiah shook his head, "much like death, the termination of someone's employment seems to attract all sorts of unhelpful euphemisms"

"Oh, I've had it with them, an all" Archibald nodded.

"Had it with what?" Josiah looked puzzled.

"Unhelpful youths!" Archibald crossed his arms and frowned, "do you know, there's this bloke down the D.I.Y. shop and he's got 'Can I Help?' written all over his T-Shirt in big, bright letters, and he couldn't be more bloody-minded if he tried!"

"Ah yes" Josiah smiled, "I rather think the addition of such epithets to the badges and garments of customer-facing staff, rather demonstrates the triumph of hope over experience on the part of the organisations concerned. However, I rather fear we may, not unusually, be at cross-purposes again, Archibald. I was referring to euphemisms, by which I mean words or phrases used in an effort to avoid saying the actual word that properly describes the situation. For example, we might say 'passed on' or 'resting', when we actually mean 'dead'..."

"Or 'fallen asleep'?" Archibald contributed, "that used to frighten the wits out of me when I was a kid, I used to try and stay awake all night in case somebody decided to bury me!"

Dead Reckoning

"Probably a wise move on your part, knowing your household!" Josiah sniggered, "But, it does go to demonstrate why such terms can be unhelpful. As I was saying, the act of terminating someone's employment seems to attract similar terms of avoidance, hence the phrase 'letting people go'"

"Yeah, I see what you mean." Archibald looked thoughtful, "Still, if it comes to that, I suppose it would be that 'last in, first out' thingy, wouldn't it?" He suggested, hopefully.

"Well, that is one system which some organisations have adopted, but it has some problematic elements"

"How do you mean?" Archibald frowned; he had been hoping that his relatively long service might make him immune.

"There are various problems. Firstly, it rather indirectly discriminates on the basis of age, as one would expect that the 'redundancy pool', which I believe is the correct term, would largely consist of those who were younger, whereas those whose jobs were preserved would, in all probability, be older"

"Well, yeah, I suppose, but if they're young they've got more chance of getting another job, ain't they?" Archibald realised he was digging a hole for himself with this line of argument.

"That might be the case, but discrimination on the basis of age is unlawful, even if that was not the primary purpose of the exercise" Josiah took another sip of tea, "Secondly, and more importantly, it rather perversely means that the organisation concerned sheds those it has most recently recruited, who presumably meet the organisation's *current* requirements, and retains those who joined the organisation many years ago, when those requirements may have been markedly different"

"You what?" Archibald looked puzzled.

"Well, for example, I.T. skills might be a prerequisite for anyone we employed today, wouldn't you agree?"

"Yeah, I guess!" Archibald looked a little shifty. His own I.T. skills were somewhat lacking.

"Whereas, employees like, for example, Mr. Strine*..." Josiah looked at Archibald, pointedly.

"Wouldn't know a P.C. if it bit him on the ar...backside?" Archibald supplied.

"Perhaps not *quite* how I would have put it, but you take my point?"

"You'd have to get rid of all them what know what they're doing and keep them what are only still here 'cause they've kept their heads down and their noses clean all these years?" Archibald suggested, "Like that Horace Dimchurch!"

"Indeed, Mr. Dimchurch was an excellent example of someone whose talents were no longer entirely compatible with the current requirements of the business"

"I shouldn't have thought they ever were!" Archibald chuckled.

"Well, be that as it may, you see the problems inherent with the LIFO system?"

"LIFO?"

"Last In, First Out" Josiah explained, patiently.

"Oh, right" Archibald nodded, "so, how else would you sort it out, then?"

Dead Reckoning

"There are various options. Possibly the most equitable would be a set of criteria based on performance, disciplinary matters, absence and so forth" Josiah waved his hands, airily.

"Ah, right" Archibald suddenly stood up, brushed off some biscuit crumbs and made for the door, "anyway, must be getting on, things to do and all that"

"Indeed, Archibald" Josiah smirked, "there is much to do and I value your dedication to your duties"

"Yeah, well, as long as you remember that" Archibald winked dramatically, tapped the side of his nose, and hastened out of the door.

"I will, indeed, Archibald" Josiah said to himself, returning to the documents littering his desk, "I will, indeed"

* Mr. Strine had become the longest-serving employee of Oakshott and Underwood, following the sudden retirement of Horace Dimchurch (see [‘The Trouble With Horace Dimchurch’](#))

Chapter Two
Doctor, Doctor

Archibald Thurble folded his arms and viewed the scene around him with ill-concealed displeasure.

"I don't reckon half of them in here have got owt wrong with them" He announced, to the world in general.

Josiah Oakshott sighed and closed, with some difficulty, the book he was attempting to read.

"I think that may be something of a sweeping generalisation, Archibald"

"Well, look at 'em!" Archibald waved a hand, disparagingly, "you can't see any reason for them being here, can you?"

"I rather doubt that people are choosing to spend their free time in the Merkin-under-Heathwood Accident and Emergency department, out of a misplaced desire for entertainment, don't you?"

"Doesn't explain why they're here, cluttering the place up" Archibald said, grumpily.

"I would remind you, Archibald, that you volunteered to drive me here. I could easily have made other arrangements"

"Well, yeah, but we've been here hours!"

"We have not 'been here hours', as you put it. We have, in fact, been here for just over an hour to date" Josiah pointed out, "which is, I strongly suspect, a fraction of the time that some other members of our cohort have been waiting"

"And that's another thing," Archibald continued, warming to his theme, "that woman over there came in way after us, and she's been seen already!"

"That is because they operate a triage system in this department" Josiah explained, patiently, "whereby patients are seen in accordance with the perceived severity or urgency of their condition"

"Then how come she's been seen and we ain't?"

"I have no idea, Archibald" Josiah shook his head, "I can only imagine that, whatever ails that poor lady, it is somewhat more serious than the possible fractured wrist for which I am awaiting investigation"

"I reckon it's a twist" Archibald frowned, "you're not telling me that it's not down to who you know. They treated her like an old friend, down at Reception"

"Perhaps she is unfortunate enough to suffer from some form of chronic illness which necessitates frequent visits here"

"Yeah, right!" Archibald responded, contemptuously.

"You do not have to wait with me, if you do not wish to, Archibald" Josiah said, testily, "I am perfectly capable of obtaining transportation home, if need be"

"Nah, you're alright" Archibald shrugged, "I'm here now, enni?"

Josiah sighed, wearily, "Aren't I?" He corrected.

"Aren't you what?" Archibald looked more puzzled than usual.

"Aren't you here!"

"Yeah, 'course I am, that's what I was saying, innit?" Archibald shook his head.

"Indeed, you are, as I'm all too well aware" Josiah opened his book again, with a wince, having erroneously used his injured hand., and then made the mistake of closing it with a snap, "And must you end your sentences with that annoying interrogative?"

"You what?"

"That 'innit' phrase that you seem to have adopted"

"Oh, that" Archibald nodded, "it's what all the kids are saying, innit?"

"With respect, you are hardly a 'kid' anymore, Archibald and it only succeeds in making you sound uncouth and ignorant"

"But, it's cool!" Archibald protested.

"Not in my view, it isn't" Josiah frowned, "I would be obliged if you would restrict your usage to when you are conversing with friends and acquaintances. It most certainly should not form part of any professional conversation. Ow!" He concluded, as he tried again to open the book.

"I can't figure out how you did that, in the first place?" Archibald observed, happy to change the subject away from his shortcomings.

"I hardly injured myself as a deliberate act of self-harm!" Josiah snapped, "I have no idea how it happened either, presumably I applied myself to the polishing of our vehicles with undue enthusiasm!"

"I don't know why you do it, at all" Archibald shook his head, despairingly, "it's not as if there aren't enough of us to look after all that sort of thing"

Dead Reckoning

"I happen to enjoy it" Josiah said, curtly, "it makes a pleasant change from staring at our accounts for hours on end"

"Things still not good then?"

"If anything, they are worse" Josiah said, sadly, "I assume you did heed my warning and avoided any mention to your colleagues concerning our current difficulties?"

"Never said a word" Archibald made a zipping motion across his mouth.

"Only, it seems to me that, whenever I venture into the workshop, a sudden, furious, industry springs up all around me" Josiah raised an eyebrow.

"You what?"

"Everyone suddenly becomes very busy, indeed" Josiah translated.

"Well, we've all got things to do, we're busy people" Archibald said, piously.

"Hmm, if you say so" Josiah turned a page in his book.

"How come there's so many people here, anyway? They can't all be accidents and emergencies, can they?" Archibald took the opportunity to change the subject, again.

"I believe it is a consequence of the difficulty some people experience in accessing primary health care"

"What's that then, when it's at home?" Archibald queried.

"I'm given to understand that it is not always easy to obtain a doctor's appointment" Josiah expanded.

"Oh, yeah, you're right there. Me Nan's always going on about it" Archibald nodded, "She gets her knickers in a right twist about this 'fastest finger first' thing"

"I beg your pardon?" It was Josiah's turn to look perplexed.

"Like off that Millionaire programme? You know, if you want to see the doctor, you have to ring up at eight-o-clock in the morning, on the dot…"

"Is that the case? Many years have elapsed since I last sought an appointment"

"Well, yeah, and you have to keep bashing the redial button if you get the 'engaged' tone, 'cause everyone's doing the same thing, ain't they?"

"I will be advised by you" Josiah shrugged.

"Oh yeah, and then, when you *do* get through, it's tough luck 'cause all of the appointments have gone to them what dialled a bit faster than what you did! So, you might be on your last legs but the bloke before you, what's got a bit of a cold, he's had the last appointment so you're up sh…the creek without a paddle"

"I had no idea that seeing a G.P. was so onerous!" Josiah shook his head in disbelief, "However, that reinforces my point about the problems in accessing primary health care and, therefore, the increased demands on the A&E departments across the country"

"How's that then?" Archibald frowned.

"Well, I have no idea whether the barriers to access to our G.P. service, which you have so eloquently described, are a deliberate attempt to ration a finite resource," Josiah closed his book, again, as he expanded on his theme, "but, if that is the case, then it has clearly failed spectacularly because the demand just shifts elsewhere within the NHS, as evidenced by the waiting times experienced here, today"

"You mean, if they can't get to see the doctor, they rock up here?"

"Indeed, or possibly, given your illustration of the difficulties inherent in obtaining an appointment, do not even make the effort to do so, but just resign themselves to the inevitable wait at A&E"

"Yeah, that would explain a lot!" Archibald looked around at the packed waiting room, "me Nan reckons it all went to the dogs during that Covid malarkey, when you couldn't see your G.P. for love nor money"

"I think that period did engender something of a shift in attitudes, both within the Health Service itself, and with its patients" Josiah agreed.

"Not half!" Archibald nodded, enthusiastically, "me Nan reckons the only thing her doctor did, during Covid, was oil the drawbridge and feed the dragon!"

"Very droll!" Josiah smirked. An urgent tingling sound indicated something coming through on his mobile phone. At the same time,

"Joshua Oakshop?" A nurse announced from the other end of the room.

"Ey up, I think you're on!" Archibald nudged his employer.

"You would think it would not be beyond the wit of man to at least get one's name right!" Josiah said, crossly.

"What was that on your phone?"

"I have not had time to look," He stood up, waved to the nurse to indicate he was coming, and briefly opened his phone, "well, I never!" He grinned, "we have an enquiry about our services, corn in Egypt indeed!" He marched off for his consultation.

"Bloody hell, I hope not" Archibald said to himself, looking seriously worried, "we had enough trouble with Spain!"

Chapter Three
I Shot the Sheriff

"You'll never guess who's waiting over there, sir" D.S. Stone remarked, with a smirk, whilst leafing through his magazine.

D.I. Wood gave him a baleful look and put his own newspaper down with such a crash that it woke the napping old lady, hunched up next to him.

"Well, let's see...how about Mahatma Gandhi and Mother Teresa after a freak trampolining accident? Am I close?"

"Er, no sir, not really" D.S. Stone shook his head.

"You do surprise me, Sergeant" D.I. Wood shook his paper out again, attracting an evil glare from his geriatric next-door neighbour.

"Shall I tell you then?"

"Well, there's a thought!" D.I. Wood said, from the refuge of his newspaper.

"It's only those two from the funeral parlour" D.S. Stone looked exceedingly smug.

D.I. Wood crashed his newspaper to his lap, causing the little old lady to utter an expletive, grab her Zimmer frame and head off to a quieter corner.

"You're having a laugh!" He looked at his Sergeant quizzically.

"No, straight up, sir. They're over there, by the window"

"Well, I can't see 'em" D.I. Wood tried to peer through the throng.

"Well, they're definitely there" D.S. Stone pointed, "look, the vulture-like one's got his arm in a sling"

"Oh yeah, I see what you mean" D.I. Wood nodded, "I wonder what's brought them here?"

"I suppose the sling is a bit of a giveaway, wouldn't you think, sir?" D.S. Stone returned to his magazine; eyebrows raised.

"Alright, alright, no need to get sarky, Sergeant" D.I. Wood glared at his companion, "I mean it's funny they should be here now, that's what I'm saying, just when we're here an' all"

"It's a small town, sir" D.S. Stone observed.

"I know that!" D.I. Wood snarled, "I was still hoping I'd seen the back of them two. I don't trust them an inch, for a kick-off"

"They were cleared of any involvement in that Frankie Knight business, sir" D.S. Stone pointed out.

"Yeah, well, you know what I thought out about that!" D.I. Wood snorted, "you're not telling me that you can haul a wanted criminal half way across Europe, in a bloody coffin for gawd's sake, and not know what you're doing!"

"I think they were just a bit..." D.S. Stone ventured.

"Thick?" D.I. Wood suggested.

"I was going to say, gullible, sir"

"Well, whatever, I still think it stinks" D.I. Wood shook his paper out again.

Dead Reckoning

"It was, erm, surprising that they put you forward for that Bravery Award, didn't you think, sir?" D.S. Stone knew he was chancing his arm but it had been niggling him for days.

"Well, not really, Sergeant" D.I. Wood squared his shoulders and tried to look heroic, "I *was* in charge of the operation and I *did* stop that conveyor"

"Yes, sir, but I was the one who threw himself at the man with the gun"

"Oh, yeah, fair enough" D.I. Wood nodded, "but he had been brained by the coffin lid coming down, so you weren't in any danger, really, were you? Any road, they've put you up for your Inspector's exam, so it's an ill wind, isn't it?"

"Only if I pass it!" D.S. Stone muttered from the safety of his magazine, and added, *sotto voce*, "then again, how hard can it be?"

"I hope we're not going to be here much longer, my foot's giving me some gyp and no mistake!" D.I. Wood took the opportunity to change the subject.

"Wonder how that happened, sir?"

"I think it might have been from that bit of action we saw" D.I. Wood rubbed his leg and winced a little, for maximum effect.

"Could be a case for compensation then, sir?" D.S. Stone asked, pointedly.

"It's a thought, Sergeant, it's a thought!" D.I. Wood attempted to look pained but stoic, at least, that was what he was aiming for. D.S. Stone thought he looked constipated.

* * * *

Josiah Oakshott, now sporting a much more professional sling than the one he had worn on the way in, weaved his way through the waiting throng, back toward his colleague, Archibald Thurble.

"I think we can be on our way now, Archibald" Josiah announced to his employee, who was currently absorbed in something on his mobile phone. Archibald visibly jumped and guiltily buried his phone in his pocket.

"Oh, there you are Mr. O." Archibald looked flustered, "what's the verdict?"

"Thankfully, the x-ray examination has confirmed the Nurse Practitioner's preliminary diagnosis that my injury is a sprain, rather than a fracture." Josiah rubbed his wrist a little, "A severe sprain, she said, mind you" He added, for effect.

"Aw, I was hoping you'd get a pot so we could all sign it and stuff"

"Which just goes to show that there is a god!" Josiah sighed, "I'm afraid that it does mean I am still unable to drive in my own right, therefore I shall have to prevail upon your good offices"

"I don't have an office" Archibald looked puzzled, "I've just got this stool in the workshop, that and a bit of shelf, so it's not very good"

"I was not referring to an office as a place of work, Archibald. I believe the definition of 'good offices' is *'services done for another'*, which, in this case, relates to you driving on my behalf"

"Oh, right-ho! Yeah, no problem" Archibald grinned.

"Which will be particularly helpful as we need to travel to the wilds of Cheshire"

"Does Cheshire have 'wilds'?" Archibald queried, "Lions and tigers and bears and stuff?"

Dead Reckoning

"I was just utilising a picturesque turn of speech" Josiah explained, "I have need of transportation to a village in Cheshire, so that I may respond to the query concerning our services which, you may recall, arrived before my appointment with the Nurse Practitioner"

"It's a bit out of our neck of the woods, innit?" Archibald observed.

Josiah frowned at the use of 'innit' but couldn't really find fault, on this occasion.

"I admit that Cheshire hardly constitutes our normal area of operation, Archibald, however, needs must when the devil drives!"

"I thought you said I was driving!"

* * * *

"I didn't think we would be sitting 'round here this long, Stoney!" D.I. Wood fumed, "Oh sod this for a game of soldiers, I'm going out for a smoke"

"But, what if they call you, sir?"

"We could be here for hours yet…days from the look of some of the poor buggers in here." D.I. Wood patted his pockets, "I need a fag, tell them you'll give me a shout"

"I'm really not sure, sir" D.S. Stone looked concerned.

"Don't be so wet, Sergeant!" D.I. Wood snapped, "they can't keep you banged up in this germ-ridden shit-hole, forever. Bloody hell, even hens have got a right to fresh air and a bit of walk around, I reckon I've at least got the right to go for a smoke!"

D.I. Wood raised himself, uncertainly and began to lurch off to the exit, when:

"Clarence Wood?" The Nurse Practitioner announced.

"Clarence?" D.S. Stone spluttered.

"Not a bloody word, Stoney, you hear me? Not a bloody word!"

* * * *

Meanwhile, somewhere in the 'wilds' of Cheshire:

"Did you send the message, mama?"

"I did, my dear"

"Has he responded?"

"Not yet, sweetheart, but he will, he will"

"Do you think he will come to us?"

"Of that, I am certain, my precious. Absolutely certain!"

Chapter Four
Footloose

"So, what did they say it was?" Detectives Stone and Wood were finally driving away from the hospital, where they had spent some considerable time in the A&E Department.

"Hmmm?" D.I. Wood was studying the leaflet that accompanied the medication he had been prescribed.

"I said, what did they say it was?" D.S. Stone persisted.

"Oh, just some blood thing. These tablets should clear it up"

"Blood thing?" D.S. Stone looked quizzically at his superior.

"Yes, that's what they reckon" D.I. Wood nodded, "they gave it some fancy name"

"Did they?" D.S. Stone gave his boss a sideways look, "wouldn't have been 'hyperuricemia' would it?"

"Yeah, that sounds about right"

"Gout!" D.S. Stone announced, with a snigger.

"What do you mean, 'gout'?"

"What I say! Hyperuricemia is an abnormally high level of uric acid in the blood, often causing a build-up of uric crystals around certain joints, such as the big toe joint, which is known as... Gout" D.S. Stone said, smugly.

"How the hell do you know all that?" D.I. Wood glared at his subordinate.

"I was looking it up while you were in with the nurse. I thought it sounded a bit like gout"

"Yeah, well..." D.I. Wood stared fixedly at the leaflet from his medication, "just don't go spreading it 'round the station, eh, or I'll never hear the last of it! Let's stick with hyper-whatsit"

"Hyperuricemia" D.S. Stone said, smugly.

"Yeah, that" D.I. Wood nodded.

"Not caused by the business in the Crem., then?"

"Well..." D.I. Wood hesitated.

"So, no chance of compo, then?"

"I wouldn't rule anything out, just yet" D.I. Wood shook his head.

"Did she tell you to knock off the booze and the fags?" D.S. Stone was enjoying himself, hugely.

"She said something about cutting down on the beer, yeah" D.I. Wood looked distinctly uncomfortable.

"And the fags?" D.S. Stone asked, hopefully.

"Well, not specifically, not for this hyper-thingy" D.I. Wood squirmed.

Dead Reckoning

"But she told you to knock them off?"

"She gave me a leaflet about giving up, yeah" D.I. Wood looked thoroughly miserable.

"Good!" D.S. Stone grinned.

"What do you mean, 'good'?" D.I. Wood snarled, "it's alright for you, isn't it, Sergeant Goody-two-shoes! What I want to know is, how come whenever you go to the quack, the answer is always to give up anything and everything you've ever enjoyed, eh?" D.I. Wood folded his arms and glared at the passing traffic, as if urging it to make something of it.

"I think moderation is the key, sir" D.S. Stone ventured.

"'*Moderation is the key*'" D.I. Wood mimicked, in a high, sing-song tone, "Moderation, bollocks! My old man was in the pub lunchtime and night, every day of the week, *and* he smoked Capstan Full Strength. Never did him any harm, I'll tell you"

"How old was he, when he died, sir?" D.S. Stone asked, innocently.

"Well...fifty eight." D.I. Wood conceded, "But he was run over by a bus!"

"On the way to, or from, the pub?" D.S. Stone raised an interrogatory eyebrow.

"Just drive, Sergeant, just drive" D.I. Wood folded his arms even tighter, and fumed.

* * * *

"Sounds alright for Cheshire" Archibald announced, turning off the traffic news on the radio.

"Good!" Josiah nodded, "it would be handy for something to go to plan, for a change" He studied the road atlas on his knee.

"Where are we heading for?"

"It's a village. I'm trying to find it on the map" Josiah peered at the book.

"The sat-nav'll get us there" Archibald pointed out.

"Well, yes, I know" Josiah responded, testily, "but there is no harm in understanding where we are going, in the context of the surrounding countryside"

"I don't see why you bother" Archibald shrugged.

"Well, that is the key difference, isn't it?" Josiah snapped, "I like to expand my knowledge, whereas you are happy to take whatever short-cut presents itself"

"That's summat else that sat-navs are good for"

"What?"

"Short-cuts!" Archibald grinned, "'course, you *can* wind up in some bloke's field, if you're not careful"

"My point exactly!" Josiah said, triumphantly, "slavishly following the directions you're given without any understanding of the context can lead you to exactly that sort of impasse"

Dead Reckoning

"Isn't that a sort of deer?" Archibald looked puzzled.

"No, that would be an impala" Josiah replied, shirtily, "I sometimes wonder if you do it on purpose?"

"Do what?"

"Never mind!" Josiah sighed and returned to his map book.

There was a strained silence, broken only by the hum of the engine and the occasional sweep of the windscreen wipers. Eventually,

"How much do you reckon you could get in a shed?"

Josiah turned to look at his employee, quizzically.

"I beg your pardon?"

"You know" Archibald insisted, "how much do you reckon you could get in a shed?"

"I fail to understand the question, Archibald!" Josiah shook his head, "there are just too many imponderables"

"Eh?" Archibald looked puzzled

"By which I mean, there are too many unknowns" Josiah sighed, "for example, the size of the shed and the nature of that which you would want to put into it"

Archibald gave his employer a long look.

"Before you say 'Eh' again, I should, perhaps, illustrate that last comment" Josiah said, having long experience of these conversations, "for example, are we referring to a shed the size of a sentry box or the Albert Hall? Are we filling it with mice or elephants? Do you take my point?"

"You mean, you could only get one elephant in a sentry box, style of thing?"

"I suspect that might be somewhat optimistic, but you get my drift?"

"Hur, it's like that 'how do you get two whales in a mini' thing, innit?" Archibald chuckled.

"I beg your pardon?"

"You go up the M50!" Archibald snorted and laughed, heartily.

Josiah looked at him, blankly.

"'Cause it sounds like 'how do you get to Wales in a mini', you see?" Archibald attempted to explain.

"Ah, I see, it's in the nature of a joke" Josiah nodded, solemnly.

"Yeah, summat like that" Archibald gave up the unequal struggle, "any road, that's why I don't get it!"

"Get what?"

"On them Traffic Reports, when they go on about a 'shed load'. How are you supposed to know how much that is?"

"Ah, light is beginning to dawn!" Josiah sighed, "it is not a unit of quantity, Archibald, it refers, instead, to a load that has been 'shed', or misplaced, from its conveyance"

Dead Reckoning

"Does it?"

"You may depend on it, Archibald"

"Oh, right" Archibald looked thoughtful, "so, it's not…"

"Whatever you are going to say, Archibald, it is not! My explanation is the correct one"

They drove on, in silence, for a while.

"Where is it we're going, again?"

"It's Evanley, in Cheshire" Josiah traced the route on the map.

"Well, it's not bad round our way, neither!" Archibald said, stoutly.

"No" Josiah rubbed his forehead, he was sure he was getting one of his migraines, a sure sign of having spent too long in Archibald's company, "I did not say it was 'heavenly' in Cheshire. I was referring to the village of Evanley. We are, as a matter of fact, to go to the Hall" Josiah said, with some pride.

"What, the Village Hall?"

"No, Archibald, I'm referring to the local Manor House, Evanley Hall. That is where we have been summoned. I believe it is a mile or two outside of the village, proper"

"Proper?"

"By which I mean, outside of the village *itself!*" Josiah snapped.

"Right!" Archibald nodded, "puts me in mind of that hymn"

"What hymn?"

"You know, that one about a *'green hill far away, without a city wall'*. Only, I used to think it meant..."

"That it didn't have a city wall" Josiah butted in.

"Yeah, when it actually means..."

"That the hill is on the *outside* of the city wall" Josiah completed.

"Yeah" Archibald said, somewhat crestfallen that his one piece of relevant knowledge had been pre-empted.

"I do apologise, Archibald, that was crass of me. I should have allowed you to complete your story"

"Nah, it's alright Mr. O." Archibald smiled, "it's just...well, you know lots of stuff like that but I only know the odd thing. Very odd, sometimes." He reflected.

"It was a very relevant comment, Archibald, and demonstrates a broader vocabulary than I had imagined. Well done!"

"Oh, I have my moments, Mr. O.!" Archibald grinned.

"You do, indeed, Archibald!" Josiah returned to his map.

Chapter Five
Driving in My Car

"So, this is Evanley, is it?" Archibald observed, as they negotiated the narrow streets, turned into chicanes by the litter of parked cars.

"Apparently so" Josiah nodded, "quite a pleasant place, it would seem. Public House, village shop, all the usual necessities of life"

"There's one of them fancy coffee shops over there, an' all" Archibald nodded in the appropriate direction.

"Ah yes, that too seems to be rapidly becoming one of the 'necessities of life'" Josiah observed, ruefully.

"I don't mind one of them frothy coffees but it's all a bit..."

"Confusing?" Josiah suggested, "I must admit that, on the few occasions that I have experienced such an establishment, I have been somewhat daunted by the variety on offer"

"Yeah, it's alright if you know what you want, innit?" Archibald nodded, "I sometimes finish up with tea because at least, that way, you know what you're going to get, don't you?"

"I imagine the owners would be somewhat disappointed by that outcome" Josiah chuckled, "in my limited experience I have only succeeded by having recourse to the knowledge of others"

"Others?" Archibald raised an eyebrow.

"By which I mean, Sam...Mrs. Knight" Josiah blushed a little, "she was rather fond of such emporiums"

"Yeah, I can see it being right up her street" Archibald nodded. "Mind you, it's not half as much of a faff as them shops where you can get them baguette thingys"

"Baguette thingys?" Josiah looked perplexed.

"Yeah, you know, there's a chain of them. They're everywhere" Archibald insisted, "I only finished up in one 'cause I thought it was the way under a busy road!"

"Ah yes, I'm aware of their work" Josiah agreed, "but I have never participated in their offering"

"I don't blame you" Archibald shook his head, "it's like being interrogated! You can't just have summat simple, there's all these questions and you have to make loads of decisions and there's all these people waiting behind you and then they get right narked, 'cause you can't make your mind up. It wears me out!"

"That does sound somewhat daunting" Josiah agreed.

"Not half!" Archibald nodded, furiously, "that's why I finish up down the chippy more often than not. I mean, you can't go wrong with a bag of chips now, can you?"

"I doubt that it would be the cause of much in the way of interrogation" Josiah grinned.

"I don't see why everything has to be so ruddy difficult!" Archibald moaned.

Dead Reckoning

"In light of our recent experiences, Archibald, I'm inclined to agree" Josiah consulted his map, "I think we should be turning out of the village, shortly. The road to Evanley Hall should be on our left"

The female voice of the sat-nav chipped in with the same information.

"Looks like she agrees with you, Mr. O." Archibald chuckled.

"I am gratified that that is the case" Josiah looked pleased with himself.

"'Course, it might have been different if it had been the bloke." Archibald frowned, "I don't trust him!" He added, darkly.

"The 'bloke'?" Josiah looked questioningly at his employee, "What 'bloke'?"

"Him in the sat-nav! It was him what was on it when we first got this and I always finished up having a barney with him"

"You *argued* with the voice on the navigation system?"

"Yeah, well, he thought he knew everything!" Archibald snorted, "But, half the time, he didn't have a clue what he was on about!"

"But...but '*he*' is just a spoken version of the generic directions emanating from the navigation system. The gender of the voice is immaterial!" Josiah protested.

"Ah, well, you sat that" Archibald shook his head, "but I know I've never gone wrong since she's took over, yet I was always yelling at him"

"I wonder, is the sky as blue in Archibald-world?" Josiah smirked.

"You what?" Archibald questioned, making a tricky left turn into a narrow lane, in response to the sat-nav instructions.

"Ignore me, Archibald, I was being facetious"

"It's a bit...grim this, innit?" Archibald commented, as they made their way, gingerly, up the pot-holed lane. Trees and bushes, hugely overgrown, cloaked the roadway in a dark tunnel, with water dripping from every branch.

"Not quite what I anticipated; I must concur"

"And that...well, that's just creepy!" Archibald nodded toward a large sign, painted in bright red paint, on an industrial pallet. It read:

"IF YOU KILL MY KITTENS, I'LL KILL YOU!"

"Indeed!" Josiah looked rather worried, "Perhaps an estate worker with a somewhat robust manner of expressing themselves?" He ventured.

"Not what you expect on your way to some stately pile, though, is it?" Archibald pointed out.

"Well, it isn't exactly what one might describe as a 'Stately Home', at least not from my limited research..." Josiah began. At that moment, the lane levelled out from its uphill climb and the dense tree canopy gave way to sunshine and blue skies. Before them, perched on higher ground and surrounded by immaculate gardens, stood Evanley Hall. A late Victorian estate house, with the odd turret and spot of castellation thrown in for good measure.

"Ah, now that is more what I anticipated!" Josiah beamed with delight.

Dead Reckoning

"Yeah, that's the business alright, innit?" Archibald nodded.

"Drive up to the front door, Archibald, if you will" Josiah was grinning like the proverbial cat.

A cattle grid, positioned between two, large stone pillars, marked the boundary between the pot-holed lane, on which they had been travelling (which swept away to the right), and the neat gravel drive that curled around the terraced lawn, fronting the property.

Josiah exited the vehicle with a spring in his step and bounced up to the large, oak door. He gave a smart 'rat-a-tat-tat' on the knocker and stood back, expectantly. Archibald emerged from the car with considerable caution, looking about with a great deal of suspicion.

"You erm, you don't think that whoever wrote that sign lives here, do you?" He asked, tugging his sleeves in his nervousness.

"I am sure that is not the case, Archibald" Josiah waved the idea away, breezily.

The door creaked open. A gentleman, dressed in a rather ill-fitting and shabby black suit peered out at them.

"How may I accommodate you?" He asked, in sombre tones.

"Good afternoon, my name is Josiah Oakshott and this" He indicated to his right, where Archibald was peering upwards in fascination at the sheer size of the house, and nudged him with some force, "is my colleague, Archibald Thurble. We are here at the invitation of Mrs. DeVille" Josiah extended his business card to the man, who held it gingerly, and with a look of some distaste. Archibald, now paying attention, looked chuffed at being described as Josiah's 'colleague'.

"One moment!" The man inspected the card, thoroughly, and then slammed the door in their faces.

"Well, I'll be...!" Archibald looked deeply offended.

"Pay no heed to it, Archibald," Josiah urged, "they have their own ways, out here in the countryside"

They stood, staring at the closed door for a few minutes, feeling rather foolish.

"Gentlemen, if you will attend on me?"

Josiah and Archibald wheeled around and saw, to their left, the man, standing at the corner of the house, beckoning to them.

"What the heck?" Archibald began.

"I have no idea, Archibald, but, as I have said, their ways are not our ways" Josiah led the procession to join the man, who was standing, tapping his foot, impatiently.

When Archibald and Josiah were within a few feet of him, he turned on his heel and marched down the side of the house and then turned smartly right. To their left, they were aware of fields as far as the eye could see, the nearest one containing a couple of stables, from which a horse watched their progress, suspiciously. To their right was the back of the house, which, like the rear of all grand homes, housed the pipework, drains and gulleys, in addition to the bins and general detritus, of a working home.

The man opened a small door and led them, up a narrow passageway, into a rather dark and dismal dining room.

Dead Reckoning

"Please wait here, gentlemen," He intoned, "my lady will be with you, presently" and strode out of the room.

"I think he's got a cheek!" Archibald fumed.

"I suspect we've been brought to the Tradesmen's Entrance" Josiah frowned, "these old houses have their own, very distinctive, ways"

"I hope this Mrs. Devil makes it worth your while, dragging us all over the country like this and then making us hang around like we were nowt" Archibald folded his arms and scowled.

"It's Mrs. DeVille, and we are very fortunate to have been asked to attend such a prestigious address, particularly as things stand at the moment" Josiah pointed out, "I am rather afraid, Archibald, that beggars cannot be choosers"

A door opened, softly, behind Josiah, as he spoke and a silky voice said "Hello, Josiah"

Josiah spun around and gasped.

"J...J...Jeanette?"

Chapter Six

There's a Ghost in My House

"You two know each other, then?" Archibald enquired, as he looked from the open-mouthed and obviously shocked, Josiah Oakshott, to the warmly smiling Jeanette DeVille.

"We do, indeed" Jeanette nodded.

"I erm…" Josiah looked lost for words and white as a sheet.

"Perhaps your…colleague…?" Jeanette began.

"Ah yes, sorry, this is Archibald Thurble" Josiah motioned in Archibald's direction, "He kindly drove me here today. As you can see, I am somewhat incapacitated" He lifted his slinged arm to illustrate his point.

"Oh dear, Josiah, I do hope you are not badly injured?" Jeanette looked concerned.

"Not at all, it is just a sprain" Josiah insisted.

"A *severe* sprain!" Archibald added, loyally.

"As I was going to say, perhaps your colleague would enjoy a little time inspecting our extensive gardens?" Jeanette asked, meaningfully raising an eyebrow.

"Ah yes, that would be a capital idea!" Josiah nodded and smiled, "Archibald, would you care to take a turn around the grounds, whilst Mrs. DeVille and I take the opportunity to renew our erm, acquaintance?"

Dead Reckoning

"You want me to go out?" Archibald looked at his employer in astonishment, "And leave you with her?"

"That was the nub and the gist of my suggestion, Archibald, yes"

"Oh, right!" Archibald looked exceedingly put out, but, nevertheless, headed back out the way he had come in. Behind him, he could hear low mutterings and then a peal of laughter.

Striding out into the rear courtyard, Archibald was conducting a monologue of misery with himself.

'Bloody marvellous!' He thought, *'I drive him all the way here, and when we do get here, we're treated like the hired bloody help by that jumped-up toerag what answered the door, and then, damn me, when the lady of the house turns up, what happens? Only that I get turfed out into the garden! Huh! It's a wonder they didn't give me a bottle of pop and a packet of crisps!'* Archibald's sulky ramblings had transported him around the back of the house and into a sort of maze, formed by a criss-cross of hedging. Head down and deep in self-pity, he marched on, oblivious to the delights of the garden. He, therefore, didn't notice when a young girl appeared from behind one of the hedges, and nearly marched straight into her.

"Bloody hell!" He yelped, finding himself about to go head-first into a slender girl, slightly taller than him, dressed all in black, with long, copper hair.

"I am sorry, did I startle you?" She asked, with concern.

"Not half!" Archibald confirmed, in an aggrieved tone, "I didn't know there was anyone else about!"

"This is *my* garden" The girl looked around her, with the pride of ownership, "and you are in my favourite spot. I like to come here when I want to be on my own"

"Oh well, don't mind me!" Archibald grumbled, "everybody's chucking me out, today" He made to march off again, but she put out a restraining hand

"Please don't go" She pleaded, "I do apologise, I did not intend to hurt your feelings. I merely meant that this is somewhere I like to come when I want to be alone with my thoughts. You must have times like that, too?"

"Well, there's a place in the stores where I like to go for a bit of peace and quiet, yeah" Archibald conceded.

"There you are, then" The girl smiled and Archibald thought she was the prettiest thing he had ever seen. Very pale and a bit odd, it had to be said, but decidedly pretty. "I'm precious" She announced, placing a palm on her chest.

"Well, I s'pose we all are to someone" Archibald hazarded, unsure of how to respond to this statement. The girl looked at him, blankly.

"I mean, my name is Precious"

"Oh, right" Archibald frowned, "that's erm…different" He suggested.

"Mama said she thought it summed me up, completely" Precious said, proudly.

"Right! Did she?" Archibald considered this latest information and decided that further comment would probably not be advisable, "I'm Archibald, Archibald Thurble, but my friends call me Archie"

"Then I shall call you Archibald" Precious stated, confidently.

Dead Reckoning

"Oh, right, I see!" Archibald said, somewhat put out.

"But I hope we can be friends" She smiled, winningly.

"Yeah, why not?" Archibald shrugged and nodded, "I'm here with Mr. Oakshott"

"That is the Funeral Director, is that correct?"

"Yeah, I'm like his right-hand man." Archibald said, proudly, "well, 'specially at the moment 'on account of how he can't use one of his hands" He giggled to himself.

"I was aware that Mama had requested a visit" Precious stated, solemnly, ignoring the attempt at humour.

"Oh, is that your mam?" Archibald nodded in the general direction of the house.

"Indeed" Precious smiled at him, "this is our home" She looked around, and smiled, warmly.

"Some place!" Archibald agreed, "so, is it just you and your mam what live here then?"

"Myself, Mama and Hames"

"Hames?" Archibald frowned.

"The butler. You must have met him! We would be lost without him"

"We were nearly lost *with* him!" Archibald commented, bitterly, "He made us come 'round to the Tradesman's Entrance"

"Ah, yes, dear Hames" Precious grinned, "he is something of a traditionalist. Pay him no heed, there is no malice in him, whatsoever"

"Yeah, well, he's got a funny way of showing it" Archibald had definitely taken a dislike to the butler.

"If you are Mr. erm..." She hesitated.

"Oakshott" Archibald supplied.

"Indeed, if you are Mr. Oakshott's 'right-hand man', then why are you out here in the garden?"

"Ah, well, they chucked me out, didn't they?" Archibald said, bitterly.

"'Chucked you out'?" Precious looked puzzled, "What do you mean by that?"

"Made me 'op it" Archibald translated, "gave me the bum's rush"

Precious looked at him, blankly, a situation that was not unusual for Archibald.

"I mean they made me come out here, in the garden, 'cause they wanted a private natter"

"Really?" Precious looked a little excited, "Do you know what they wanted to talk about?"

"No idea" Archibald shook his head, "it was just obvious they knew each other, probably from way back, I'd guess"

"How thrilling!" Precious clapped her hands together.

"Not if you're stuck out in the garden, like a kid shoved outside a pub!" Archibald grumbled.

"A pub?" Precious looked puzzled.

"Yeah, you know, a boozer" Archibald made a drinking motion.

"You have me at a disadvantage" Precious looked perplexed.

Dead Reckoning

"You know, where people go to have a drink"

"Do you mean..." Precious looked around her, as if afraid that someone might hear, "alcohol?" She whispered.

"Yeah, that's it" Archibald nodded, "Back in the day, when kids couldn't go into pubs, they used to be parked outside with a bottle of pop and a packet of crisps, that's what I meant"

"I'm afraid I have no knowledge of such establishments" Precious said, seriously, "Mama does not approve of..." She lowered her voice, again, "alcohol"

"Oh well, takes all sorts" Archibald conceded, generously, "Me Nan's the other way 'round, she don't approve if you *don't* drink your own weight in it"

"Your 'Nan'?" Precious queried.

"Yeah, you know, me grandmother, although she'd go barmy if you called her that. She lives with me and me Mam"

"That must be...cosy" Precious suggested, after some thought.

"Well, it keeps her out of trouble...sometimes" Archibald said, thoughtfully.

"But I must not detain you" Precious pulled a pocket-watch on a chain from around her waist and consulted it, "goodness, just look how long we have been chatting! Come, I will escort you back to the House"

"Oh, ta! I wasn't taking any notice of how I got here, to be honest, so I wasn't looking forward to finding me way back" Archibald admitted.

"It is something of a labyrinth" Precious agreed, leading the way. Shortly they found themselves at the rear of the House.

"Please feel free to go in" Precious urged, "I am sure they will have concluded their business, by now"

"Aren't you coming?" Archibald asked, as he made to go through the door.

"No, I think I will enjoy the fresh air for a little longer" She turned to go, but then turned back, "It was really good to meet with you, Archibald" She treated him to a devastating smile that turned his legs to jelly, "I do hope we can meet again"

"Yeah, me an' all" Archibald managed, and then she was gone.

He made his way back into the Dining Room. Josiah and Jeanette DeVille were sitting side by side at the table, laughing and clearly enjoying each other's company. Archibald coughed, diplomatically, to make them aware of his presence.

"Ah, Archibald! Your timing is excellent" Josiah beamed at him, and started to get up, "I had just said, to Mrs. DeVille, that we really should be going"

"Right you are, Mr. O." Archibald nodded, "I've just been chatting to that young girl, out the back, like" Archibald jerked a thumb in the general direction of the garden.

"A young girl, you say?" Mrs. DeVille queried.

"Yeah, name of Precious. Your daughter" Archibald said, to remove any doubt.

"You are mistaken, Archibald" Mrs. DeVille said, seriously, "I have no daughter. There *was* a young girl of that name, here at the House, many years ago, but she died in tragic circumstances"

"You what?" Archibald yelped.

Chapter Seven
Ha! Ha! Said The Clown

Archibald stared at them aghast, rapidly growing panic filling all of his senses. He could not read anything from Josiah's expression, his face was a blank. Mrs. DeVille, just looked at him quizzically.

"You mean, I've been chatting to a g...g...ghost, all this time?" Archibald asked, horrified.

Josiah was the first to break, stifling a giggle he managed to say,

"Oh, Archibald, I'm so sorry. Do forgive us, it was just our little joke!" Then dissolved into helpless laughter. Mrs. DeVille followed him, but her laughter was just that little bit more manic.

"Hahahaha" She took a deep breath, "ahahaha" and continued in that vein for a little longer than was entirely comfortable. Even Josiah glanced at her with some concern.

"Well, thanks a ruddy lot!" Archibald folded his arms and looked decidedly hurt, "you frightened the sh...the life out of me there. What a lousy thing to do!"

"Oh really, Archibald, it was just an innocent jape, surely you can see the funny side?" Josiah asked, hopefully.

"No, actually, I can't. If anyone wants me, I'll be out in the car" Archibald stalked out of the house.

"Oh dear!" Josiah looked distinctly uncomfortable.

"He is your employee, Josiah," Jeanette DeVille pointed out, "you should not allow him to speak to you in that manner"

"Well, he might be my employee," Josiah agreed, "but that does not give me *carte blanche* to ridicule him in any way I see fit. Moreover, we have, recently, been through some trying times together, so I should have had more regard for his feelings."

"Nevertheless, it does not do to allow the hired help to get ideas above their station" She drew closer to Josiah and placed a hand on his arm, "let me get Hames to show you to your car"

"There's no need, Mrs. De…Jeanette" Josiah blushed, a little, "I'm perfectly capable of finding my own way back"

"Not at all. Wouldn't hear of it. HAMES!!" She bellowed.

The butler slithered through a side door and looked at her, attentively.

"Be so kind as to show Mr. Oakshott back to his vehicle, if you will, Hames"

"Of course, ma'am" Hames stepped over to the rear door, opened it, and indicated for Josiah to proceed. "And the other gentleman?" Hames enquired.

"Mr. Furrball has already left the building" Jeanette said, sharply.

"It's Thurble, not Furrball" Josiah corrected.

"Whatever!" Jeanette waved his interjection aside, "You see, Josiah, THAT is how one should deal with staff"

Dead Reckoning

"I think the employment relationship between Archibald and myself is somewhat different in nature" Josiah said, picking up his hat and gloves and heading for the door. "Will I...will I see you again?" He asked, nervously.

"I am quite sure that you will" Jeanette smiled at him, warmly, and briefly held his hand.

With a spring in his step, Josiah marched with Hames, toward the car, where a hunched-up Archibald Thurble could be seen sitting behind the wheel.

"Thank you for waiting, Archibald. We can leave now" Josiah said to his grim-looking employee.

Silently, Archibald guided the vehicle back down the gravel drive. Josiah turned to look back and saw Jeanette DeVille and Precious standing at the front of the grand house, waving. He wound down his window and waved back, a beaming smile on his face.

As they, once again, crossed the cattle grid, and entered the dark and dingy country lane, a middle-aged woman with wild hair and a tatty housecoat, jumped out in front of them, carrying a shotgun. Archibald stood on the brakes in time to avoid her and Josiah fought to get his window back up but she spotted it and grabbed the glass with a grimy hand.

"You ain't seen my kittens, 'ave yer?" She spat.

"I assure you, my good lady, we have seen no animals whatsoever, on our travels" Josiah shrank back from her foul breath.

"That right, be it?" She looked at them both, suspiciously, "not even up at the 'ouse, like?"

"Especially not up at the House" Josiah insisted, fighting to get the window up, "now, if you could step aside, we will be on our way"

"You wanna be careful of 'er" The woman nodded back toward Evanley Hall, "'er and that brat, they ain't quite right, if yer know what I mean?"

"I think you are perfectly correct that someone here is not, as you say, right" Josiah tried a winning smile, "and now, may we proceed?"

The woman stood aside and nodded,

"BUT YOU WATCH OUT FOR MY KITTENS, YOU 'EAR ME?" She yelled, as the car pulled away.

Archibald tried to drive as quickly as possible down the lane, despite the numerous potholes.

"I tell you, I've about had it up to here with this place, I have straight!" He muttered as they lurched and banged their way down the lane.

"You mean that lady's unfortunate interjection?"

"I mean, everything! Particularly you and her taking the doo-dah!" Archibald nodded back toward the Hall.

"I did apologise for our ill-considered prank, Archibald"

"Oh yeah, but *she* didn't, did she?" Archibald said, sulkily, "She just p…killed herself laughing!"

"When all is said and done, Mrs. DeVille is a client and we need to be attentive to her needs"

"Client, is she?" Archibald asked, glancing at Josiah, "put any business our way then, has she?"

"Well, no, not on this occasion." Josiah looked rather uncomfortable, "but, as you know, our business is about establishing relationships over the long term, rather than quick wins. An association with such an established and well-respected family, will pay dividends for us, over time"

"Didn't sound like that woman with the gun had much respect for them"

"I imagine she lives on the Estate" Josiah mused, "you would expect a little resentment, under those circumstances. These rural communities always have their fair share of eccentrics"

"I don't know about 'eccentric', she was off her nut, if you ask me!" Archibald, thankfully, heaved the car out of the rutted lane and back onto the main road. "How come you know this Mrs. DeVille, then?"

"Ah, yes" Josiah steepled his fingers and sighed, "you may recall, some time ago now, when you were enquiring if I had ever been engaged or married, that I said that there had been someone, once?"

"Yeah, I remember" Archibald nodded.

"Well, Jeanette, Mrs. DeVille, she was that someone" Josiah blushed, slightly and fiddled with his gloves.

"Oh, right" Archibald considered this latest news, "and how long ago was all this, then?"

"Some considerable time ago" Josiah sighed, "I would guess, perhaps eighteen or nineteen years, something like that"

"Right!" Archibald nodded, and then a thought struck him, "how old would you say that Precious was?"

"I don't really know" Josiah frowned, "I would imagine she is still quite young. I'm really not good at guessing people's ages, particularly the younger generations"

"Not, eighteen or nineteen then?"

"I suppose she could well be, oh!"

"Just a thought!" Archibald smirked.

They drove on in silence, with Josiah looking increasingly thoughtful and Archibald grinning like the proverbial cat, delighted to have got one up on his employer.

As they pulled in to the gates of Oakshott and Underwood, they could see Mr. Strine, the oldest and longest-serving employee, hopping from one foot to the other, at the main door. Josiah exited the car to let Archibald garage it properly and headed toward Mr. Strine.

"Is all well, Mr. Strine?" He asked, hopefully.

"All under control, Mr. Oakshott, don't you go worrying yourself about that" Mr. Strine managed a faint smile, "only, there's someone here to see you. I've put them in your office, I hope that's all right?" He asked, nervously.

"That is absolutely fine, Mr. Strine. Thank you so much for deputising in my absence"

Dead Reckoning

"Always happy to help, Mr. Oakshott, you know that" Mr. Strine continued to hop from one foot to the other, "only, I couldn't deputise for this, if you take my meaning"

"I'm not entirely sure that I do, Mr. Strine, but, no matter, I will deal with it, whatever it is"

"Right you are, Mr. Oakshott" Mr. Strine opened the main door for his employer and then scampered away.

Shaking his head, as he reflected on this last conversation, Josiah opened his office door with a sense of relief to be back on familiar ground. He was, therefore, surprised to see a woman, standing, with her back to him, by his desk, silhouetted by the light from the stained-glass window. She turned at the sound of the door opening and smiled.

"Hello, Josiah!" She said, softly.

"Samantha?" Josiah gasped.

Chapter Eight
I Heard It Through The Grapevine

"What the h…what the dickens are you doing here?" Josiah asked, eyes wide in amazement.

"Nice to see you, too, Josiah" Samantha smirked, "I do work here, you may recall?"

"I DON'T think so!" Josiah said, firmly.

"Really?" Samantha raised an eyebrow, "Have you formally dismissed me?"

"Well, no, but…" Josiah spluttered.

"And, have I resigned?"

"No, not as such, but I should have thought it would be obvious to anyone…"

"I'm afraid it is not obvious to me, Josiah" Samantha smiled, sweetly.

Archibald sidled in and, aware that this conversation could be very interesting indeed, pulled out the visitor's chair and made himself comfortable.

"Oh, but you have hurt yourself?" Samantha noticed the sling he was sporting.

"It is nothing, just a simple sprain" Josiah shrugged.

"A *severe* sprain" Archibald pointed out, loyally.

Dead Reckoning

"Are the police aware of where you are?" Josiah crossed to the window and peered out, cautiously.

"The police have no need to know where I am, I have been released on Unconditional Bail"

"Oh!" Josiah looked crestfallen, "Well, that's as may be, but you cannot be here"

"Why not?"

"Well, you're…you're a wanted felon!"

"Don't be ridiculous, Josiah, I am nothing of the sort. In fact, my solicitor is of the opinion that I may well avoid criminal charges, completely"

"WHAT?" Josiah looked perplexed.

"After all, I haven't *really* done anything wrong…" Samantha began.

"You must be joking!" Josiah spluttered, "How can you possibly say that? Your convict of a husband burst out of one of our coffins!"

"I had nothing to do with that, Josiah, as you well know. I was as surprised as everyone else when he appeared." Samantha folded her arms and gave him a steely look, "In fact, if we are going to bandy accusations, it could be argued that you and Archibald are even more culpable, given that you transported Frankie across the continent and then smuggled him back into this country"

"She's got a point, there, Mr. O." Archibald observed, nodding enthusiastically.

"Fine!" Josiah fumed, "But what about the stash of loot you were hiding for him? Eh? What about that?" Josiah looked triumphant.

"That is an issue and I was, undoubtedly, foolish to allow that to happen..." Samantha looked thoughtful.

"Ha!"

"But, ultimately, I had no knowledge of its contents" Samantha shrugged.

"You *say* that..." Josiah sneered.

"I DO say that!" Samantha nodded, "do you really think, if I had known that I had many thousands of pounds sitting at the bottom of my garden, that I would have been living with my parents, scrimping and saving? Why, with the fake passports, I could have taken myself anywhere in the world, and no-one would have been any the wiser!"

"She's got a point there too, Mr. O." Archibald nodded.

"Archibald! Will you stop scoring this as if it were a tennis match!" Josiah snapped.

"Look, Josiah, I quite understand why you are so upset. I would be too, under the circumstances, but I played no part in Frankie's escape, or his return. The police, who have released me from custody, seem to accept that, so perhaps you should, too? Obviously, I now need to consider my future."

"And what do you expect to happen?" Josiah looked at her, quizzically.

"I'm a realist, Josiah." Samantha sighed, "I appreciate that it will probably be quite some time before I could hope to serve as a Celebrant again, given the bad publicity, but I see no reason why I could not work 'behind the scenes', as it were"

"No, no, absolutely not!" Josiah shook his head, violently.

"She's got..." Archibald began.

Dead Reckoning

"If you say, 'She's got a point there' once more, Archibald, it won't just be Mrs. Knight here who will be looking for directions to the Job Centre!" Josiah snarled.

"Humph!" Archibald scowled and looked away from them, in a marked manner.

"Josiah, I think, if you looked at this dispassionately, you would realise that I have done nothing wrong" Samantha said, quietly.

"NOTHING WRONG?? What about becoming engaged to me when you were still married? How about that?"

"That is a fair point," Samantha conceded, "I should not have done that. In my defence, the marriage was so long ago, when I was still very young and foolish, and I had not seen Frankie for so many years, that I had more or less forgotten all about it, and him"

"But, you were not *free*..." Josiah insisted.

"No, you are quite correct. I should have been honest with you, but I did not want to trouble you with something that was of no importance, well, not as far as I was concerned, anyway. My plan was to end my marriage quietly and without fuss, long before we made any arrangements. That is still my intention"

"You need not trouble yourself!" Josiah snapped, waving a hand in the air, "our relationship is over"

"Oh, Josiah!" Samantha sighed, and took a step toward him, "Don't you think it would be a terrible waste to allow something as good as we had, to just…slip away?"

"Not necessarily! In fact, I think it is only fair that you should know that there is someone else" Josiah said, with a hint of bravado, stepping back to ensure a *cordon sanitaire* between him and Samantha.

"Is there?" Archibald looked astonished.

"Yes, there is!" Josiah said, defiantly.

"I see" Samantha frowned and took a deep breath, "If that is the case, Josiah, then, obviously, I would wish you every happiness" Samantha shook her head, sadly, "and with regard to my employment…?"

"I will consult with my legal advisor and I will contact you as soon as I have a response"

"Fine!" Samantha nodded, "We will talk again, Josiah"

"Indeed! Now, if you will forgive me, I have much that needs my attention" Josiah crossed the room, and opened the door, pointedly. Samantha and Archibald trooped out and the door closed, firmly, behind them.

"Thank you, Archie. I really appreciate your support" Samantha touched him, lightly, on his arm, as they walked down the corridor.

"Oh, it's nowt" Archibald blushed, "he was right upset after all that palaver at the Crem., you know?"

"Yes, I can imagine" Samantha nodded, "So was I! I would not have wished that situation on anyone"

"I think he was shocked, more than anything" Archibald confided, "but I think finding out you were still married, well, that was the straw that broke the camel's how's-your-father"

"I know" Samantha said, quietly, "what's all this about there being 'someone else'?"

"Oh, don't ask me!" Archibald protested, flapping his arms in exasperation, "it's him you need to talk to"

Dead Reckoning

"But, it's *you* that I'm asking, Archie" Samantha nudged him and winked, "Go on, be a pal!"

"Well..." Archibald sighed, "we've been to see this posh sort, up in Cheshire, this afternoon. Turns out that him and her used to be an item, back in the day"

"Is that so? He never mentioned anything before" Samantha raised her eyebrows.

"No, I know, but that's what he reckons" Archibald nodded, "She was supposed to be a potential client, and they're few and far between, at the moment, but that all went out the window as soon as she put in an appearance. They were getting on like an' house on fire, an' all. All whispering and private jokes and stuff"

"I see" Samantha said, quietly.

"But, if you ask me..." Archibald looked around, to check that no-one was listening, "I reckon she's a bit...strange"

"Strange?"

"Yeah, odd, a bit peculiar like" Archibald scratched his head and looked worried, "she gave me the willies, to be honest"

"I don't like the sound of this, Archie" Samantha frowned. "Why would she suddenly turn up, out of the blue, at this time? How did she know how to contact him and why hasn't she done so, before?"

"Must have seen it in the papers, I suppose" Archibald mused, "it was all over the Advertiser, they loved it!"

"Well, yes, I suppose there's that but why wait until there was an article in the news? Surely, if she wanted to make contact again, she could have done so any time, it can't be that hard to track down a Funeral Director, can it?"

"There's summat else, an' all" Archibald looked around, again, "she's got a daughter, Precious"

"Precious?" Samantha looked surprised.

"Yeah, that's what I thought," Archibald nodded "but she was all right, to be fair, only, she's like eighteen, nineteen, summat like that"

"Ok" Samantha nodded.

"Guess how long it's been since Mr. O. and her were together?" Archibald asked, pointedly.

"NO!" Samantha looked shocked.

"I was winding him up about it, on the way back" Archibald said, "but he went a bit quiet, so I reckon he must think there's something in it"

"Gosh! This is a mess, isn't it Archie?" Samantha looked very thoughtful.

"Yeah, I know." Archibald nodded and looked glum, "I wish we could turn the clock back. Nowt's gone right since we came back from Spain!"

"We've got to keep an eye on him, Archie" Samantha frowned, "he's very vulnerable, just now. I don't want to see him get hurt"

"Me neither" Archibald agreed, looking thoughtful, "he's a pain in the ar...backside at the best of times, but he'd be bloody awful if owt else goes wrong"

They walked together, down the corridor, both deep in thought.

Chapter Nine
Standing in the Shadows of Love

Archibald Thurble was enjoying a few quiet moments, alone in the stockroom, with a cup of tea and a biscuit. He was perched, precariously, on a stool, with his tea and biscuits arranged on the shelf that he had configured into a sort-of makeshift desk. He was just in the act of dunking his biscuit, with all the careful thought and precise manipulation that such action required, when;

"Hello, Archie!" Samantha Knight was standing beside , clutching a laptop under her arm.

Archibald gave a yelp and dropped his biscuit into the mug.

"Oh bug..." He began, and then thought better of it. "You made me jump!" He grumbled, whilst attempting a recovery operation with a teaspoon.

"Sorry, Archie" Samantha grinned, "am I interrupting your tea-break?"

"No, it's ok" Archibald shrugged, "what are you doing here? Does Mr. O. know?" Archibald looked around, wildly, to see if his employer was on the rampage.

"Oh, he knows, Archie" Samantha sighed, "that's why I'm here. Have you got room for another?"

"I doubt it" Archibald shook his head, sadly, "that one's taken up most of the mug" He surveyed the scene moodily.

"I wasn't talking about another biscuit" Samantha chuckled, "I meant, could you make room for me on the shelf, here?"

"Here?" Archibald looked at her with astonishment, "You want to sit here?"

"Well, I've got to work somewhere and there really isn't any spare office space, so Josiah suggested I should commandeer a bit of your shelving" Samantha looked around at the available space, dubiously.

"You're still working here, then?" Archibald tried to hide his surprise, without a great deal of success.

"I am indeed, and I have to say that Josiah is less than pleased about that fact" Samantha grinned, "I did try to warn him but he wouldn't listen. I suspect that the legal advice he has received has told him that, whilst he *could* dismiss me, he would probably find it a very expensive undertaking (if you'll excuse the pun) if I subsequently took him to an Employment Tribunal" Samantha put her laptop down on the shelf.

"Oh heck, he'll be dead narked about that" Archibald shook his head, "so, what's going to happen now?"

"Well, I think he's hoping that I'll be convicted of something and that will give him an excuse to dismiss" Samantha looked thoughtful, "but I think he's going to be disappointed, if I am to believe what my solicitor has told me. Anyway, in the meantime, he has graciously allowed me to return to work, but there's nowhere for me *to* work, as I obviously can't continue to share his office"

"Here, have my stool" Archibald jumped up and moved the furniture around, "you'll need somewhere to sit. There's a power point just up there" He indicated a dusty and grimy outlet a little further along the wall, and tried, with the back of his sleeve, to clean a bit of the shelf for her.

"That's very sweet of you, Archie, but you mustn't concern yourself" She beamed at him, "I'm a big girl, I can take care of myself."

Dead Reckoning

"Well, I don't think it's right, you being treated like this!" Archibald said, stoutly.

"Oh, it's nothing" Samantha perched on the proffered stool and opened her laptop, "he's been hurt and so he's lashing out. I can understand that" Samantha watched the laptop going through its start-up routine.

"Yeah, I can see as how he's narked" Archibald nodded, "but he shouldn't be taking it out on you"

"I can manage, Archie, don't you worry" Samanth winked, "but I am bothered about this new lady in his life. Not that I'm jealous…" She blushed, a little.

"No, course not" Archibald shook his head.

"…but, there's something not quite right about all that, I can just feel it" She looked thoughtful, "Actually, Archie, you could do me a favour"

"Yeah, whatever"

"I think he's got something planned for later" She confided, "I don't know what it is, but he was looking very chipper, when he got off the 'phone, before talking to me. Could you take him his tea, and see if you can find out what's going on?"

"I'll have a go, but you know what he's like" Archibald shrugged, "for every time he's in the mood to chat, there's another where he'll just ignore you"

"I know, but be a pal and try, will you?"

Which is why, a quarter of an hour later, Archibald was attempting to knock on Josiah Oakshott's door, whilst juggling a cup of tea and a plate of biscuits.

"Come!" Josiah intoned.

"I've got your tea, Mr. O." Archibald edged around the door and made his way carefully to the desk, fiercely concentrating on the task in hand.

"Ah, the cup that cheers!" Josiah beamed at his employee. "Thank you, Archibald. Very thoughtful of you"

"No problem, Mr. O." Archibald was somewhat startled by his employer's apparent good humour. "Everything alright, is it?" He asked, pointedly.

"Everything is capital, Archibald, absolutely capital!" Josiah grinned, broadly, and settled back in his chair, tea in one hand, biscuit in another. "I must admit to feeling better than I have done for some time" He added.

"Well, that's good then, innit?" Archibald settled himself in the visitor's chair, unbidden.

"It certainly is, Archibald" Josiah nodded, munching happily.

"Anything in particular, cheered you up?" Archibald raised a querying eyebrow.

"Well, as a matter of fact, yes!" Josiah nodded and took another reflective bite from his biscuit, "I received news today, not too long ago, in point of fact, that Jeanette, Mrs. DeVille that is, will be joining me for dinner this evening"

"She's coming all the way down here for a bite to eat?" Archibald looked suitably surprised.

"Well, not entirely" Josiah blushed a little, "she has other business to attend to, I would imagine, but she has graciously accepted my invitation"

"Oh, right" Archibald nodded, "what are you knocking up for her, then?"

Dead Reckoning

"Oh, goodness, no!" Josiah chuckled, "I am not cooking dinner for her. We will be dining at L'eau Bleu, the new restaurant in town. I have been fortunate to secure a reservation at short notice"

"That's that new French place, innit? Got a lot of *'avec'* in everything?"

"It does specialise in French cuisine, yes" Josiah agreed, "I am very much looking forward to sampling their wares"

"Be a bit pricey that, won't it?"

"The cost is immaterial, Archibald, when you are dealing with a lady of Mrs. DeVille's taste and discernment" Josiah snapped.

"If you say so," Archibald helped himself to a biscuit, much to Josiah's annoyance, and munched reflectively, "what was she before she was a DeVille then?" He enquired.

"Before she was a...oh, I see what you mean!" Josiah frowned, "She was born a Mountjoy, a very distinguished family that goes back many generations. Evanley Hall is the family seat, bought and much modified by her grandfather, Shepherd Mountjoy"

"Shepherd?" Archibald looked astounded.

"Yes, it's an old family name, apparently" Josiah looked a little embarrassed, "he was a noted Naval designer and engineer, you know?"

"Was he?" Archibald looked doubtful.

"Oh yes. For many years" Josiah nodded, "I believe he had the Hall extensively modified to accommodate his experiments"

"I didn't know that was a proper job, if you know what I mean?" Archibald mused.

"I'm sorry?" It was Josiah's turn to look puzzled.

"Well, you wouldn't think there would be much call for it, would you?" Archibald expanded, "I mean, once you've done one or two…"

"Once you've done one or two? What are you talking about, Archibald? There's endless variety in naval design"

"You could have fooled me!" Archibald responded, scattering biscuit crumbs in all directions.

"What?" Josiah looked perplexed, "Destroyers, cruisers, battleships…aircraft carriers, for heaven's sake!"

Archibald looked at him, blankly.

"They have to be designed! They don't just appear, by magic!" Josiah waved his arms in agitation.

"Ships?" Archibald asked.

"Yes, of course, ships" Josiah nodded, "what did you think I meant…oh, hang on" A sudden realisation dawned on Josiah, "you thought I was referring to the design of the human navel, the belly-button if you will, were you not?" He sighed.

"Well, yeah, that's why I thought there couldn't be much to it, 'cause they're pretty much all the same, so once you've knocked one or two out…"

"No, Archibald" Josiah pinched the bridge of his nose and sighed deeply, "Shepherd Mountjoy designed ships and various craft for the Royal Navy"

"Ah, right" Archibald nodded, "you can see how he might have made a few bob doing that"

"Indeed, I believe Shepherd Mountjoy single-handedly revived the family fortunes"

Dead Reckoning

"Not bad going for a bloke with just one arm, is it?" Archibald stole another biscuit whilst his employer's focus was elsewhere.

"Who said he only had one arm?" Josiah looked perplexed. "You're sure you're not thinking of Nelson?"

"No, 'course not" Archibald looked suitably affronted, "you did, just now! You said he did it 'single-handedly'"

"By that, I did not mean...oh, never mind" Josiah sighed, "was there anything else, Archibald, before my supply of biscuits vanishes forever?"

"No, not really" Archibald shook his head, "only that I see Ms. Knight's back"

"MRS. Knight," Josiah began, putting particular emphasis on her marital status, "has indeed returned to our employ, pending the outcome of the ongoing police enquiries. I trust this has not discomfited you in any manner?"

"No, it's fine by me" Archibald shrugged, "I've always rated Ms. Knight. It's just, she's sharing my shelf in the stock room"

"Ah, yes, regrettably office space is at something of a premium in these premises" Josiah looked a little guilty, "however, should the police decide to press charges and if she were to be subsequently convicted of any crime or misdemeanour, then her employment would be terminated forthwith and you would, again, have sole use of your shelf"

"Well, I hope that they don't!" Archibald said, stoutly, "She's alright is Ms. Knight. You know where you are with her, unlike some I could mention"

"Meaning what?" Josiah looked at his employee, sternly.

"Nothing" Archibald eased himself out of the chair and slunk toward the door, "I was just sayin'"

"I think any future commentary might be best reserved for an internal monologue" Josiah snapped.

"You what?" Archibald asked, opening the door.

"Keep it to yourself, Archibald, and shut it!"

"Shut it?"

"The door, Archibald" Josiah snarled, his good mood now irretrievably evaporated, "I meant the door"

Chapter Ten
My Girl

"Psst, Archie!" Samantha hissed from her perch beside him, on the shelf in the stock room.

Archibald Thurble, engrossed in polishing some brass coffin handles, carried on without responding.

"Archie!" Samanth hissed, somewhat louder this time.

Archibald visibly jumped and spun around.

"What?"

"Are you doing Josiah's tea, this morning?" She whispered.

"Well, I don't know" Archibald looked thoughtful, "'cause you reckoned I shouldn't be just a 'tea boy', didn't you?"

"That is true, Archie, and I still think that…"

"There you are then!" Archibald looked triumphant.

"…but, don't you want to know what happened last night?" Samantha tilted her head and looked at Archibald, pleadingly.

"Not particularly" Archibald shrugged.

"Oh, come on! Be a pal"

"It's *you* that wants to know" Archibald pointed out, "why don't *you* take him his tea?"

"And how likely do you think it would be that he would tell me about his 'date'?" Samantha made the 'inverted comma' sign with her fingers, and raised an eyebrow.

"Yeah, fair point" Archibald nodded, "Alright, I'll do it" He added, wearily.

Which is why, once again, Archibald found himself knocking on Josiah's door, tea and biscuits in hand.

"Come in, Archibald" Josiah boomed.

Archibald edged his way in, set the tea things on the desk, and immediately clamped a hand over his mouth and nose.

"Oh my God!" Archibald said, in muffled tones, "Has there been a gas leak or summat?"

"Gas leak?" Josiah looked puzzled, "We do not have gas here, how could there be a…ah, I think I might have an explanation" He looked a little sheepish.

"Worrisit then?" Archibald asked, hand still covering his face.

"Ah, well, as you know, myself and Jeanette, Mrs. DeVille that is, had dinner at L'eau Bleu last night"

"Yeah" Archibald agreed, still muffled.

"And French cuisine is somewhat noted for its use of garlic," Josiah blushed somewhat, "the chef at L'eau Bleu having a particular penchant for that ingredient"

"Strewth!" Archibald backed away and carefully moved the visitor's chair some way from the desk.

"I appreciate that it can be a little anti-social" Josiah admitted.

Dead Reckoning

"Not half!" Archibald nodded, "What did that Mrs. Devil think?"

"It's DeVille" Josiah snapped, "and, as she had also partaken of the same cuisine, I very much doubt that she was aware of any lingering odours"

"Just as well you're not seeing her today, then" Archibald said, from a safe distance.

"As a matter of fact, I am!" Josiah looked rather smug, "She will be joining me for luncheon"

"Luncheon?" Archibald looked puzzled, "what's that, when it's at home?"

"It is the correct and proper term for 'lunch', which is a foreshortened version of that same word"

"Oh, right" Archibald conceded, "Hold up, though, is she coming back, just for that?"

"No, in fact she stayed over last night" Josiah admitted, coyly.

"She...she stayed over?" Archibald looked shocked.

"Oh, no, not with me!" Josiah chuckled, "She took a room in town"

"Oh, right" Archbald looked relieved, "only, I was going to say..."

"Would that have offended your sensibilities, Archibald?" Josiah smirked.

"Well...it's just a bit...you know...on your first date, and stuff" Archibald looked decidedly embarrassed.

"I do take your point, Archibald, and you can rest assured that nothing untoward happened between us" Josiah smiled, happily, at the memory.

"I should think not!" Archibald said, primly.

"Was there anything else? Only, I do have work to do as, I am sure, do you" Josiah pointed out.

"No, no, nothing else" Archibald took the hint and made for the door, "you're not going to that Blue place for lunch, are you?"

"No, Archibald" Josiah smiled, "I think the local tearooms will suffice, for a light luncheon"

"That's a relief!" Archibald grinned and made his way out.

* * * *

"What did he say?" Samantha asked, as soon as Archibald reappeared.

"Well, it's like he said, he took that Mrs. Devil to that French place and they had a ton of garlic between them, if the air in the office is owt to go by!" Archibald reported, "Oh, and she stayed over"

"She what?" Samantha looked shocked.

"Not with him, like" Archibald explained, "she stayed in town, somewhere"

"Oh, thank heavens for that" Samantha sighed.

"Yeah, but he's taking her out for 'luncheon' an' all, today" Archibald said, gloomily.

"It's all a bit…intense, wouldn't you say?" Samantha looked concerned.

"I dunno what to make of it, to be fair" Archibald shrugged.

"I wonder," Samantha looked thoughtful, "if we were to stroll into town, in our lunch break, whether we might catch a glimpse of them, what do you say, Archie?"

"Oh no, leave me out of it" Archibald shook his head, firmly.

"Oh come on, be a sport!" Samantha grinned, "I'll stand you a bag of chips"

"Go on then" Archibald agreed, reluctantly.

Which is why, a little while later, Samantha and Archibald were walking out of the premises, together, when Archibald came to a sudden stop. Samantha looked at him with concern but then became aware that a slender, rather tall girl, dressed all in black, with long copper hair, was standing on the pavement, directly before them.

"Bloody hell!" Archibald exclaimed.

"Hello, Archibald" Precious said, sweetly.

"What the...what erm, what are you doing here?" Archibald asked, ungraciously.

"Mama wishes to go shopping, later, and she asked me to join her" Precious explained, "Dear Hames kindly drove me in" She indicated a dilapidated vehicle, parked across the road, that might once have been a luxury car. Hames, in the driver's seat, glowered at Archibald. "I wondered if we might have a bite to eat?" Precious asked.

"You want to go for summat to eat? With me?" Archibald looked astounded.

"You really should do that, Archie" Samantha said, firmly, "forgive me, I'm Samantha Knight" Samantha extended her hand to Precious, who looked at it in distaste and made minimal effort to shake it.

"Precious DeVille" She nodded, perfunctorily.

"Well, you youngsters should cut along" Samantha said, with forced jollity, "I'll take myself off into town" She strode off, looking back at Archibald from time to time.

"Well, she seemed...nice" Precious offered, with very little sincerity, "where might we eat?"

"Oh, erm, well, I dunno!" Archibald looked puzzled, "Do you like doughnuts?"

"I don't believe I have ever tried such a thing"

"Only, there's a shop, just down the road, what does doughnuts and coffee and stuff" Archibald explained, "we could go there?"

Precious looked unconvinced but nodded, reluctantly.

Ten minutes later they were ensconced at a table. Before them, a box of doughnuts each and a coffee in a cardboard cup.

Precious looked at the food offering, doubtfully, and prodded one with a well-manicured fingernail.

"The girl behind the counter seemed to know you" She ventured.

"Ah yeah, that's Fanny, she owns the place now" Archibald nodded, attacking his first doughnut, "her dad, Dick, used to run it but he had health problems and stuff"

"I'm not surprised!" Precious delicately tore a morsel from one of her doughnuts and consumed it, thoughtfully.

"He had this slogan, did Dick" Archibald chuckled, "It's not a proper doughnut if it ain't been made by a Dick"

"How...different!" Precious responded, carefully.

"'Cause, that's all changed now, what with his daughter taking over" Archibald explained.

"One would hope so" Precious agreed.

Dead Reckoning

"Like it says on the box" Archibald pointed at the lid, "'They're only doughnuts if they look like Fanny's!'"

"Very...memorable" Precious agreed, tearing off another slight morsel.

"Yeah, it's catchy, right enough" Archibald concurred, eating with gusto, "but I'm not sure it means what she thinks it does. People could take it the wrong way, style of thing" He went on to explain.

"I imagine that could be a possibility...whatever that might be" Precious said, seriously. "I do hope you have no objection to my joining you, today, Archibald? I do realise it was somewhat...presumptuous of me to just appear in the way that I did. Hames was very dubious about my proposal"

"Nah, it's no bother" Archibald responded, cheerfully, "we could have gone to the chip shop, only...well, I've got a bit of history there, so perhaps best not" He blushed a bit.

"History? Really? How intriguing!" Precious smiled, "You must tell me all"

"Oh, well, one of these days, eh?" Archibald answered, sheepishly.

"You think we might meet again, then?" Precious teased.

"Oh, no, I wasn't presuming owt" Archibald flustered, "I just meant...you know..."

"I am sure we *will* meet again, Archibald" Precious beamed in his direction, "Mama is somewhat...fond of Mr. Oakshott, so I do not see how it could not be so"

"Yeah, it's an ill wind, innit?" Archibald grinned.

"Is it?" Precious looked puzzled, "perhaps it's the doughnuts?" She suggested.

Chapter Eleven
What Becomes of the Brokenhearted

Archibald Thurble staggered back into the premises of Oakshott and Underwood, with a digestive system full of doughnuts and a beaming smile on his face. The smile could have been attributed to the doughnuts but might also have been strongly associated with the peck on the cheek he had just received from a departing Precious DeVille!

"You look pleased with yourself" Samantha observed, from her perch on a stool in the Stock Room.

"Do I?" Archibald grinned.

"You certainly do!" Samantha nodded, "Any connection with Ms. DeVille, by any chance?"

"We had doughnuts and coffee," Archibald beamed, "it were great!"

"I'm sure it was" Samantha snapped, turning around and typing on her laptop, furiously.

"It's just...well, it's nice to have someone interested in *me*, for a change" Archibald said, in a hurt tone.

"Oh, I'm sorry, Archibald" Samantha sighed, "you're quite right, I shouldn't be mad at you." She closed her laptop and smiled at him. "You've every right to have whichever girlfriend you want. It's just...well...don't they strike you as a bit...I don't know...'Addams Family'?"

"Who?" Archibald looked puzzled.

Dead Reckoning

"Jeanette DeVille and her daughter and that creepy butler of theirs"

"No, I know who you mean, I meant, who is this Addams Family?"

"Haven't you come across them? They're a bit...gothic, and weird" Samantha tried to explain.

"Gothic? Is that like being Goth-y?" Archibald frowned.

"Well, in a manner of speaking, yes, I suppose it is" Samantha nodded.

"I don't think Precious is 'weird'" Archibald stated, loyally, "and she's not a Goth"

"She wears black clothes and has black painted fingernails" Samantha pointed out.

"Yeah, but that's just her style. She's not a Goth like them what hang around that Games shop in the town centre. They look like they've lost a bob and found a tanner. You can have a laugh with Precious...a bit"

"Well, ok, not her so much" Samantha conceded, diplomatically, "although just turning up like that, with her butler in tow, driving the limousine, that's a bit...different, isn't it?"

"I don't know. It's never happened to me before!" Archibald shrugged.

"Well, that's my point! You can't imagine either of the Ryder sisters from the chip shop just turning up like that, now, can you?" Samantha pointed out, referring to Archibald's two previous girlfriends.

"No, and look where that got me!" Archibald folded his arms and looked fed up.

"Yes, that's a fair point" Samantha nodded, "I'm sorry, Archie. I'm honestly not trying to rain on your parade. I just have my doubts about that family"

"You're sure you're not just...jealous?" Archibald risked a sideways glance at his colleague.

"Yes, quite probably" Samantha nodded, again, "Josiah and Preciious's mum seemed quite cosy down at the Country Manor tea rooms" She added, miserably.

"I wouldn't know" Archibald shrugged, "we were in Fanny's Doughnuts" A sudden thought struck him, "You didn't go in, did you?"

"No, I just walked past...a few times" Samantha admitted.

"Look Ms. Knight" Archibald sighed, "don't you think it's perhaps time to, I don't know, let go and move on? Eh?"

"Yes, I should, I know" Samantha agreed, glumly, "but I can't! Not just yet. Not until I'm sure there's no hope and this 'Jeanette DeVille' is definitely the one for him. There's just something not quite right about all of this, I can feel it in my water"

"Ah, me Nan has those" Archibald nodded.

"Has what?"

"Feelings in her water" Archibald explained, "she has to have pills for it, else her feet swell up like footballs. 'Course, on the other side of the coin, she knows every toilet in Merkin-under-Heathwood"

"A diuretic?" Samantha commented.

"No, she can eat sweet stuff all she likes" Archibald shook his head, "just as well, considering the amount of lager she gets through"

"You know, there are times when I can see why Josiah is, like he is" Samantha grinned.

* * * *

Dead Reckoning

The object of their discussion was humming a merry little tune, when Archibald arrived with the tea and biscuits a little later that afternoon.

"You sound chipper, Mr. O." Archibald observed, with a grin.

"I would be forced to agree with you, Archibald" Josiah took an appreciative sip of his tea, and nodded, "things are definitely on the up!"

"This you and Mrs. DeVille is it?" Archibald asked, flopping down into the visitor's chair.

"Not entirely," Josiah frowned at his employee sitting down without invitation, "the other aspect that has pleased me is that we have seen a definite uptick in trade over the past week or so, with more enquiries coming in on a daily basis. If this trend continues, then I think we could legitimately hope to see a return to our former trading position"

"So, no redundancies then?" Archibald asked, hopefully.

"I would sincerely hope not, Archibald, no" Josiah selected a biscuit and munched, thoughtfully.

"But this Mrs. DeVille business, that's got to have perked you up, hasn't it?" Archibald asked, slyly.

"I would be less than honest if I did not admit that my meetings with Jeanette...Mrs. DeVille, have, indeed, had a positive effect on my demeanour"

"I saw her daughter, this lunchtime" Archibald admitted, a little bashfully, "we went for a bite to eat"

"Ah, Precious!" Josiah nodded, "How nice. I had no idea you had extended an invitation, Archibald"

"Nah, I didn't" Archibald shook his head, "she just turned up. I took her up Fanny's"

"You did what?" Josiah looked aghast.

"Fanny's Doughnuts" Archibald explained, "I took her up there for lunch"

"Oh, thank goodness!" Josiah said with considerable relief, mopping his brow with a handkerchief, "I think I may have misconstrued...never mind, I'm delighted you have made acquaintance with Miss DeVille, once more"

"Yeah, she's alright, is Precious" Archibald nodded. "You planning to see any more of her mam then?" He asked, archly.

As this question coincided with a particular train of Josiah's thought, he blushed deeply before replying.

"As a matter of fact, Mrs. DeVille has invited me to dine with her at the Hall this Saturday evening"

"Oh, smashing" Archibald grinned, "do you need me to drive you up there, or owt?"

"Thank you, but that will not be necessary, Archibald" Josiah sipped at his tea, "Mrs. DeVille has made arrangements to send a car for me"

"I s'pose that'll be that butler of theirs, that Hames, don't you reckon? He seems to do all sorts!"

"I have not enquired" Josiah surveyed the biscuit selection.

"I reckon so. It was him what brought Precious down today, to meet her mam. They're off shopping, aren't they?"

"I understand they had plans of that nature, yes" Josiah confirmed.

Dead Reckoning

"A bit of posh nosh then, is it? On Saturday, I mean"

"I believe her table is justly renowned" Josiah said, smugly.

"Oh, right" Archibald looked perplexed, "antique, is it?"

"I mean that the standard of cuisine, emanating from her kitchens, is known and famed throughout Cheshire"

"Is it?"

"So I am reliably informed"

"Well, that'll be nice then, won't it?" Archibald brushed some biscuit crumbs from his trousers (much to Josiah's annoyance) and stood up to go.

"I thought I may have glimpsed Mrs. Knight passing the tearooms, earlier" Josiah ventured, "would you know if that was the case?"

Archibald, who had reached the office door and was just about to make his escape, hovered in the doorway.

"Erm..." He replied.

"Has she not spoken with you concerning this?"

"Well..." He began, waiting for inspiration to strike.

"In fact, I thought that I noticed her on more than one occasion" Josiah mused.

"Did you?" Archibald was aware that he was breaking into a cold sweat, "I erm...ooh, I think someone shouted me!" He improvised and made a speedy exit.

"Must be desperate, whoever they are" Josiah mused to himself, archly, snaffling another biscuit.

Chapter Twelve
Stop Her On Sight (S.O.S.)

D.I. Wood was perusing a motoring magazine, well, mostly motoring. He clutched 'Babes & Bumpers', whilst sitting sideways at his desk, with his gout-inflamed leg resting on a spare chair. From time to time, he munched a biscuit, thoughtfully, before flicking to the next page. A brief tap on the office door preceded the arrival of his colleague, D.S. Stone.

"Anything?" D.I. Wood enquired, without looking up from his periodical.

"Not a lot, sir" D.S. Stone consulted the papers he was carrying, "biggest thing is a robbery at a jeweller's"

"Much taken?"

"Not a heck of a lot. They've reported a necklace worth a few thousand pounds stolen"

"Hardly worth the bother, then" D.I. Wood flipped over to another page.

"Well, possibly, but the owner does reckon he's a chum of the Chief Constable" D.S. Stone pointed out.

"Cobblers!" D.I. Wood threw his magazine onto the desk, "all that means is he's seen her from afar at some Chamber of Commerce finger buffet, you mark my words." He bit into a biscuit, savagely, "'Friend of the Chief Constable' my arse!"

"Don't you think it would be wise to take a look, even so?" D.S. Stone looked distinctly worried.

"It's just shoplifting on a slightly bigger scale" D.I. Wood reached for his coffee, "you wouldn't turn out for someone nicking a couple of apples and a banana, would you?"

"Well, no, but..."

"There you are, then" D.I. Wood selected another biscuit, "there's no difference, except for a couple of noughts on the end"

"I still think..." D.S. Stone began.

"You fretting about your promotion, Stoney?" D.I. Wood raised an eyebrow.

"Hadn't crossed my mind, sir" D.S. Stone replied, primly.

"Yeah, right" D.I. Wood sneered, "and the band played 'Believe Me If You Like'"

D.I. Wood looked at him blankly.

"Doesn't matter, Sergeant" D.I. Wood shook his head, "just an expression. If it's going to fret you, we'll go and take a look at this jeweller's but don't expect me to waste much time on it, alright?"

"Whatever you say, sir"

* * * *

"I take it she's gone back home?" Samantha Knight asked, as she studied her laptop.

Archibald Thurble, sitting a few feet away from her perch in the stock room, frowned.

"Who?" He asked, eventually.

"Mrs. DeVille" Samantha replied, with considerable contempt.

"I should have thought so" Archibald nodded.

"Hmph!" Samantha contributed, with a snort.

"He's going over to hers on Saturday" Archibald nodded in the general direction of Josiah Oakshott's office.

"Yes, so you told me" Samantha said, through clenched teeth.

"Spot of posh nosh, he reckons" Archibald said, expanding on his theme, "she's got a famous table, or summat"

"He's welcome to it!" Samantha snarled. "I suppose you'll be taking him up there, so's you can see your Precious?"

"No, she's 'sending a car for him'" Archibald said, in what he thought was a posh voice, denoting the phrase with his fingers.

"Oh, is she?" Samantha frowned, "that makes him a bit of a hostage to fortune, doesn't it? I wonder if he's thought about that?"

"Eh? What do you mean?" Archibald looked puzzled.

"I mean, Archibald, that he won't be able to leave whenever he wants to. I'm sure it sounds great, but it might be a different story when he wants to come home"

"You're just jealous!" Archibald chuckled.

"Maybe I am!" Samantha nodded, "but that doesn't change the fact that he will be stuck up there, in the wilds of Cheshire, with no way of getting home. I think he ought to have more sense!" She seethed.

"If you say so" Archibald sniggered and returned to his work.

* * * *

Dead Reckoning

"Could you describe for me, exactly what happened, sir?" D.S. Stone enquired, whilst D.I. Wood perused the premises of Scrivener & Scrapes, High Class Jewellers, with a bored expression.

"As I said, in my original report" Mr. Scrivener replied, with more than a touch of peevishness, "a lady, of some refinement, came into our establishment yesterday afternoon, and asked to view a rather fine necklace that we had on display..."

"Ok, thank you sir, could you describe her?" D.S. Stone asked.

"I regret not" Mr. Scrivener replied, mournfully.

"CCTV?" D.I. Wood interjected, nodding toward the blinking red light on the ceiling by the corner of the store.

"Regrettably, and strictly *entre nous,* that is not currently functioning" Mr. Scrivener admitted and looked distinctly uncomfortable.

"Give me strength!" D.I. Wood muttered.

"Can you remember anything about her?" D.S. Stone persisted.

"I am unable to help you in that respect, Sergeant, because I did not attend to the lady in question. Perhaps it would be helpful, at this juncture, if I called upon my assistant, who *did* attend to her needs?" Mr. Scrivener suggested.

"You think?" D.I. Wood sneered, *sotto voce.*

"That would be helpful, sir" D.S. Stone nodded.

"Mr. Hamble, could you spare me a moment?" Mr. Scrivener called through the archway leading into the stock room, behind.

"Hamble?" D.I. Wood looked surprised.

Lawrence Hamble oozed into the room, much to the astonishment of the detectives.

"Stone the flaming crows, Stoney! Look who it is!" D.I. Wood chuckled.

"Detective Inspector, Sergeant" Lawrence nodded to each, in turn.

"You know these gentlemen, Mr. Hamble?" Mr. Scrivener looked startled.

"Mr. Hamble had occasion to help us with our enquiries, a little while ago" D.S. Stone rushed to explain, before D.I. Wood could get a word in.

"Really? I do not recall this being mentioned on your Curriculum Vitae, Mr. Hamble" Mr. Scrivener looked sharply at his employee.

"To be clear, Mr. Scrivener, Mr. Hamble was never charged with any crime and was released without a stain on his character" D.S. Stone scrambled to explain.

"His missus, however..." D.I. Wood observed, dryly.

"We are separated" Lawrence explained, blushing furiously.

"By a few thousand miles, would be my guess" D.I. Wood sniggered.

"Perhaps Mr. Hamble would be kind enough to provide a description of this lady you mentioned?" D.S. Stone attempted to get the inquiry back on track.

"Ah yes, she was an attractive, dark-haired lady, of medium height and build" Lawrence explained, "dressed in a rather old-fashioned manner. She seemed very self-assured"

"That narrows it down" D.I. Wood said, under his breath.

"And she was the only person in the shop, at the time of the theft?" D.S. Stone continued.

Dead Reckoning

"Well, originally, yes" Lawrence nodded, "but, as I was showing her the necklace, this young girl came in. She was a bit...odd"

"Odd? In what way, sir?"

"I think they call them 'goths' these days, don't they?" Lawrence looked from D.S. Stone to D.I. Wood, "She was dressed all in black, even had black fingernails"

"I see" D.S. Stone made a note, "what happened then?"

"Well, the lady asked if we had any other necklaces like the one, she was inspecting. I said we had but they were in the stock room and I would have to go and fetch them" Lawrence explained.

"Leaving her and this 'goth' with the original necklace?" D.I. Wood asked with a raised eyebrow.

"Well, yes" Lawrence admitted, miserably.

"Mr. Hamble acted perfectly correctly" Mr. Scrivener intervened, "we expect our staff to make a judgement on the risk attached to any particular client and I am sure that his evaluation of this specific customer was a sound one"

"Dropped a bollock there, didn't you?" D.I. Wood muttered.

"Thank you, Mr. Scrivener" Lawrence gave his employer a weak smile, "unfortunately, subsequent events have rather cast some doubt on my judgement"

"In what way?" D.S. Stone asked.

"Well, when I returned, from the stock room, and I couldn't have been missing for more than a couple of minutes, the lady was slumped over the counter, clearly distressed and the strange girl had disappeared completely." Lawrence explained, with some agitation, "I asked her if she was alright and she said that the 'goth' girl had snatched the necklace she was examining and run off. She was understandably shocked by the event"

"Yes, of course, sir" D.S. Stone nodded, "did either you, or your customer, see where the 'goth' girl went?"

"No, I went straight to the shop door and looked both ways along the High Street, but there was no sign" Lawrence said, miserably.

"What about this *lady*?" D.I. Wood asked, putting emphasis on the 'lady', "What happened to her?"

"Ah, yes, well, I found her a chair so that she could sit down, as she was clearly distressed" Lawrence said, "I fetched her a glass of water and, at that point, this gentleman bustles in who said he was her husband and wanted to know what I had done to his wife!"

"Really? What did he look like?" D.I. Wood asked.

"He was dressed rather formally...and a bit shabbily, if I'm going to be honest" Lawrence recounted, "not the sort of person I would have associated with this particular lady. Anyway, I explained about the robbery and he insisted on taking his wife away, immediately, so that she would not come to any further harm"

"Did he now?" D.I. Wood grinned.

"Was there anything else you needed to add, sir?" D.S. Stone asked.

"Oh, come on, Stoney, don't make a meal of it" D.I. Wood hissed.

"No, I think that's everything, Sergeant" Lawrence nodded.

"I would say, Inspector, that this has been a most trying of experiences for Mr. Hamble" Mr. Scrivener patted his employee on the shoulder, sympathetically, "I do hope you can apprehend this 'goth' girl at the earliest juncture?"

"We will put out a description and do everything we can, sir" D.S. Stone said, keenly.

"I wouldn't hold your breath" D.I. Wood muttered.

"I beg your pardon, Inspector?" Mr. Scrivener asked.

"I said we'll leave no stone, left" D.I. Wood explained, "unturned, that is, sir" He turned to his colleague, "Come on, Sergeant, let's leave these good people to their business" He spun on his heels and said, "Thank you gentlemen, we'll be in touch"

Back in the car, D.I. Wood let out a deep sigh.

"What a waste of time and effort that was!" He exclaimed.

"Did you think so, sir?" D.S. Stone looked up from his notes.

"'Course it was, Stoney" D.I. Wood said, edging out into the traffic, "a couple of grand's worth of necklace goes missing, they reckon, but it won't really be worth that much, that's just what they can sell it for and it's odds-on the insurance will cough up for it, anyway. That's if he keeps schtum about the CCTV being buggered, of course…"

"Ah yes, I wondered about that" D.S. Stone nodded.

"I wouldn't wonder too much" D.I. Wood shook his head, "you can either see conspiracies in everything or accept that people are bloody stupid, most of the time. My money's on stupidity, nine times out of ten"

"Do you think we should fingerprint the counter?"

"Don't be wet, Sergeant!" D.I. Wood spluttered, "this was yesterday. How many customers have they had since then, eh? Let alone that they'll have cleaned it this morning, don't you think? Nah, the forensics boys won't thank you for sending them on *that* wild goose chase"

"Ok, so I'll send out a description of this 'goth' girl, shall I?"

"Werl, you can" D.I. Wood conceded, "but, if I was you, I'd be sending out descriptions of all three of them"

"All three?"

"You didn't seriously think that they weren't all in on it, did you?" D.I. Wood scoffed.

"*All* of them?" D.S. Stone looked astounded.

"That would be my bet" D.I. Wood looked pleased with himself, "and then there's the fact of Lawrence Hamble turning up, out of the blue"

"Oh, surely he's got nothing to do with it, has he?"

"Who knows?" D.I. Wood shrugged, "but it's a hell of a bloody coincidence, don't you think?"

They drove on, each deep in thought.

Chapter Thirteen
Farewell Is a Lonely Sound

Archibald whistled, tunelessly, as the hearse which had, until recently, contained the late Edwin Brood and which now comprised just Archibald and his employer, Josiah Oakshott, edged its way down the road, along with the rest of the traffic caught in the jam.

"Ever thought about it?" Archibald asked, conversationally.

Josiah, who was, at that moment, deeply involved in a train of thought that strongly featured Jeanette DeVille, started guiltily.

"Thought?   Thought about what?"

"You know, funerals and stuff" Archibald explained, without really explaining anything.

"Given our occupation, I think of little else!" Josiah snapped, annoyed that his reverie had been broken.

"I think I used to know her!" Archibald chuckled.

"Know whom?"

"That Little Else you were on about" Archibald wound a window down to let a little air through, "she used to knock around with my Nan. Tiny little woman, could drink her own weight in stout, you know who I mean?"

"I am delighted to report that I have never made the lady's acquaintance" Josiah said, with a shudder, "and I fail to see how she relates to your original question"

"Original question?" Archibald furrowed his brow and thought, furiously, "Oh yeah, I was just thinking about funerals and stuff, and I wondered if you'd thought about yours?"

"Well, yes, I have given the matter some thought" Josiah nodded.

"It's not gonna involve 'orses and plumes and stuff, is it?" Archibald asked, suspiciously. He could still feel the bruise from an unfortunate incident, involving one of the hired horses, from a rather grand funeral a few weeks ago.

"No, that would not be my preferred style" Josiah replied, although, if he was honest with himself, he could see the attraction, "I think something…dignified, understated even, simple but classic"

"I could pass the hat around, at work, and we could get one of them floral tributes" Archibald grinned, "you know, like them that spell out 'MAM' or 'DAD' and stuff. We could get one with 'MR O' done out in chrysanth's or summat, what do you reckon?"

Josiah shuddered.

"Whilst I understand, and am entirely grateful for, the kind thought, I think that such a tribute would hardly fit with my 'simple but classic' motif, if you take my meaning?"

"Oh! No chrysanth's then?"

"A simple but stylish wreath would be more than sufficient" Josiah said, firmly, "however, I feel absolutely fine and in top form, so such plans are not, unsurprisingly, foremost in my mind. How about you, Archibald, do you have any plans?"

"Well, no, not to be honest" Archibald edged the hearse forward a few inches, "I can't say I've really thought about it"

Dead Reckoning

"Hardly surprising" Josiah nodded, "you're a relatively young man with your whole life ahead of you. It would be somewhat concerning if you were fixated on your funeral arrangements"

"I suppose, if I've thought about it at all, I reckon one of them burials at sea could work"

Josiah looked at his employee with some surprise.

"A burial at sea? Do you have naval connections?"

"Nah" Archibald shook his head, dismissively, "they cut all that stuff off when I was born, well, that's what me Mam said, any road"

"I mean, did any members of your family serve in the Navy?"

"She said she wouldn't go through all that again, not for a big clock!" Archibald continued with his reminiscence.

"Why would you want a burial at sea?" Josiah snapped, in an attempt to drag the conversation back to its original topic.

"Eh?" Archibald looked temporarily confused, "Oh, right, yeah, well it looks like it could be a bit of fun"

"Fun?" Josiah looked astounded.

"Yeah, you know, what with all that sliding down into the water, and stuff!"

"You do appreciate, Archibald, that this is not in the nature of a waterpark ride?"

"Well, yeah but…"

"And that, even if it were so, you would not, consciously, be taking part in the proceedings?"

"Well, I suppose so" Archibald conceded, grudgingly.

"So, a burial at sea would confer no particular benefit on you, personally and would not fit with any family tradition of service. On the whole, it would be somewhat difficult to think of a less appropriate ceremony, do you not think?"

"I don't see why it shouldn't be a bit of fun, an' all" Archibald grumbled, sulkily.

"There are many and varied ways of taking your leave from this world," Josiah pointed out, "you are by no means confined to the twin options of burial or cremation. I understand that one possibility is that of having your ashes fired into space, or into the atmosphere, certainly" Josiah made a mental note to find out more about this.

"Oh yeah!" Archibald brightened up, considerably, "that would be a laugh, wouldn't it?"

"I would, however, draw your attention to my earlier remarks concerning you not, consciously, being part of the proceedings"

"Well, yeah" Archibald said, somewhat deflated, "mind you, what goes up must come down, don't they reckon?"

"It is a function of gravity that has been commented upon"

"Well, there you are then!" Archibald grinned, "with a bit of luck, I could come down on Bilston, that'd serve 'em right"

"Most original" Josiah nodded and smiled, "I don't think I have ever been party to a vindictive committal, before"

* * * *

"I've finally got the CCTV back from the High Street" D.S. Stone announced, triumphantly, as he barged into D.I. Wood's office.

"Good for you!" D.I. Wood snarled, his toe had been throbbing quite a bit, lately, despite the medication, and he was not feeling particularly well disposed toward humanity in general and D.S. Stone in particular.

"I've been going through it, and they're there, all right" D.S. Stone continued, undaunted.

"Who are?"

"The people that Mr. Hamble said had been in the jeweller's"

"Really? Bugger!" D.I. Wood said, with feeling.

"Why, what's wrong with that?" D.S. Stone looked perplexed.

"What's wrong with it? What's wrong is that I'd hoped he'd made it all up and had it away with the necklace himself, that's what!" D.I. Wood shifted his leg, slightly, to a more comfortable position on the stool that was supporting it.

"Lawrence Hamble?"

"Yes, Lawrence Hamble!" D.I. Wood snapped, "he was mixed up in that Frankie Knight business, however you dress it up, so why not get a bit light-fingered with the jewellery stock, eh?" (See 'Bring Out Your Dead')

"He was cleared of any involvement, sir" D.S. Stone reminded him.

"'*He was cleared of any involvement, sir*'" D.I. Wood mimicked his Sergeant, "doesn't mean he wasn't up to his neck in it, not from where I'm sitting, anyway"

"How's the foot today, sir?"

"It's just fine and dandy, thank you, Sergeant" D.I. Wood snapped, "what are you implying, eh?"

"Nothing sir" D.S. Stone responded, innocently, "just wondered"

"So, what's on the CCTV then?"

D.S. Stone opened his tablet and started to play the video.

"You can see, here sir, that the 'goth' looking girl comes out first, and heads toward the camera…"

"Can we get a better look at her?" D.I. Wood peered at the screen.

"I'm afraid not, sir." D.S. Stone shook his head, "she appears to be wearing some sort of shawl, or something, around her head and that's partially covering her face"

"Knew what she was about, then" D.I. Wood commented, grimly.

"Possibly," D.S. Stone concurred, "we've been unable to get any form of visual identification, I'm afraid. Shortly after, the other two come out of the jeweller's at a trot, just here, do you see?"

"Yeah, I can see them" D.I. Wood nodded.

"Only they head in the opposite direction, away from the camera, so, again, we can't get any firm identification"

"Anything on any of the other cameras?"

"No sir, they seem to drop off the radar" D.S. Stone closed his tablet.

"What, all three of them?"

"Yes sir, there's no further sighting of any of them" D.S. Stone confirmed, sadly.

"Well, that's than then!" D.I. Wood brushed his hands together, dismissively, "we waste no more time on this, Sergeant. We've got better things to do than waste our days chasing necklaces that might never have been nicked, in the first place"

"Never been nicked?" D.S. Stone raised his eyebrows.

"Yeah, that's right" D.I. Wood nodded, "it could be an inside job. I'm still not ruling out Laurence *'I had nothing to do with it'* Hamble. Or, it could be that Scrivener bloke doing an insurance swindle. Either way, it's not worth us wasting our valuable time on it"

"Well, yes, possibly, but…"

"Oh flaming hell, now what?" D.I. Wood snapped, irritably.

"Well, I've been going through the National Crime Database…" D.S. Stone began.

"Isn't there a life you should be living, Sergeant?"

"I'm sure there is, sir" D.S. Stone responded, with feeling, "but I think I've found something"

"What?"

"Six months ago, in Leeds, a virtually identical theft from a High Street jeweller's. They never caught the culprits, but the descriptions are a good match for our gang"

"Bugger!" D.I. Wood said, with feeling, "That's all we're short of!"

Chapter Fourteen
A Night To Remember

"It's Saturday, Archie" Samantha Knight announced, listlessly, to her work companion, one hand propping up her chin as she gazed, blankly, at the laptop screen.

"Takes a good 'un to get past you, don't it?" Archibald Thurble chuckled from the depths of the sports pages of his newspaper.

"You know what I mean!" Samantha snapped.

"Yeah, you're on about Mr. O., again" Archibald nodded.

"Well, yes, and with good reason!"

"What are you doing here, any road, on a Saturday? He can't have you in for overtime, surely?"

"No, I just thought I'd come in and...well, I suppose I hoped I might have the chance to have a word with him"

"Mr. O.?"

"Josiah, yes" Samantha nodded, "I think he's making the most terrible mistake. I just have this dreadful feeling about it all"

"He's not going to take any romantic advice from you, now, is he?" Archibald pointed out, with a grin.

"No, I know" Samantha sighed, "I feel so helpless!"

"I don't know why you're getting yourself in such a state" Archibald shrugged, "he's only going for a posh nosh at her place"

Dead Reckoning

"Yes, but he's not driving himself…" Samantha began.

"Well, he can't, can he, not with his…" Archibald raised a wrist.

"I know, but he could have asked you to drive him. Instead, he's going to be held hostage by Cruella DeVille and her henchman! She was the villain in '101 Dalmatians'" Samantha explained.

"Oh yeah!" Archibald nodded, "I remember now. I can't watch that film, makes me cry every time. I think it's that bit where the pup goes "I'm hungry, mother"" He gave the pup a creditable American accent, "does me 'ead in, that does" He shook his head. "Any road, I think you're putting it a bit strong; he's just going for a bite to eat and then he'll come home. Nowt to it!"

"Well, call it 'woman's intuition' or rampant jealousy, or anything you want! I just have a bad feeling about it all" Samantha scowled and attacked the laptop keyboard as if she held a personal grudge.

* * * *

Saturday evening saw the subject of their conversation pacing up and down his hallway, formally dressed and in a state of some agitation. Whilst, on one hand, he had been eagerly awaiting this night, he was also acutely aware that it might well be a crucial stage on the journey to resuming his relationship with Jeanette DeVille, and he wasn't entirely sure how he felt about that.

If he was honest with himself, he was beginning to regret having agreed to be driven to Evanley Hall. On the whole he would have felt much more comfortable with Archibald doing the driving but Jeanette wouldn't hear of it.

A sharp rap on the front door made him jump. He proceeded to open it and there stood the lugubrious figure of Hames, Mrs. DeVille's butler, chauffeur and general factotum.

"Good evening, sir" He said, funereally, and bowed slightly, "I have come, on Mrs. DeVille's instructions, to take you to the Hall"

"Ah, yes, thank you Hames" Josiah briefly checked his appearance in the hall mirror, frowned at what he saw but shrugged and locked the door behind him. In the meantime, Hames strode down the steps to the waiting car and stood with the rear door open.

"Thank you, but I would be quite happy to sit in the front" Josiah offered.

"That would not be seemly, sir" Hames frowned and gestured toward the back seat.

"Oh, right!" Josiah felt distinctly uncomfortable but settled himself into the car, anyway.

The limousine may have seen better days, from its internal appearance, but it moved smoothly enough into the Saturday evening traffic.

"It's been a particularly pleasant day, has it not?" Josiah ventured, as a means of starting a conversation.

"Most acceptable, sir" Hames agreed.

"I must say, I've been looking forward to this evening. I gather Mrs. DeVille is renowned for her hospitality" Josiah went on.

"I have heard it said, sir" Hames nodded.

There was a long pause as they drove out of town and Josiah struggled to think of anything else to say.

Dead Reckoning

"Not much traffic about, for a Saturday evening, is there?" He suggested, at a loss for anything else.

Hames twisted around in his seat and regarded his passenger, seriously, then turned back.

"With respect, sir" He intoned, "it is neither necessary, nor desirous, that you should engage me in conversation"

"Oh, fine!" Josiah responded, deeply embarrassed. He slumped back in his seat and watched the countryside speed past, thinking how much more pleasant it would have been to be chatting with Archibald, however inane the conversation.

After about an hour of this awkward silence, the limousine finally turned into the dark, potholed and overgrown lane leading up to the Hall. Almost instantly, a ragged figure, carrying a shotgun, jumped out in front of them, causing Josiah to jump in his seat. The woman held her position, in front of the car, bringing them to a halt. She then lurched around to the driver's door and Hames, with an audible sigh, wound down the window.

"You ain't seen my kittens, 'ave yer?" The apparition enquired.

"Jeannie, you know you are not supposed to do this, don't you now?" Hames said, not unkindly.

"Is 'e going up the big 'all?" She nodded toward Josiah, cowering in the back seat.

"That really is none of your concern, Jeannie" Hames said, firmly.

Jeannie scuttled around to Josiah's window and knocked on it with the shotgun. Despite himself, he wound the window down a little.

"Yes?" He said, hoarsely.

"You b'aint be goin' up there, be yer? Not with 'er?" The woman nodded toward the Hall beyond.

"I have the honour of being invited for dinner, yes" Josiah smiled, weakly.

"No good'll come of it, you mark my words!" The woman shrieked, "You get yoursel' away, while yer can!"

Hames suddenly appeared beside her, grabbed her by the elbow and steered her back toward her rundown cottage.

"Now, come on Jeannie, this will NOT do" He said, determinedly, "time for your pills, I shouldn't wonder"

"I don't want none of yer potions, d'yer 'ear me!"

"One moment, if you please, sir" Hames said, with some difficulty, to Josiah, as he pushed a struggling Jeannie onward, "I would wind up your window, if I were you, sir" He suggested.

Josiah did as he was asked and watched Jeannie disappear into the cottage, closely followed by Hames. There were some crashes and bangs before Hames reappeared, looking somewhat dishevelled, and locked the cottage door with a key he produced from his coat pocket.

"I'm so sorry you had to see that, sir" he said, flatly, taking his place in the driver's seat.

"You've locked her in?" Josiah observed.

"For her own good, sir, as I'm sure you will agree" Hames nodded, and restarted the car, "She is a poor soul, but we do our best, sir"

"Does she work for the estate?"

Dead Reckoning

"Heavens no, sir!" Hames gave a slight smile, "not for many a long year. She will be fine, once she's had her pills"

The car eased its way along the road and up the gravel driveway, coming to rest by the grand front door. Hames nipped smartly out of the car and, with a flourish, opened Josiah's door.

"If you will walk this way, sir?" He motioned to the huge, oak door, which swung open at that moment.

Josiah, somewhat unnerved by recent events and the silent car journey, eased out of the limousine and stumbled toward the door. The darkness of the entrance hall, in contrast to the early evening sunlight, temporarily clouded his vision but he soon made out Jeanette, standing by the grand staircase looking immaculate. To her right, was Precious.

"Josiah, how nice of you to come" Jeanette smiled, sweetly, "Precious, you know, of course" She indicated her daughter.

"Miss DeVille, a pleasure to meet you again" Josiah bowed slightly. Precious blushed and, to Josiah's surprise, attempted a curtsy.

"Hames, please help Mr. Oakshott with his coat and gloves" Jeanette instructed.

Josiah felt Hames grip his coat collar, lightly, from behind, but then there was an odd sensation, as if his elbows were being pinned behind him. That, however, was nothing compared to the sharp knock on the back of his head, incredible pain and a blinding light.

For Josiah Oakshott, the evening had come to an unexpected close.

Chapter Fifteen
Monday, Monday

Samantha Knight dumped her handbag and laptop case onto the shelf which constituted her office, in the store room, and looked around for her partner-in-crime, Archibald Thurble. At this time on a Monday morning, she expected to find him hunkered down in a corner somewhere, gradually coming to terms with the start of a working week, but he was nowhere to be seen.

Deciding that the day could only be improved by the addition of coffee, she headed for the kitchenette. The crashing and banging that preceded her arrival, indicated that this was where the object of her search was *in situ*.

"Archibald? Is that you?" She called out.

"Yep, and before you say anything, I'm on it!" Archibald crashed the filled kettle onto its stand and flicked the switch.

"You're on it? What is this 'it' that you're on?"

"I know what you're going to say, and I'm doing it" Archibald folded his arms and glared at the kettle, which resolutely declined to boil, instantly.

"Well, you're one ahead of me there, Archie" Samantha shook her head, "even I don't know what I'm going to say!"

"You're going to say '*Why don't you take Mr. O. his tea and biscuits and find out what happened on Saturday night*', "Archibald did a reasonable impression of Samantha, "that's what you're going to say, and I'm already on it"

Dead Reckoning

"So I can see!" Samantha said, with a grin, and then frowned, "Actually, I'm not sure that I want to know what happened on Saturday night" She admitted.

"You're joking!" Archibald looked astonished, "I thought you'd be gagging to know"

"I think I could live without the gory details" Samantha said, sadly, "but I would like to know that he's ok"

"Like I say," Archibald said, adding the now boiling water to the individual brown teapot, "I'm on it"

"You're a gem, Archie" Samantha grinned.

"Me mam says I'm a treasure" Archibald nodded.

"I'm sure she does, Archie"

"Yeah, she reckons I ought to be buried"

Archibald trotted off with the tea things as Samantha headed back to the store room to set up her makeshift desk. A few minutes later, Archibald reappeared, a look of panic on his face.

"He's not there!"

"What?" Samantha looked puzzled, "You mean Josiah?"

"Mr. O., yeah, he's not there" Archibald nodded, frantically.

"Perhaps he's just stepped out, for a moment?" Samantha suggested.

"No, there's no coat, no briefcase, nothing!" Archibald flapped his arms, "He's not there!"

"Come on, let's take another look" Samantha led the way back to Josiah's office. Knocking, timorously, on the door, she poked her head into the dark and deserted office. She stepped inside, closely followed by Archibald. The tea things had been set on the desk, but otherwise there was no sign of any habitation.

"He's not here" Samantha announced.

"What did I tell you!" Archibald flapped his arms, again, and looked exasperated.

"Have you checked if his car is in the yard?"

"No!" Archibald looked pleased with this sudden flash of inspiration and shot off to investigate. Moments later, he returned. "It's not there!" He announced, glumly.

"Well then, I think, by a process of elimination, we can definitely say – he's not here!" Samantha put her hands on her hips and reviewed the empty office. "This isn't like him. Someone should go and see if he's alright" She looked at Archibald, pointedly.

"Oh no!" Archibald held his hands up and shook his head, violently, "don't look at me! I'm not going, no way!"

"Oh, come on, Archie, be a pal" Samantha said, pleadingly, "he could be ill, or anything"

"He could be with that Mrs. DeVille an' all, and I don't want to run into her, thanks very much!" Archibald folded his arms and looked resolute.

"Ring him, then" Samantha suggested.

"I'm not ringing him!" Archibald looked aghast at the suggestion, "you ring him!"

"I can't, can I? If he saw it was me, he probably wouldn't answer and, given where I am in the 'pecking order' here, I can hardly be checking up on the boss, now can I?"

Dead Reckoning

They both looked thoughtful.

"I know!" Archibald said suddenly, obviously delighted with his idea, "We'll get Mr. Strine to ring him, he's sort of next in line, isn't he?"

"Well, good luck with that!" Samantha shook her head, "I don't think Mr. Strine does initiative"

"I'll go an' ask him" Archibald hurried off whilst Samantha slumped into Josiah's chair. After a few minutes, and some raised voices in the distance, he returned. "He won't ring him" he said, sulkily.

"Told you" Samantha shook her head, "Ok then, Archibald, it's down to you and me"

"What is?"

"We're going to have to go round there" Samantha stood up and straightened her jacket. With a determined air, she marched to the office door. "Coming, Archibald?" She raised an eyebrow and a dejected Archibald set off in her wake, grumbling fit to burst.

A little while later, they were standing at the bottom of the stone steps leading up to Josiah Oakshott's Victorian terraced town house.

"We should ring the bell" Samantha said, with more confidence than she actually felt.

"You ring the ruddy bell" Her companion suggested, grumpily.

Samantha frowned at him.

"Oh, I know! Is his car in the garage?" She asked, suddenly.

"Good idea! I'll go and look" Archibald grinned, delighted to do anything that didn't involve ringing the doorbell. A few minutes later, he returned, brushing dust from his jacket and trousers and looking distinctly fed up.

"Is it there?" Samantha asked.

"Yeah, it's there" Archibald nodded, "I had to stand on this box to look through the window, didn't I? Then it only went and fell to bits, didn't it?" He said, bitterly.

"Right then, nothing for it, we've got to ring the bell" Samantha took a deep breath, marched up the stairs and pressed the bell push, firmly. In the distance they could hear the bell chiming, as it echoed around the hall. Samantha skittered back down the stairs and rejoined Archibald. They both waited, with bated breath, for the door to open and reveal the furious countenance of their employer, but nothing happened.

"I suppose I could try it again?" Samantha said, doubtfully.

"You'd have thought he'd have heard that, wouldn't you?" Archibald observed.

"Hmm, I'll give it one more go" Samantha jogged up the steps and tried again. Once more the chimes echoed around the empty hallway and, once more, absolutely nothing happened.

Samantha and Archibald looked at each other.

"That's that then, I guess?" Archibald went to start walking back.

"Well..." Samantha began.

"What?" Archibald responded, with deep suspicion.

"It's just...I do still have a key!" Samantha admitted, with a blush.

"A key?" Archibald looked astonished.

Dead Reckoning

"Yes, I never quite got around to giving it back to him, and he didn't ask, so I sort of...hung on to it" She admitted.

"We can't just break in!" Archibald said, wide-eyed.

"Well, it's hardly 'breaking in' if I've got a key, is it?"

"I dunno!" Archibald flapped his arms and shook his head, "It's Mr. O.'s place. He'd have a fit!"

"Yes, that's one way of looking at it" Samantha conceded, "but, think about it, what if he was lying unconscious in there, eh?"

"Do you think he is?" Archibald looked astonished.

"I don't know, that's the point!" Samantha shrugged, "Unless we go in, we'll never know. Come on!" Samantha rummaged through her handbag and produced an old door key. She marched back up the steps and turned the key, carefully. Archibald, meanwhile, was busily scanning the street for irate neighbours or suspicious police officers.

"Come on, we're in!" Samantha announced, edging the door open. Archibald followed, reluctantly, tugging his jacket sleeves at a frenetic rate, as he always did at times of high anxiety.

The hallway was dark and empty.

"You try the Living Room, I'll check the Kitchen" Samantha whispered.

"I'm not going nowhere" Archibald shook his head, firmly, "not on me own, I'm not. He'd have my guts for garters!"

"Alright, we'll BOTH check the Living Room and the Kitchen, then" Samantha sighed.

Samantha eased open the Living Room door, which creaked, causing them both to jump. The room itself, lit only by the weak light leaching in through the front window, seemed exceptionally gloomy. It was also devoid of any sign of Josiah Oakshott. The Kitchen, at the end of the Hall, was similarly empty.

"There's a cup and saucer on the draining board, but nothing else" Samantha observed, picking the cup up, "and its bone dry, which means it's been here some time. I think he made himself a drink before he went out on Saturday and then, nothing since"

"Well, maybe, but we don't *know* that, do we?" Archibald pointed out.

"I'm going to check upstairs; you wait down here in case he comes back" Samantha announced.

"Oh, thanks a lot!" Archibald spluttered.

"There's nothing to worry about" Samantha reassured, "if he does turn up, I'll take the blame. After all, I couldn't be much less in his favour now, could I?"

"Yeah, that's a point" Archibald nodded, "makes a nice change from it always being me what's in the cart!"

"I'm glad I have my uses" Samantha smirked as she made her way, gingerly, up the stairs.

Archibald dithered in the hallway, jumping a foot in the air at every creak and bang.

Eventually, Samantha reappeared.

"Right, I've been in every bedroom and there's no sign. His bed's not been slept in and everything's very tidy. I don't think he's been here since Saturday" Samantha looked worried.

"Oh well, not a lot we can do then, is there?" Archibald said, with a degree of relief, and headed for the door.

"Well, not here, no" Samantha agreed, "that's why we need to go to the Police Station"

"You're having a laugh!" Archibald looked astonished.

"No, Archibald, I'm not" Samantha looked around at the dark and deserted house, "I don't think there's much to laugh at, here, do you?"

Chapter Sixteen
Can't Get Used to Losing You

"You'll never guess who's downstairs!" D.S. Stone grinned at his boss, who, with his leg up on one chair, looked less than comfortable.

"Lots of blokes in uniforms, am I close?"

"Oh, come on, humour me!" D.S. Stone pleaded.

"I don't have to humour you, Stoney. I'm your boss, if anything, you should be humouring me!" D.I. Wood eased his leg off the chair and winced as his foot touched the floor, "Those bloody pills from the hospital don't make any bloody difference" He grumbled.

"You have to remember to take them" D.S. Stone pointed out, primly.

"I DO remember to take them!" D.I. Wood glared at his subordinate, "Well, most of the time, anyway"

"Are you going to guess?"

"No, I am not going to guess, Stoney. If you've got something to tell me, either spit it out or clear off!" D.I. Wood snarled.

"It's only that woman, Frankie Knight's missus" D.S. Stone looked smug.

"Bloody cheek! What the hell's she doing here?" D.I. Wood snapped, and then looked hopeful, for the first time for weeks. "Has she come to confess?"

"No such luck!" D.S. Stone shook his head, "She wants to report a missing person"

"She's got a nerve! If it's Frankie she's lost, tell her to try HMP., they've got him banged up somewhere"

"No, it's not Frankie. She's lost that bloke who runs the Funeral Director's" D.S. Stone studied a piece of paper he was holding, "Josiah Oakshott"

"Oh, bugger me, not them again!" D.I. Wood raised his eyes to the ceiling, "You can tell her to get stuffed, I'm not chasing around after those two and that's final!"

"Do you want me to have a word, sir?"

"If you must!" D.I. Wood winced with pain, again, and adjusted himself in his chair, "but don't waste any time on this, Stoney. Get the details and chuck her out. Bloody nerve of her, coming in here, large as life!"

"I'll go and see what it's all about" D.S. Stone made a discreet exit.

* * * *

"I don't like it in 'ere" Archibald grumbled, as he fidgeted next to Samantha on the plastic bench.

"I'm not a big fan, myself" Samantha shook her head, "and don't forget, I was here for a lot longer than you were!"

"Yeah, but…" More fidgeting, "I didn't reckon I'd be back here, already!"

"Neither did I" Samantha looked around, gloomily, "but, needs must, as they say"

"Who do?" Archibald looked puzzled.

"Who do what?"

"Say that what you said, about that 'knees rust' stuff"

"No, it's not 'knees rust', it's 'needs must'" Samantha pinched the bridge of her nose, and reflected on the amazing patience of Josiah Oakshott.

"Oh, only I thought it explained all that creaking and groaning what goes on"

"What would explain what?" Samantha shook her head.

"That 'knees rust' lark" Archibald explained, "you should hear me Nan's knees, they make a hell of a racket when she tries to get up. Not that she *can* get up, not most of the time"

"I think it's from a saying, '*needs must when the devil drives*'" Samantha said, searching her memory.

"Drives what?"

"Pardon?" Samantha looked pained.

"What is it, what the devil drives? Only I'd have thought it'd have been tricky, what with his tail and all that. You'd have to put a hole in the seat or summat, don't you reckon?"

"I can't really say I'd thought about it" Samantha rubbed her brow, "to be honest, Archie, I don't know much about the saying. I'm sure Josiah could give you chapter and verse"

"Yeah, he would an' all" Archibald grinned, "not that he's been his usual self, not lately any road. What with that Mrs. Devil and stuff"

"Perhaps it's her that the saying's about" Samantha winked, "she did insist on him being driven, didn't she?"

"D'you think?" Archibald was wide-eyed with amazement.

"Erm, probably not" Samantha conceded, "but it is a thought, isn't it?"

Dead Reckoning

"Mrs. Knight, how can I help you?" D.S. Stone had appeared whilst they were deep in conversation.

"Oh!" Samantha jumped, a little, "Sorry, didn't see you there! Detective Sergeant Stone, isn't it?"

"Yes, it is. So, what's brought you to us, today, eh?"

"I told your Desk Sergeant, we seem to have lost Mr. Oakshott" Samantha explained.

D.S. Stone opened a manilla folder and consulted the single sheet of paper within it.

"Yes, so I see." He nodded, "it says here that you *think* he's been missing since Saturday?"

"Yes, that's correct" Samantha agreed.

"He went off on a date" Archibald supplied.

"Did he?" D.S. Stone raised an eyebrow, "And you think he hasn't been home, since?"

"I don't think so" Samantha shook her head.

"Mrs. Knight, with the best will in the world" D.S. Stone sighed, and settled himself beside Samantha, "Mr. Oakshott is a grown man. He's quite entitled to have the odd romantic liaison. Very odd, I would imagine" He commented, "Anyway, if that's what he wants, that's what he wants. It might be surprising, but there's no accounting for tastes, is there? And, bear in mind that you don't know *for sure* that he hasn't been back since last Saturday, do you?"

"Well, not for sure, no..." Samantha conceded.

"There you are, then!" D.S. Stone smiled a reassuring smile, "For all you know, he could be anywhere around Merkin-under-Heathwood, living the high life. Even if he hasn't been home…"

"He hasn't, I'm convinced of it" Samantha said, determinedly.

"Well, even if he hasn't, my guess would be that he's just having a rather good time and hasn't noticed how long he's been away. I would bet good money that he'll turn up, any day now, with lipstick on his collar, a faraway look in his eyes and a happy smile on his face." D.S. Stone resisted the temptation to pat her hand, but it was a close-run thing. "You mark my words, it happens all of the time" He concluded, although he was unable to think of a single instance.

"But, it's just not like him. He wouldn't go missing! You know what he's like, his work is his world!" Samantha sniffled.

"He's always there, that's right enough" Archibald nodded.

"Romance does funny things to people" D.S. Stone pointed out, blushing slightly at the memory of how Chantelle had taken him for a mug on the ferry, "particularly these late-blossoming romances. I wouldn't worry too much about it, if I were you" He got up to leave.

"So, you're not going to do anything?" Samantha glared at him.

"No, Mrs. Knight, we're not" D.S. Stone shook his head, "if he hasn't shown up, say, by the end of the week, let us know and we might make a few more enquiries but, for now…"

"Well, thanks a lot!" Samantha jumped up from her seat, grabbed Archibald by the elbow, and stormed out.

"You're welcome!" D.S. Stone shouted after her, sarcastically.

Out on the street, Samantha dabbed her eyes and took a deep breath.

"Well, Archibald, it looks like we're on our own"

"He did say he'd do summat if he wasn't back by the end of the week" Archibald pointed out.

"Anything could have happened, by then!" Samantha snapped.

"I don't know what else we can do?" Archibald flapped his arms.

"I think I do" Samantha said, grimly.

Chapter Seventeen
Words

Samantha Knight marched into the premises of Oakshott and Underwood, strode down the corridor and swept into Josiah Oakshott's office. Behind her trailed a perfectly miserable Archibald Thurble.

"Right, Archie" Samantha announced, placing her handbag firmly on Josiah's desk, "this is what we're going to do"

Archibald peered around the office in the obvious hope that Mr. O. would magically appear from somewhere.

"He's not back, then?" He said, after a swift perusal.

"No, and I didn't expect him to be" Samantha shook her head, sadly, "did you?"

"Well, I sort of hoped..." Archibald trailed off and shrugged his shoulders.

"Despite what the police say, I think something's happened to him" Samantha said, firmly, "but, in the meantime, we've got to prioritise. That means appointing someone to run the place in Josiah's absence"

"That'll be Mr. Strine, won't it?" Archibald suggested.

"Well..." Samantha began, settling herself in Josiah's chair, "yes, I would agree, at least as far as the operational side of the business goes. Actually managing funerals and so on, you know?" Samantha nodded, "but, when it comes to sales and customer relations..." She looked at Archibald, quizzically.

"Yeah, he's not the best with people" Archibald conceded.

Dead Reckoning

"So, in Josiah's absence, I'm going to assume control"

Archibald's eyebrows shot up. "Are you sure that's a good idea? I mean, what will Mr. O. say?"

"Nothing, not at the moment anyway. He's not here, is he?" Samantha opened a file on the desk and studied it, "Besides, I ran the place whilst you two were galivanting in Spain, with no problems." She stared at Archibald who was tugging his sleeves with obvious agitation, "Look, Archie, there are a number of potential clients due to come in over the next few days to discuss funeral details, we can't take the risk of losing them, just because Josiah has gone AWOL"

"AWOL?" Archibald looked deeply puzzled, his lips moved as he tried to spell out the word, "Is that like some sort of owl?" He asked, eventually.

"No, Archie" Samantha sighed, "it's an acronym"

"Is it?" Archibald looked thoughtful, "is that good, or bad?"

"It's neither" Samantha shook her head, "it means a word that's made up of the initial letters of other words"

"Why would you want to do that?"

"Well, it saves saying all of those other words" Samantha's patience was beginning to wear a bit thin. "Like BURMA"

"BURMA? Isn't that a country, or summat?"

"Yes, well, it was at one time, but..."

"I don't know why they have to go around mucking about with the names of things" Archibald grumbled, "why can't they leave stuff alone?"

"I'm not really sure of the history" Samantha admitted, "but, anyway, I wasn't talking about the country..."

"Yes, you was!" Archibald asserted, "you were on about Burma, I heard you"

"No, Archibald!" Samantha rubbed her forehead and began to see Josiah's point of view, "we were talking about acronyms, and I made the mistake of mentioning 'BURMA', which was an acronym that people used to put on the back of envelopes, to their sweethearts"

"Why would they put the name of a country on a...love letter, style of thing?" Archibald asked, with obvious embarrassment.

"Because, in this instance, it stands for something"

"What, like 'faith, hope and charity', that sort of thing?" Archibald dredged from his memory.

"Pardon?" It was Samantha's turn to look puzzled, "Oh, you're thinking of a sort of motto, aren't you?"

"Am I?" Archibald frowned.

"Yes, but that's not what I meant" Samantha took a deep breath, and tried again, "Each letter of BURMA stands for another word..." There was a knock on the door and she automatically said, "Come in"

"What are them, then?" Archibald asked.

"Be Undressed and Ready My Angel" Samantha explained, with a sense of deep trepidation.

Mr. Strine, who had just walked in, looked shell-shocked.

"Sorry, miss, sorry, Archie" He flustered, "I 'ope as 'ow I'm not interrupting nowt?" He looked, frantically, from one to the other.

Dead Reckoning

Samantha placed her head in her hands and counted to ten.

"No, Mr. Strine, you are not interrupting anything" She assured him, "I was just explaining to Archibald, here, that I will be assuming control of the business during Mr. Oakshott's unforeseen absence"

"Right!" Mr. Strine nodded his head, slowly, "Fair enough." He pondered for a moment, and then looked concerned, "You don't want me to get undressed an' all, do yer?"

"No, that won't be necessary, Mr. Strine" Samantha giggled, and realised that she was borderline hysterical.

"It's a country. Only, it's not now" Archibald attempted to explain.

"What is?" Mr. Strine asked, now thoroughly confused.

"Burma!" Archibald answered, laconically.

"Oh, I know about Burma" Mr. Strine said, darkly, "me dad fought there in the last lot. He reckoned it were sticky"

"Ah well, that explains it then," Archibald nodded, "'cause Mrs. Knight reckons you stick it on the back of envelopes"

"Do yer?" Mr. Strine looked surprised, "What, like RSVP?"

"Oh god, no" Samantha muttered under breath, "don't start him off again"

"Russervup?" Archibald attempted this new word.

"Yeah," Mr. Strine nodded, "it's foreign for 'are yer comin', or what?'"

"Yes, that, sort of, sums it up" Samantha nodded, grateful for a simple explanation.

"I don't see why they 'ave to make everything so ruddy complicated!" Archibald grumbled.

"Yer 'ave to 'ave a bit of foreign" Mr. Strine said, confident in his expert knowledge, "makes stuff look sophisticated, ain't that right, Mrs.?"

"You've probably got a point, Mr. Strine" Samantha nodded, "now, are you happy to continue to oversee the operational side of the business?"

"Erm…" Mr. Strine looked bewildered.

"By which I mean, are you happy to take care of running the funerals and all the funeral preparation, if I look after dealing with prospective and existing clients?" Samantha gave him her best winning smile.

"Oh, right!" Mr. Strine looked relieved, "yeah, that sounds fine and dandy, miss"

"Then that's all sorted, then" Samantha said, with a sigh. "If you will excuse us, Mr. Strine, I need a brief word with Archibald"

"Right, right" Mr. Strine nodded and backed towards the office door, then, turning to Archibald, he whispered "you keep an 'and on yer 'a'penny, my lad, if'n yer know what's good for yer" before scuttling for the exit.

"Now, Archie…" Samantha began.

"I'm not gettin' undressed!" Archibald said, stoutly. "I know all about what that 'Sexual Harris' meant and I'm not 'aving none of it. I'm right there with the U2 lot"

"Sexual Harris?" Samantha had the distinct impression that this conversation was getting ever further away from her.

"Yep, that Australian bloke, went to jail for it, and I don't have to put up with it" Archibald said, firmly.

Dead Reckoning

"You wouldn't mean 'sexual harassment' by any chance, would you?"

"Yeah, that's the bunny!" Archibald nodded.

"Well, I can assure you that I have no intention, now or at any time in the future, of sexually harassing you, Archibald, so you can relax on that score. You've lost me with the reference to U2 though, I must say"

"It's a wotsit…a sisterhood, innit?"

"Really? I thought it was a rock group but…oh, hang on, you mean MeToo, don't you?"

"Well, yeah, it's you what I've been talking about!" Archibald looked even more puzzled.

"No, not 'me too', I mean the movement 'MeToo'" Samantha looked at Archibald who was quivering with a mixture of apprehension and self-righteousness, "Archie," she said, as sympathetically as she could manage, "I can assure you, I have absolutely no interest in you divesting yourself of your garments"

"Well, you say that now…" Archibald began, in a hurt tone.

"I say it now and I will continue to say it, Archie" Samantha smiled warmly at him, "now then, what we need to sort out is what we're going to do about Josiah?"

"Well, you heard the cop…the policeman" Archibald tugged a sleeve, again, "he can't do nothin' 'til the end of the week"

"*He* can't, no" Samantha nodded, "but, that doesn't mean to say that *we* can't do something"

"Like what?" Archibald asked, with some trepidation.

"Ah, now that's what I was coming to, Archie" Samantha beamed and steepled her fingers.

Chapter Eighteen
My Girl and Me

Archibald Thurble burst out of the door of, what had until recently been, Josiah Oakshott's office, launching himself into the corridor beyond. With ragged breaths, he yelled into the office behind him,

"No, I won't!"

And slammed the door shut.

Mr. Strine, who had been observing events from a few yards away, sidled up to Archibald.

"You alright, Archie, me lad?" He asked, solicitously, eyes flicking from side to side.

"No!" Archibald responded, shaking his head and breathing heavily.

"What's she done to yer, lad?" Mr. Strine looked very concerned, "'cause I'll tell yer, whatever it is, me and the lads are behind yer, all the way!" He said, emphatically, then, after a moment's thought, added, "'cept Egbert, 'e says 'e'll be in front of yer, on account of 'ow 'e's not adverse to a bit of sexual 'arassment, if there's some going"

"It's…it's nothing like that" Archibald gulped.

"I 'ope yer kept yer 'and on yer 'a'penny?" Mr. Strine frowned.

"I don't know" Archibald shook his head, "I don't know if I've got one, or even where it is!" He wailed.

"Ah well," Mr. Strine nodded, "in that case, yer prob'ly all right" He conceded. "So, what's she want yer to do then, eh?"

"She wants..." Archibald gulped and tried to contain his emotions.

"Go on, lad" Mr. Strine encouraged, "I'll have the lads out on strike, if need be"

"She wants...she wants me to visit my girlfriend" Archibald managed, at last.

Mr. Strine looked at him, blankly.

"Visit yer girlfriend?" He said, eventually.

Archibald nodded.

"Don't get me wrong, Archie, me lad" Mr. Strine rubbed his grizzled chin, "and I may 'ave got the wrong end of the stick, 'ere, if yer know what I mean. But, speakin' as I find, that don't seem to be too much to ask, if yer get me drift?"

"I don't want to go!" Archibald wailed, again.

"Well, she's *your* girlfriend" Mr. Strine shrugged his shoulders, "I suppose you know best, all I can say is, if it was my girlfriend...werl!" A faint light of fond memory appeared in Mr. Strine's eyes.

"You don't...you don't know where she lives!" Archie gulped.

"Well, no, 'course I don't" Mr. Strine shook his head, deeply aware that this conversation was definitely getting away from him, "why would I? She's your girlfriend!"

The office door opened, at that moment, and Samantha Knight appeared.

"Ah, Archibald, Mr. Strine" She nodded to each, in turn.

Dead Reckoning

"Mrs." Mr. Strine attempted to tug a missing forelock, "Archie 'ere reckons as 'ow yer tryin' to force 'im to visit 'is girlfriend" He realised, even as he was saying this, just how ridiculous it sounded.

"Well, I think the word 'force' is, perhaps, a little strong" Samantha began, smoothing down her skirt.

"You said as 'ow it was the right thing for the business!" Archibald said, accusingly.

"Well, yes, I think it is" Samantha nodded.

"What, 'im seein' 'is girlfriend?" Mr. Strine looked thoroughly confused.

"In this case, yes," Samantha agreed, "not because of *who* she is, but because of *where* she is"

"And where's that, then?"

"The same place that Josiah went to, last Saturday"

"Ah! I see!" Mr. Stine nodded, sagely.

"Why can't you send 'im, instead?" Archibald sniffled, jerking a thumb in Mr. Strine's direction.

"Ah, now, let's not be too 'asty, Archie!" Mr. Strine said, hurriedly, "just 'ang on a moment, it is *your* girlfriend, when all's said an' done!"

"You said you were right behind me!" Archibald pointed out.

"Well, yeah" Mr. Strine nodded, "but that was afore I 'ad all the facts"

"Archie, all you have to do is to go and see Precious..." Samantha began but was interrupted by Mr. Strine stifling a giggle, she frowned at him and ploughed on, "and just see if she's got anything to say about Mr. O. If not, then there's no harm done and that's an end to it"

"Does 'e get to use a company car?" Mr. Strine asked.

"Of course!" Samantha nodded, "expenses and everything"

"Seems to me, you'd be a fool not to, young Archie" Mr. Strine urged, "'Ow often is it yer get to see yer girlfriend, all expenses paid, eh?" He nudged Archibald with his elbow, and leered.

"Alright!" Archibald snapped, "I'll go! But if she says nowt about Mr. O., then I'm straight back home"

"Of course, Archie" Samantha patted him on the shoulder.

"Are you coming with me?"

"Well, I would, but we've got potential clients coming in all day, today. I need to be here, I'm afraid." Samantha gave him a weak smile.

"How about 'im?" Archibald nodded toward Mr. Strine, who jumped back as if someone had delivered an electric shock.

"Same problem, Archie. I need Mr. Strine to oversee the practical side of preparing our clients for their funerals" Samantha said, much to Mr. Strine's relief.

"So, I've got to go on me tod?" Archibald looked thoroughly miserable.

"It's yer girlfriend, Archie, this..." Mr. Strine looked at Samantha, questioningly,

"Precious" Samanta supplied, Mr. Strine stifled a snort and continued,

"Yeah, 'er. What's there to be worried about?"

"It's not just 'er though, is it?" Archibald thrust his hands deep into his pockets and looked dejected.

Dead Reckoning

"If you're in any doubt, you just come straight home" Samantha patted his shoulder again, but he shrugged her off.

"Easy for you to say!" He grumbled.

"Look, you've got your phone, haven't you?" Samantha asked. Archibald nodded, sulkily, "Well, there you are then! Any trouble at all, you just ring me, and Mr. Strine and we will come running, won't we, Mr. Strine?" She beamed at her colleague, who backed off, considerably.

"Ah, now, don't get me wrong, 'course I would" Mr. Strine held his hands up and continued to back along the corridor, "only, I got this knee, see? I wouldn't be no good if it comes to no runnin'" He explained, and vanished back into the workshop.

"Well, *I'll* come running then" Samantha grinned.

"I'm not 'appy" Archibald grizzled.

"I know you're not, Archie, and I do value your help with this, honestly I do" She gave him a hug.

"You're not after me 'a'penny, are you?" Archibald muttered, from the depths of the hug.

"I think we can safely say that I'm not, Archie!" Samantha released him from the hug and winked.

Chapter Nineteen
Love Potion No. 9

Archibald folded his arms over the top of the steering wheel and rested his chin on the result. There wasn't really much else to do, given the stationary nature of the traffic. He sighed and watched a bit of sweet wrapper, caught by the wind, spiralling and dancing across the carriageways.

In some ways, he wasn't too concerned about being stuck in a traffic jam. At least it put off the awful moment when he would, eventually, arrive at Evanley Hall and have to decide what the heck it was that he was going to do. On the other hand, he could think of better things to do than be stuck in a black limousine that was getting steadily warmer as the day progressed.

Bored, he pressed the button on the radio, something he would never have dared to do if Josiah Oakshott had been present.

"Ok" said a cheerful radio voice, *"well you've got thirty seconds to say your 'hello's', starting from…now…"*

"Oh, for…" He remembered where he was and modified his language, "…pete's sake!" He stabbed at the button and the radio fell silent. 'Why do they have to do that? It's so ruddy boring!' He grumbled. He remembered that Mr. O. had said that, people like to hear their names read out on the radio, but he wasn't convinced. 'If he'd have said 'Archibald Thurble' amongst all that lot, I'm not sure I'd have noticed' He reflected. He calculated that thirty seconds must have elapsed, so he tried the radio again:

Dead Reckoning

"particiipantsmustbe18oroverfulltsandcsapplyandcanbefoundonourweb sitewww.conartists.com..."

A voice gabbled. He stabbed the button again. 'How come, whenever you turn on a commercial radio station, it's always during an advert?' He moaned, 'and where do they get these people who can talk that fast? Or do they just say it normally and then speed it up?' The verbal equivalent of small print and just as understandable, he thought. He decided to give it one more go:

"and make sure you answer within five rings and, don't forget, you must say 'Give Me The Dosh' and we will transfer £250,000 straight to your bank account..."

"Flamin' hell!" He chuntered, and switched off the radio, once more. 'I reckon it's cruel' He thought, 'I mean, what if you heard it ringing and just didn't make it in time, eh? What would you feel like? Or you did pick it up and then just said 'Hello' out of habit! You'd never be able to live with yourself, would you? I mean, they picked your ruddy phone number out of the hat, so you've won the ruddy raffle when all's said and done, so why should you have to jump through all these hoops to claim the prize that should be yours in the first place?' He suspected that Mr. O. would have an answer, although he knew the answer he'd get if he ever found out he'd been listening to the radio, in work's time, in a company vehicle.

"About flamin' time!" He announced, as the cars in front started moving, again. Soon, he was speeding along, once more and, although he looked everywhere, there was no evidence of any reason for the hold-up.

Half an hour later, he was negotiating the narrow streets of Evanley village, again. Everything looked quite bright and cheerful, in stark contrast to his mood. He even thought, it must be nice to live in a neat and tidy place like this. Not that his Nan would be too chuffed, given that the pub seemed to have shut down. Easing out of Evanley itself, he came to the turn off, down the narrow and overgrown country lane, that led to Evanley Hall.

His mood, already pretty dark, took a dramatic turn for the worse as he spied the hand painted notice:

"IF YOU KILL MY KITTENS, I'LL KILL YOU!"

In bright red, amidst the gloom of the overhanging trees.

'I wonder if anyone has?' He thought, grimly.

For reasons that he would have been hard pushed to articulate, he decided against driving right up to the Hall, as he and Mr. O. had done on their first visit, and decided instead to park up on the lane and walk up. Locking the car, close to the ominous sign, he could hear a fearful banging and clattering coming from the small, decrepit cottage, partially hidden by the overgrown garden in front of it. He scuttled up the lane, looking back over his shoulder from time to time, in the direction of the din.

Finally, across the cattle grid and onto the gravel drive, he breathed a sigh of relief. The Hall was imposing and definitely daunting but was as nothing compared to that dark track he'd just come from. That gave him the willies!

He looked at the grand front door but decided against that.

Working his way around the house, hugging the wall as if trying to escape rather than enter, he made it, eventually, to the garden. There, as he had hoped, he spied Precious, at work with some secateurs.

"Ha! Take that you devil!" He heard her say, as a shoot fell to the ground.

He coughed, politely, and said, "Precious?"

She jumped and turned toward him, with a very startled look.

"Archibald!" She gasped, eyes wide with astonishment, "What are you doing here?"

"I just thought I'd come and see you?" Archibald lied, and shrugged.

"You shouldn't be here!" She looked panic-stricken and her eyes flitted from side to side.

"I thought you'd be pleased" Archibald said, in a hurt tone.

"I am, of course I am" Precious said, without much conviction, "but Mama does not approve of uninvited guests"

"Well, I don't have to come in, or owt" Archibald flapped his arms, "I'm fine out here, honest!"

"Yes, but…NO!" She suddenly yelled, looking over his shoulder.

Archibald whirled around, but there was nothing and no-one behind him, although he had the impression that someone had just slipped behind one of the bushes.

"Who was that?" Archibald asked.

"No-one!" Precious shook her head, "No-one at all. Come with me, we must take tea"

"Where do you want to take it?" Archibald frowned.

"Oh, you are funny!" She tapped his shoulder with her secateurs, playfully, and led the way toward a pergola where there was small table with a teapot and two cups and saucers.

"You expecting someone?" Archibald nodded toward the table.

"Oh no, I…" She blushed a little, "I have little tea parties, you see. Just me and my doll, Jeannie" She reached down, under the table, and produced a doll, about three foot in length, with wild hair and a crazed expression. It looked like something that Archibald had only ever seen in nightmares and horror movies. "You must think me foolish" She blushed again.

"No, no" Archibald shook his head, "like me Nan says, it wouldn't do for us all to be the same"

"I'm sure that's very wise" Precious sat down and indicated for Archibald to do the same. "Shall I be 'mother'" She enquired.

"Well, I dunno!" Archibald looked puzzled, "Depends what you've been up to, I suppose?"

"Oh, you are a one!" Precious giggled, "Do you take sugar?"

"Just a couple, please" Archibald nodded.

Precious reached into one of her voluminous sleeves and produced what looked very much like a test tube. She uncorked it and poured a little of the white powder into Archibald's cup.

"Looks like a test tube?" He noted.

"It does, doesn't it?" Precious held it up, as If noticing for the first time, "Well, drink up!" She raised her cup and took a dainty sip. Archibald took a swig from his.

Dead Reckoning

"Have you seen owt of Mr. O.?" He asked, replacing the cup on the saucer.

"Mr. O.?" Precious frowned, "you mean, your employer?"

"Yeah, he came up here for dinner with your mam and we haven't seen him since." Archibald was aware of a buzzing in his ears.

"How peculiar!" Precious sipped her tea.

"You don't know where he went to, do you?" That buzzing was much louder, now, and Precious was looking decidedly fuzzy.

"Well, all I can say is that he's not here, right now, is he?" Precious gave a nervous little laugh, "Are you feeling alright, Archibald?"

"You're looking a bit fuzzy!" Archibald slurred.

"Ah yes, that would be the powder" Precious nodded, "Night, night, Archibald" Her sweet smile was the last thing he saw, as he slid from the chair onto the lawn, below.

Chapter Twenty
Trapped

It was difficult, no, it was impossible, to know how long he had been there. Yes, there had been periods of relative dark and light which might, he supposed, have corresponded to days passing but they might just as easily have been figments of his imagination.

He knew that he had slept, occasionally, but he also knew that he had been unconscious, more than once, and separating one from the other was no mean feat.

He tried to lick his lips with his parched tongue, with little success. He sighed, but immediately regretted it when the dust and odours, from the sacking covering his head and face, blew back into his nose and mouth.

The intriguing thing was that he had the sense that there was someone else there, with him, in the room (wherever and whatever that was). He had nothing to substantiate that feeling, no noises, no sounds of breathing or motion, just a sense of 'not being alone'.

He strained to hear something, anything, but it was difficult to detect over the constant dripping of a tap in the distance which had been his only, infuriating, companion for all of his stay here.

There had been noises, earlier. The sound of people moving about, purposefully but quietly. The sound of a chair being scraped across the floor. He had called out "Hello!", but there had been no acknowledgement, no reply.

Dead Reckoning

Nevertheless, the idea that there was someone else there nagged at him. He had to find out. He called out;

"Is there anybody there?" and a familiar voice responded,

"Oh bloody hell! I am dead then, 'cause they're trying to reach me by séance!"

"Hello Archibald" Josiah said, with mixed feelings of relief and sadness.

"Mr. O.? Is that you?"

"I'm afraid it is, Archibald. Are you similarly restrained?"

"Eh?"

Josiah sighed, regretted it, and said, "Are you blindfolded, with your hands and feet bound?"

"Well, yeah, summat like that. I've got some sacking or summat over me face, smells like old socks to be honest, and I can't move me hands nor me feet, so I guess they're tied up. I'm sitting on some sort of chair"

"Yes, that accords with my position" Josiah nodded, pointlessly.

"Do you know where we are?"

"No idea, I'm afraid" Josiah shrugged, out of habit.

"Smells a bit, in 'ere, don't it?" Archibald observed.

"Ah, that might have something to do with me" Josiah was pleased, for once, that the sacking covered his blushes.

"How do you mean?"

"I'm afraid that there are no toilet arrangements, wherever we are. Some time has now passed since my incarceration and, in the words of the poem, "there are some things we all must do"

"Oh, right, got you?" Archibald said, wishing he'd never mentioned it, "how about food, water, stuff like that?"

"I have not been fed" Archibald said, mournfully, "as for water, had it not been for your girlfriend, Precious, popping in occasionally with a glass, I rather fear that I might have been dead by now. She allows me a couple of sips, at the most, then she has to hurry away, before she gets caught. At least, that is the impression I have gained"

"So, she's in on it?"

"I have no idea!" Josiah shrugged, again, "I know not who my captors are, nor why I am being held captive, albeit that I have my suspicions. How do you come to be here, Archibald?"

"Ah, well, Ms. Knight, Samantha, she wanted me to come to see if I could figure out what had happened to you…"

"That was kind of her, and you" Josiah coughed and retched, slightly. The effort of talking, after all this time, when his mouth was dry as a bone, was telling on him. "A kindness which I feel my behaviour, of recent date, has hardly warranted"

There was a silence, before, "Eh?"

"By which I mean that I have not behaved well to either you, or Mrs…Samantha, recently"

"Yeah, well," Archibald shrugged, "she said I could crack on that I was there to see Precious, so that's what I did. Only, I reckon that Precious put summat in my tea, 'cause the next thing I know, I'm waking up in 'ere, wherever that is?"

"It would appear that you had a somewhat gentler, if no less incommodious, abduction than I. My incarceration commenced with a

Dead Reckoning

sharp blow to the back of my head, which has left me somewhat the worse for wear, I fear"

"Any idea who's doing all this?" Archibald asked, warily.

"As I said, I have my suspicions" Josiah replied, darkly, "the apparent ease of access by Miss DeVille would seem to indicate a degree of involvement. I thought, given her small acts of charity to me, that she might be an unwilling participant but now, given your abduction, I am less sure"

"So, her and that Mrs. DeVille then, do you reckon?"

"And/or the butler, Hames, or possibly all three!" Josiah admitted, "I am at a loss to comprehend what possible motive there could be, if my suppositions are correct"

"What do you think they're planning to do with us?" Archibald asked, a little fearfully.

"I really do not know" Josiah sighed, "on the one hand, that I have continued living and breathing, albeit with some difficulty, has to inspire a degree of hope. On the other, that they now have both of us in captivity, a situation which is unlikely to go unnoticed by the outside world, may lead them to do something…rash"

"Oh bugger!" Archibald said, with heartfelt emotion.

* * * *

Samantha swept into the Company yard, turned a corner and nearly crashed into Mr. Strine having a surreptitious smoke.

"Oh sh…" He began, sparking a bout of energetic coughing, cigarette ash and flying embers, "sorry Mrs., no harm done, eh?"

"Have you heard from him?" Samantha barked.

"Who?" Mr. Strine wheezed.

"Archie, of course!"

"Oh, young Archie, well, no, not since you sent 'im off to see 'is girlfriend"

"Have you checked that he's not on site?"

"Checked…?" Mr. Strine looked confused.

"Oh, for heaven's sake!" Samantha brushed past him and strode into the premises. She hurriedly checked all of Archibald's usual haunts, but came up empty. None of the other employees could recall seeing him, either. She summoned Mr. Strine to Josiah's office.

"Well, Mr. Strine, it would appear that Archibald has not reported for work today. I have checked both the works' phone and my mobile, and there are no messages or missed calls, how about you?"

"Me, what, Mrs.?"

"Have you checked your mobile phone?"

"Oh, I don't have no truck with any of that modern nonsense" Mr. Strine shook his head, vehemently.

"No, I don't suppose you do!" Samantha cradled her head in her hands, "right, well, in that case, I need to have another word with the police. Can you hold the fort?"

"Hold the…, oh, right, yeah, I'm with you" Mr. Strine grinned, "you leave it with me, Mrs., you've got nowt to worry about!"

"I wish that were the case, Mr. Strine, I really do" Samantha said, glumly

Chapter Twenty-One
Missing You

"We've got someone downstairs who wants to see us!" D.S. Stone grinned at his boss, D.I. Wood, who was currently partially hidden by a motoring magazine.

"If it's Santa Claus, tell him he's too early and if it's the Easter Bunny, tell him he's too late!" D.I. Wood turned a page, sighed and tried to get his leg, and inflamed foot, into a more comfortable position.

"Nope, neither of them" D.S. Stone looked smug, "it's only Frankie's missus, again!"

D.I. Wood put down his magazine and stared at his colleague, sternly.

"You're having a laugh, aren't you?"

"No, straight up, she's downstairs again and wants to see us"

"She's got a bloody nerve!" D.I. Wood snarled, "I suppose this is about her boyfriend going walkabout, again! Does she think we're her private bloody detective agency? You did kick it into touch last time you spoke to her, didn't you? Didn't give her any false hope, or nothing?"

"I said we *might* make a few more inquiries if he hadn't shown up by the end of the week"

"Did you?" D.I. Wood raised an eyebrow.

"I didn't make any promises" D.S. Stone reassured, hastily, "and, anyway, it isn't the end of the week yet, is it?"

"No, more's the pity" D.I. Wood massaged his leg and dreamed of a couple of days on the sofa.

"Shall I go down and see her again?"

"No, *I'll* have a word" D.I. Wood started to ease himself up from his seat, and then thought better of it, "tell you what, get her brought up here. I don't see why I should be putting myself out for the likes of her!"

D.S. Stone made a diplomatic retreat.

* * * *

"Mr. O.!" Archibald whispered, and then, when there was no response, "MR. O.!" somewhat louder.

"Hmm?" Josiah started, a little, and tried to focus on what was being said, "what did you say?"

"You were talking and then you, sort of, drifted off…" Archibald observed.

"Oh, I'm sorry Archibald, that seems to keep happening" Josiah shook his head, sadly, dislodging odd bits of grain and dust in the process from the sack covering his face, and reviving a raging headache that he had been trying to ignore. "Was I saying anything interesting?"

"You were saying what happened when you got to the Hall, last Saturday"

"Oh yes, I recall now" Josiah sighed, "well, I came in through the main door, Jeanette and Precious were waiting in the Hall to greet me, all dressed in their finery, I thought we were going to have a simply splendid evening…"

"Right!" Archibald nodded, "and then what?"

There was no answer from his companion, just the sound of gentle breathing and the steady drip of water from a tap, somewhere.

"Mr. O.!" Archibald tried again, "MR. O.!" but there was no response, this time.

* * * *

"Mrs. Knight to see you" D.S. Stone announced, and retreated to the safety of a corner of the office.

"Ah, Mrs. Knight, you're becoming a regular visitor" D.I. Wood said, grimly.

"Inspector, Sergeant" Samantha nodded to each, in turn.

"If this is about Mr. Oakshott, I think my Sergeant did point out that it was rather too early to be instigating any formal inquiries"

"It is not about Mr. Oakshott, well, not directly" Samantha shook her head, "it concerns Archibald"

"Archibald?" D.I. Wood frowned.

"The one you call 'Lurch', sir" D.S. Stone supplied.

"Thank you, Sergeant, I'm aware of who we are talking about" D.I. Wood snapped, "what seems to be the problem with Mr. Thurble?"

"He's missing, too" Samantha blushed a little.

"HE'S missing?" D.I. Wood looked at her in astonishment.

"Yes, I'm afraid so" Samantha nodded, miserably, "and it's all my fault!" She began to sob. D.S. Stone raced forward with a chair and helped her to sit down, despite the glares from his superior. She placed her handbag on the desk and retrieved a handkerchief from it.

"Have *you* abducted Mr. Thurble?" D.I. Wood asked.

"No, of course not!" Samantha snapped, "why would I do such a thing?"

"Then, I'm somewhat at a loss as to why you think it's all your fault!" D.I. Wood raised his hands in puzzlement.

"It's because I sent him to find out what had happened to Josiah, Mr. Oakshott" Samantha explained, "on the pretext of going to see his girlfriend, Precious"

"Let me be quite clear about this," D.I. Wood eased himself upright in his chair, winced with the pain, opened a manilla folder and read from it, "Mr. Oakshott went to see his girlfriend last Saturday and you haven't seen him since?"

"That's correct" Samantha nodded.

"You have since despatched Mr. Thurble to go and see his girlfriend, and this was when?"

"Yesterday" Samantha replied, glumly. "Monday"

"And he hasn't returned?"

"No"

"Do you, perhaps, see something of a pattern developing here?" D.I. Wood raised an eyebrow, "two men go off to meet their new girlfriends and neither return? I fail to see what you find odd about this state of affairs, Mrs. Knight"

"It's just not like Josiah, his work is everything to him" Samantha replied, testily, "and I sent Archibald specifically to see what he could find out about Josiah's disappearance. He would have contacted me, somehow"

Dead Reckoning

"Don't you think that it is more likely that they are having the time of their lives, and you're just a bit jealous, isn't that the long and the short of it?" D.I. Wood frowned at her.

"It's nothing like that!" Samantha shouted, causing a few people in the outer office to stop in their tracks, "There's something odd going on, I'm sure of it! Archibald didn't go to see Precious gleefully, I had to force his to go, he was very reluctant"

"Mrs. Knight" D.I. Wood covered his face with his hands and breathed, deeply, "you do appreciate that my superior would do his fruit if I suggested sending officers to see why two blokes, who had gone to see their respective girlfriends, hadn't returned, you do see that, don't you?"

Samantha shrugged and made no comment.

"Where is it that you think they are, anyway?" D.S. Stone, enquired.

"Evanley Hall" Samantha said, and when D.I. Wood looked at her blankly, added, "it's in Cheshire"

"Ah well, then" D.I. Wood beamed and eased himself back in his chair, "not our patch!"

"But, you must be able to do something!" Samantha pleaded.

"Out of my hands, I'm afraid, Mrs. Knight" D.I. Wood looked pleased with himself, "like my Sergeant here said, when you saw him only *yesterday*, if either or both of them are still missing at the end of the week, then we *might* ask the local plod if they'll make a few inquiries, but we can't make any promises." He slammed the folder shut, with an air of finality, "Now, if there's nothing further, Sergeant Stone here will escort you off the premises"

"That's it, is it?" Samantha glared at D.I. Wood.

"That, as you so accurately say, is, indeed, it, Mrs. Knight" D.I. Wood confirmed, pulling some papers toward him, "don't let me detain you, further"

"If you would come with me, please?" D.S. Stone tentatively took Samantha by the elbow, but she shook him off.

"There are two men who have been, almost certainly, abducted, and you're going to do NOTHING?" She yelled.

"Good day, Mrs. Knight" D.I. Wood murmured, apparently engrossed in the documentation before him.

"This way, please" D.S. Stone insisted, as a couple of uniformed officers appeared at the door.

Samantha grabbed her handbag, snorted and stalked out of the office.

"I'm sorry we couldn't be of more help, Mrs. Knight" D.S. Stone said, apologetically, as they made their way downstairs and to the main door leading on to the street.

Samantha turned to glare at him. D.S. Stone opened the door for her and smiled, weakly.

Just at that moment, Samantha noticed a couple of grainy, black and white photos, on the noticeboard by the door.

"What are these?" She asked.

"Oh, those" D.S. Stone peered at the photograph, "they're CCTV images of some people who we would be interested in talking to about a jewellery robbery a few days ago"

"Are they, now?" Samantha turned to him, in triumph, "well, you might be interested to know that, in my opinion, she" she stabbed a finger toward the image of a young girl in the foreground, "looks an awful lot like Precious, Archibald's girlfriend and she" She stabbed finger at the image of an older woman walking away from the camera in the other photo, "is remarkably like Josiah's Mrs. DeVille! Do you think I might get your boss's attention, now?"

She fixed him with a steely stare and a grim smile. D.S. Stone swallowed hard and wished the ground would open up beneath him.

Chapter Twenty-Two
Here Comes the Rain Again

"There had better be a good reason why that woman is sitting outside my office, once again, Sergeant, after I specifically told you to escort her OUT OF THE BUILDING!" D.I. Wood was clearly not happy.

"There is, sir" D.S. Stone nodded, miserably, "she saw the photo of those three, you know, the ones we're looking for in that jewellery theft." He took a deep breath and soldiered on, "she reckons it could well be that bunch up in Cheshire"

"What? You mean where she's sent her boss and Lurch to be with their girlfriends?"

"Yes, that's right" D.S. Stone looked at his superior, gloomily, "Shall I bring her in?"

"This had better be on the level, Stoney, or on your head be it" D.I. Wood hissed.

* * * *

Archibald heard some light footsteps, apparently coming down stairs. A few moments later, the sacking covering his face was lifted, gently, away and Precious was standing before him, holding a glass of water.

"Here" She whispered, "drink this. But hurry, I shouldn't be here!"

Archibald blinked in the sudden half-light and scowled at her, but leant forward to sip, gratefully, from the glass. Eventually, he leant back to take a breath.

"What did you do to me?" He managed, between gulps.

Dead Reckoning

"I'm sorry, I really am" Precious sounded close to tears, "I know it probably doesn't seem like it, but I was trying to do you a favour!"

"Ha!"

"I mean it" Precious insisted, "if I hadn't drugged you, well, it would have been the same as Mr. Oakshott"

"I'm worried about him" Archibald frowned at her, "he's not answering when I talk to him and his breathing doesn't sound right"

"I'll go and look" Precious said, then, hearing heavy footsteps behind her, she quickly dragged Archibald's sacking back over his head.

"What are you doing down here?" A dark voice asked.

"Just giving them a sip of water" Precious said in a trembling voice, "they need to have water"

"You're too soft" The voice sneered. "They'll get water, don't you worry!"

"There's something the matter with the older one" Precious went on, "I don't think he's conscious"

"That won't do" The voice grunted. There was the sound of footsteps heading past Archibald to the other side of the room, "She wants him conscious"

"What are you doing?" Precious asked, fearfully.

There was the sound of a tremendous slap, and then a groan.

"Oh!" Precious shouted.

"What's happening?" Archibald cried out.

"Like I said, she wants him conscious" The voice said, flatly, "Tell him to shut up, unless he wants some. Have you got your stuff together?"

"Yes" Precious replied, timidly.

"Good, now get out of here"

There was the sound of two sets of feet heading back up the stairs, and then silence, apart from the constant sound of dripping water.

"Mr. O.?" Archibald tried.

"Yeth, Archibald?"

"Oh brilliant, you're back!" Archibald could hardly contain his excitement.

"I'm not shure that bwilliant ith a word I'd uthe" Josiah said, with difficulty, "I theem to 'ave a fat lip, do you know why?"

"There was a bloke here" Archibald said, glumly, "I think he hit you"

"Right, right!" Josiah sighed, "to be expected, I thuppothe"

"I think you were out of it" Archibald explained, "I'd been trying to get you to answer for ages!"

"Thmall merthieth, then, Archibald, thmall merthieth"

"He said that 'she' wanted you conscious" Archibald reported.

"Who doeth?"

"I don't know" Archibald said, miserably, "not Precious, that's for certain. I don't think she's too happy about all of this"

"Hmm, under the thircumthtanthes, I'm not thure that 'conthious' is where I want to be!" Josiah mused.

Dead Reckoning

* * * *

"Right then, *Mrs*. Knight" D.I. Wood managed to turn her marital status into a sneer, "On a scale of 1 to 10, how sure are you that you know who these three are?" He tapped the photos on his desk, impatiently.

"For this one walking toward the camera, I would say '8', possibly '9'" Samantha glared back at him, "for the other two, because they're facing away from the camera, the best I would say is '6'"

D.I. Wood sighed and shook his head.

"I'm not sure that's enough for us to go haring off to Cheshire on some wild goose chase"

"I'm as sure as I can be, that this girl is Archibald's girlfriend, Precious" Samantha said, firmly, "the scarf around her head makes it a bit difficult but the clothes, how she holds herself, they all lead me to believe this is her"

"Yes, but…" D.I. Wood shrugged.

"Look, if I'm right and this *is* her. Then it follows, like night follows day, that these two must be Mrs. DeVille and, I would imagine, her driver. We know that Precious said they were going shopping together, maybe this is their idea of shopping?" Samantha drummed her fingers on the desk, much to the Inspector's annoyance.

D.I. Wood looked like a man who had bitten into a ripe peach, only to discover it was a lemon. He sighed deeply and said:

"Right, Stoney, get on to the local plod in Cheshire and tell them they'll be having the pleasure of our company. See if you can get them to part with a couple of uniforms, just in case things get a bit hairy, will you?"

"Will do, sir!" D.S. Stone hurried out of the office.

"I'm telling you, Mrs. Knight, that if I find you've fed me a cock and bull story just to get your boyfriend back, I'll fit you up with something, good and proper, even if it's only 'wasting police time'" D.I. Wood said, menacingly.

"You won't be wasting your time, Inspector, I'm sure of that" Samantha matched him glare for glare.

* * * *

"Are you...are you alright, Mr. O.?" Archibald asked, hesitantly.

"Well..." Josiah chuckled, "tha' depends on wha' you mean by 'alwight'"

There was the sound of a number of feet coming down the stairs. Then there was the unmistakeable voice of Jeanette DeVille.

"Well, gentlemen" She began, "we're so sorry to love you and leave you, but we have to go"

"You're letting us go?" Archibald asked, hopefully.

"Ha! Not quite, young man" Jeanette giggled, "no, I'm afraid you two will be staying here. I'm sure you'll be excellent company for each other"

"I don't know why you're doin' thith, Jeanette" Josiah managed, with difficulty.

"No, no, of course you don't!" Jeanette screamed. She rushed over and pulled Josiah's sacking away, roughly. He blinked in the dim light. All he could see was Jeanette's contorted face, glaring at him, and two other dim figures standing by the stairs in the distance. To his left, he could make out Archibald slumped on a chair, his face covered by a sack.

"Do you know who I am?" Jeanette was still ranting at him.

"Of courthe" He nodded, "You're Jeanette"

"Am I? Did she ever tell you, back when you were cosying up together, that she had a sister? Eh? No, I'll *bet* she didn't" 'Jeanette' hissed in Josiah's ear, "I wasn't the *pretty* one, I wasn't the *bright* one, I was the one who was shoved down in the kitchen to do all the drudge work!"

"A thithter?" Josiah shook his head, and regretted it as a wave of pain hit him, "no, I didn't know"

"Did I get a pretty name, like Jeanette? No, I did not!" She continued to whisper in his ear, "I was named after a bloody dusting mop! Nenette, they called me, because they thought it sounded *cute*! Bastards!"

"Nenette?" Josiah muttered, and looked puzzled, "Then...I don't underthtand, what'th happened to Jeanette?"

"She's...somewhere else" Nenette whispered, grimly.

"We should be going" A dark voice behind her, said.

"Yes, you're right" Nenette nodded. She dragged Josiah's sack back, over his face, viciously. "Like I said, gentlemen," She announced to the room, "we're sorry to love you and leave you, but leave we must. But, don't worry, we'll leave you a little something to remember us by" She giggled for rather a long time. There was a metallic clanking and banging and then the sound of footsteps heading back upstairs.

"Do you think they've gone, Mr. O.?" Archibald asked, after a while.

"I hope tho" Josiah replied.

"Good!" Archibald sighed with relief, "Somebody will come looking for us, soon, I'm sure they will"

"I really hope they hurry up, Archibald" Josiah said, tremulously.

"Why's that, Mr. O.?"

"You may have notithed, that the drip of water hath turned into a guth?"

"A guth? Oh, you mean a gush?"

"Yeth, a guth" Josiah confirmed, "and, there theemth to be water collecting around my feet, how about you?"

Archibald raised each foot and put it down, experimentally. He was rewarded with a splashing sound and a distinctly damp feeling around his ankles.

"Yeah, you're right!" Archibald nodded, pointlessly, "what's that all about?"

"You remember me telling you about Jeanette'th grandfather, that he wath a naval dethigner?" Josiah chuckled, "you thought I meant…"

"Belly buttons, yeah, I remember" Archibald chuckled too.

"Well, if ath I thuthpect, we're in the thellarth of Evanley Hall…"

"Fellers? Oh, you mean, cellars?"

"Yeth, them" Josiah sighed, "well, if thath where we are, old Theperd Mountjoy had them made waterproof, tho he could ecthperiment with thip dethign"

"Ecthperiment with…oh, right, you mean he could play with his boats down 'ere and stuff?"

"That'th it!" Josiah hesitated before continuing, "tho, you thee, a guthing tap and water collecting around our feet, it'th not a good thign, do you thee what I mean?"

"Erm, well…" Archibald thought, furiously, "you mean, this place is going to fill up with water?"

"Yeth!"

"And we're tied to these chairs so we can't get out?"

"Yeth, got it in one!" Josiah agreed, miserably.

"Oh bloody hell, Mr. O., what are we going to do?" Archibald whimpered.

"Get rather wet, I thuthpect, Archibald" Josiah managed a weak little smile.

Chapter Twenty-Three
The Jean Genie

"There's a turn coming up, on the left" Samantha announced, "looks like some sort of track leading up to the Hall itself"

"Glad you're making yourself useful, Mrs. Knight" D.I. Wood said, sarcastically, from his position in the rear of the car, where he was managing to rest his aching leg and throbbing foot by lying across the seat.

"At least *she* can read a map!" D.S. Stone muttered.

"What was that, Sergeant?"

"I said, I hope you're alright at the back?" D.S. Stone improvised, making the turn into the lane.

"Look, there's a car parked up there, by that rundown cottage" Samantha pointed ahead, "I'm sure that's…it is, it's the car that Archibald took!"

"Pull up and go and have a look, Sergeant, will you?" D.I. Wood asked.

Sighing, D.S. Stone parked behind the limousine. As soon as he opened his door, they could all hear a fearful hammering, banging and yelling coming from the cottage. D.S. Stone quickly checked the limousine.

"No-one in the car, and it's all locked up" He reported back, "but there's a hell of a row coming from that cottage"

"Perhaps someone needs help?" Samantha suggested.

Dead Reckoning

"Strewth! I don't know why we did all them months in Training College when we could have just asked Mrs. Knight here!" D.I. Wood sneered, "I'm still not sure why you're here with us?"

"If you recall, sir, Mrs. Knight is the only one who can positively identify our suspects," D.S. Stone pointed out, "always assuming we find them?"

"Yes, well" D.I. Wood huffed, "You stay here, we'll go and take a look at this cottage"

D.I. Wood eased himself out of the back of the car, rather gingerly, and limped up the cottage pathway with his Sergeant. He knocked, loudly, on the cottage door, which only served to increase the volume of oaths and yells from inside.

"From the commotion, I'd say we've got just cause to effect an entry, wouldn't you, Sergeant?"

"Yes sir, but..." He tried the door handle, "the door's locked and there are no open windows"

"Have to give it a bit of a kick then, Stoney" D.I. Wood grinned.

"Me? Why don't you?"

"Don't be so wet, Sergeant!" D.I. Wood snarled, pointing at the foot he was nursing in an over-large trainer, "just look at me! Do you really think I'm up to kicking doors down, eh?"

"Well, no" D.S. Stone conceded, "but I was on crutches for weeks last time I tried"

"Put your shoulder to it, then" D.I. Wood suggested, "looks rotten, shouldn't take much"

"I'm not doing that!" D.S. Stone folded his arms and glared at his superior, "I'll be in physio for months if I try anything like that!"

There was the sound of a pot being dragged over stone.

"Would this help, gentlemen?" Samantha held a key up, "it was under the flowerpot"

"Right, well, yes, that would be one way forward...Sergeant!" D.I. Wood took the proffered key and handed it to his colleague. "I thought I told you to stay in the car!" He hissed at Samantha.

"I wanted to see if it was Archie, or Josiah" Samantha hissed in reply.

They opened the door and immediately took a step back as the stench hit them. A host of flies took the opportunity to make a break for freedom, as did a couple of cats.

"Hello! Is there anyone there?" D.I. Wood shouted through the handkerchief he had quickly pressed to his face. The commotion from the door to the right of the small hallway, continued. "After you, Sergeant" D.I. Wood nodded.

D.S. Stone opened the door, cautiously. The stench was even worse here and a flurry of cats escaped into the hallway.

"Don't you go lettin' my cats gerrout!" A voice screamed.

"Are you alright, madam?" D.S. Stone asked.

"'Course I ain't alright, yer barmpot!"

"See if you can put a light on, Sergeant, so as we can see where we're treading, at least" D.I. Wood mumbled through his handkerchief.

D.S. Stone scrabbled either side of the doorway and, eventually, a very dim ceiling light sputtered into existence. Looking around, they could see that the small room was cluttered with furniture that was far too large for the space. Every surface was littered with unwashed plates and cups, along with empty packets and tins. Such space as there was,

Dead Reckoning

between these items, was filled with cats of all descriptions, pacing around and mewing pitifully.

"I ain't been able to feed 'em, that's why they're all upset" The woman sitting on the dining chair by the fireplace, explained. On closer examination, it was obvious that she had been tied, hand and foot, to this chair.

"Get her untied, Sergeant" D.I. Wood commanded, "then get the paramedics to come and have a look at her" He looked around the room with disgust, "Better get Social Services as well"

D.S. Stone set to, quickly, with a penknife, and D.I. Wood worked his way around the room in order to face the woman.

"CAN YOU TELL ME YOUR NAME, MADAM?" He shouted.

"I AIN'T DEAF, NOR DAFT!" She shouted back, "You tell me your'n and I'll tell yer mine" The woman tried to rub some feeling back into her wrists as they suddenly became free.

"I'm Detective Inspector Wood, this is my colleague, Detective Sergeant Stone" D.I. Wood produced his Warrant Card, "we heard your cries and thought you might need assistance"

"Nah, I allus tie meself up of an evenin'" She reached down to rub her ankles, now free from the restraining rope.

"Your name, please, madam?"

"Perhaps I could open a window a little?" Samantha suggested, trying not to retch.

"Don't you be lettin' none of my cats out!" The woman yelled.

"Your name?" D.I. Wood's patience was wearing very thin.

"It's Jeannie" The woman mumbled.

"Ok, Jeannie, nice to meet you. Jeannie what?" D.I. Wood persisted.

"Just Jeannie" Jeannie shrugged and shuffled on her seat. "I know it smells in 'ere, but I ain't been able to do nowt about the cats' litter, you see?" She looked up at D.I. Wood, pleadingly, "Nor about meself, for that matter" She added, in a small voice.

"How long have you been tied up like this, Jeannie?" D.S. Stone asked, putting away his penknife.

"Well now, lemme see" Jeannie looked thoughtful, "what day be it today?"

"It's Tuesday, madam, Tuesday afternoon" D.I. Wood supplied.

"Sa'urday, 'e did this to me, last Sa'urday" Jeannie said, after a few moments thought. "Could I 'ave a drink of wa'er, d'ye think?"

"Sergeant?" D.I. Wood snapped.

D.S. Stone looked around, hopelessly, for something approaching a clean mug or glass. He finally found a mug with marginally fewer stains than most and went to fill it from the tap, dangling from a loose pipe, above the sink in the corner of the room. He handed it to Jeannie, who grabbed it and drank heartily.

"Perhaps you could put the kettle on, get a few things washed up?" D.I. Wood suggested to his Sergeant, who was conversing in an undertone on his 'phone. D.S. Stone looked less than pleased at the suggestion.

"I can do that" Samantha rolled up her sleeves, "does she know anything about Josiah or Archie?"

"Thank you, Mrs. Knight, but *I* will conduct this investigation, if you don't mind!" D.I. Wood snapped, and turned to the woman, "Jeannie, who did this to you?"

"It were 'im, up there" She nodded in the general direction of the Hall.

"Who would that be?"

"Calls 'isself, 'Ames" She sniggered, "reckons 'e's 'er driver or summat" She tossed her head, "'e ain't no driver!"

"Would this be the man?" D.I. Wood produced the CCTV image from his pocket.

"I can't see, I ain't got me specs" Jeannie screwed her eyes up.

"Where are they?" D.S. Stone looked around the mess. Jeannie shrugged.

"When this man tied you up, was there anyone with him?" D.I. Wood persisted.

"'Ar there was" Jeannie nodded, "'e 'ad a bloke in the car with him. Posh sort. Well dressed, yer know?"

"Josiah!" Samantha gasped.

"Was that 'im?" Jeannie looked troubled, "'e looked, I dunno, like someone I might 'ave known, once, if yer know what I mean?"

"He had been here before, about a week ago, with his assistant, Archie" Samantha explained.

"Had 'e? Ah well, that'd be it then, I s'pose" Jeannie replied, thoughtfully.

Chapter Twenty-Four
The Tide is High

"This man, the 'posh sort' in the car, did he help tie you up?" D.I. Wood asked.

"Inspector!" Samantha protested.

"I have to ask" D.I. Wood snapped.

"Nah, it were just 'im from the 'All" Jeannie shook her head, "Bastard!" She added for good measure, and spat into the fireplace, which did nothing to aid the ambience.

"Who else is at the Hall, Jeannie?"

"'Im, 'Er, an' some chit of a girl what reckons she's their daughter, but, if you asks me, I'd say she ain't no daughter of there'n!" Jeannie chuckled.

"This girl who's a ..." D.I. Wood began.

"She said 'chit', Inspector" Samantha clarified.

"I know, I know!" D.I. Wood glared at her, "this girl, Jeannie, does she look like this?" He produced the other CCTV image from his pocket.

"I tole yer, I ain't got me specs, I can't see nuffin'"

Samantha rifled through her handbag, "Here, try mine" She suggested. Jeannie held them, tentatively, and looked at them warily. "Give them a go, Jeannie, they can't hurt you, can they?" Samantha smiled warmly at her.

Dead Reckoning

Jeannie, grudgingly, put the spectacles in place, and peered at the photograph.

"Ar, that be 'er" She nodded, "daughter! Pfft! Good specs these"

"You can keep them, Jeannie, if you can tell me what happened to the man in the car, and did you see or hear anyone else recently?"

D.I. Wood scowled at Samantha but waited to hear the answer.

"I dunno what 'appened to 'im in the car, on account of me being tied up, yer see?" Jeannie looked at Samantha as if she wasn't all that bright, "but, if 'e went up to that 'All, it wouldn't 'ave gone well fer 'im, I know that much"

"And did you see or hear anyone else, perhaps yesterday?" D.I. Wood asked.

Jeannie nodded, "There were a car, I thought it were comin' 'ere. I yelled and 'ollered but...nothin'. I could tell, from the shadow like, it were parked out there, still is, I reckon"

Samantha produced some tea, in a recently washed mug.

"Thank you, Jeannie" She smiled, "you can keep the glasses"

* * * *

"I reckon..." Archibald began, through gritted teeth, "I reckon, with a bit of luck, I can drag this sacking off, if I can get it between me teeth"

"A worthwhile endeavour, Archibald, I'm thure" Josiah commented, "although, whether it will change anything, I rather doubt"

"Got to try, Mr. O.!" There was the sound of snuffling and growling, and then, "Hey, I did it! I got it off!" There was no doubting the pleasure in Archibald's voice.

"Well done, Archibald!"

"This water's come up a lot in a short time, hasn't it, Mr. O.?" Archibald said, in a worried voice, after enjoying the novelty of being able to see his surroundings.

"That wath my concluthion, Archibald, I mutht admit" Josiah nodded.

"Now I can see, I reckon I could shuffle this chair of mine over to you"

"I would counthel againtht that courthe of action, Archibald" Josiah said, seriously.

"Why not? I might be able to help you. You don't look in a good way, Mr. O." Archibald said with concern.

"That ith kind of you, Archibald, and I apprethiate your conthern but, conthider thith, if your chair were to topple, ath you thuffled it, what would happen then?"

"Well, I'd get a bit of a soaking!" Archibald chuckled.

"A bit more than that, Archibald!" Josiah pointed out, "remember, you are tied to the chair. If it fell over, you would be unable to right yourthelf and you would be underwater, with all that entailth"

"Under…, oh heck, yeah, I see what you mean" Archibald looked gloomily at the rising water, "but, I've got to do summat!"

"You might try praying" Josiah suggested, "I can't think of anything elthe"

* * * *

"So, now what?" Samantha asked D.I. Wood, as Jeannie noisily enjoyed a mug of tea.

Dead Reckoning

"Once this lady's been attended to, we'll go up to the Hall and see if there's anyone there who can help us with our enquiries." D.I. Wood looked around at his surroundings with some distaste, "I'll be glad to get out of here, I know that much. Never did like cats!"

"Paramedics are on their way, sir, not sure about Social Services, I left a message" D.S. Stone reported.

"You really need to keep on top of things, when you're feeling a bit better!" Samantha suggested to Jeannie.

"Oh, I do that, don't you worry yer sen" Jeannie said, proudly, "I kin look after mesel', an' me kitties, long as I don't get messed about by them up there" She jerked her head in the direction of the Hall.

"We'll go up and have a word with them" D.I. Wood said, slowly and with excessive enunciation.

"'E thinks I'se barmy, yer know" She sniggered, "yer can git yersels up there, if yer a mind to…"

"Thank you, madam" D.I. Wood said, sarcastically, bowing a little.

"…burrit wunna do yer no good!" Jeannie took another draught of tea.

"Why do you say that, Jeannie?" Samantha asked, scowling at the Inspector.

"I 'eard their car goin' out jest afore ye came and nearly bust me door down!"

"We were helping you, you ungrateful…" D.I. Wood spluttered.

"Thank you, Inspector!" Samantha snapped, "you say their car went out, Jeannie?"

"Ar, that be right" Jeannie nodded and slurped some more, "if'n the car goes out, ye can betcher bottom dollar they've all gone"

"Perhaps they're taking Josiah and Archibald home?" Samantha suggested, hopefully.

"Sergeant, see if you can get any APNR data on it" D.I. Wood commanded.

"I'll have to get their registration before I can do that, sir" D.S. Stone grumbled.

"Well, get it found out, Sergeant" D.I Wood snapped, "it can't be beyond the wit of man to track down their registration!"

"At least, we could go up and have a look?" Samantha mused.

"Ah, could be a bit tricky" D.I. Wood looked sheepish, "you see, if they *have* gone out, then we can't ask for permission to enter the premises"

"Can't we just break in?" Samantha looked astonished.

"Of course not!" D.I. Wood snapped, "we can't just break into people's houses!"

"We nearly did here" D.S. Stone grumbled, rubbing where he *might* have had a shoulder injury.

"And, as you well know Sergeant, that was because we heard sounds of distress and, therefore, had a reason for breaking in" D.I. Wood frowned at his subordinate. "To gain access to the Hall, we would need a warrant, which I doubt we would get"

"But...but...we've got to do something!" Samantha looked exasperated.

"Let's see what comes back from the ANPR" D.I. Wood shoved his hands in his pockets and headed out of the door.

"And, in the meantime...?" Samantha flung her hands up in the air.

"We wait for the paramedics, somewhere that's a cat-free zone, preferably"

* * * *

"I think I thould mention thomething, Archibald" Josiah suggested, in a tired voice.

"What's that, Mr. O.?"

"Well, with the water rithing, ath it ith..." Josiah began.

"Writhing?" Archibald frowned.

"Yeth, rithing...getting higher" Josiah explained.

"Oh yeah, got you!" Archibald nodded.

"Well, you thee, becauthe there ith a dithparity in our heightth..." Josiah continued.

"Dithparity?"

"You're taller than me" Josiah sighed.

"Oh, well, I'm younger" Archibald explained, "we're getting taller, it's summat to do with diet, they reckon. Which beats me 'cause I've never been on a diet! Now me mam, she is all the time, and she's smaller than me, so it don't make sense now, does it?"

"*Anyway*, be that ath it may," Josiah continued with a sense of exasperation, "you are taller and, therefore, the water ith likely to affect my thurvival earlier than yourth, if you thee what I mean"

"Eh? Oh, yeah, I think so" Archibald frowned and concentrated really hard, "but, it won't matter though, 'cause we're sitting down!"

"That'th irrelevant!" Josiah snapped.

"No, I don't think so" Archibald shook his head, "I'd be taller if we were standing up, but we aren't!"

"*Nevertheleth*, your tortho…you are head and thoulderth above me, even thitting down" Josiah tried to explain.

"I don't see how shampoo's going to help?" Archibald was seriously confused.

"Put thimply, the water will drown me thome time before it doeth the thame to you"

"Oh, don't say things like that, Mr. O.!" Archibald pleaded.

"It'th a matter of fact" Josiah sighed, "tho, before that happenth, I juth wanted to thay how proud I am to have worked alongthide you, and how thorry I am that it hath come to thith" There was the sound of a stifled sob.

Archibald looked at his employer and the ever-rising water. He looked down at the chair to which he was tied. He frowned, tried to swallow the lump in his throat, and said in a low voice,

"Bugger this for a game of soldiers!"

And then, against his employer's express instructions, Archibald began to shuffle his chair, with immense difficulty, in Josiah's direction.

Chapter Twenty-Five
Bridge Over Troubled Water

D.I. Wood leaned against the car, drawing heavily on a cigarette and easing the weight from his troublesome foot. Samantha paced up and down, muttering to herself and looking grim. D.S. Stone appeared from within the cottage, closely followed by Jeannie, who was trying to contain an Escape Committee of cats.

"Sir, I have some news from the ANPR" D.S. Stone announced, looking rather smug.

"Oh, well done, Stoney! You managed to track down the reg. then?"

"Only 'cause he asked me, didn't 'e?" Jeannie cackled, "Get back in there, yer buggers!" She yelled at her escaping cats.

"Is that right, Sergeant?" D.I. Wood looked at his subordinate, quizzically.

"The erm...lady did have some pertinent information" D.S. Stone agreed, coyly.

"Ok, so what have you got?"

"Well, I think we can safely assume that they're not taking Mr. Oakshott and his colleague, back home," D.S. Stone explained, "they were tracked heading north."

"Right, get the Traffic lads onto them, pronto!"

"Ah, well, unfortunately, we've lost them, at the moment" D.S. Stone said, sheepishly.

"Then we need to get up to the Hall!" Samantha exclaimed, "If they're not taking them home, they must have left them there"

D.I. Wood shifted his stance on the car, uneasily.

"I'm not sure we've really got probable cause to break into somewhere like Evanley Hall"

"What more do you need? Josiah and Archibald are missing and the perpetrators have done a bunk!" Samantha folded her arms and glared at the Inspector.

"Well..." D.I. Wood looked distinctly uncomfortable, as he considered how his superiors might react to him breaking into a stately home.

"Perhaps Mrs. Knight and I could just have a look around the outside of the House?" D.S. Stone suggested, diplomatically.

"Yes, all right, no harm in that, I suppose" D.I. Wood drew on his cigarette, thoughtfully, "But don't go getting all 'Sweeney' on me, ok? Take a careful look and report back, yes?"

"Indeed, sir" D.S. Stone nodded and indicated to Samantha to follow him up the drive.

"Bloody waste of time!" D.I. Wood grumbled, rubbing his troublesome leg.

"That playin' yer up?" Jeannie nodded toward his leg.

"Thank you, ma'am, yes" D.I. Wood winced.

"Want me to tek a look?" Jeannie cocked her head.

"I am not a cat, madam!" D.I. Wood drew himself up.

Dead Reckoning

"Suit yersel', only I know me stuff e'en if you dunner" Jeannie sniffed and turned to head back into the cottage, "wossit s'posed to be then?" She turned and asked.

"Gout!"

"Gerroff!" Jeannie chuckled, "betcher it inna."

"You don't think so?" D.I. Wood couldn't help being intrigued.

"Nah, never gout!" Jeannie shook her head, "come back in 'ere, let's 'ave a butcher's"

* * * *

Samantha and D.S. Stone began working there way around the Hall, starting with the main doors, which were unsurprisingly locked and bolted, they made their way to the left, edging around by the kitchen and back door (also locked and bolted).

"Josiah! Archibald!" Samantha shouted, aware that it sounded like she was trying to find a lost pet.

"I can't hear anything, I'm sorry Mrs. Knight" D.S. Stone looked glum.

"They've got be be here, somewhere!" Samantha shook her head, "hang on, can you hear running water?"

D.S. Stone stood, silently, and concentrated.

"Yes..." He answered, eventually, "I think I can!"

* * * *

Archibald, with immense effort, had finally got his chair within spitting distance of Josiah's. He realised he had seriously underestimated how difficult it would be to move a chair against the weight of water surrounding them.

"Mr. O., are you ok?" He asked.

"It'th pfft, it'th getting clothe now, Archibald" Josiah sputtered. Archibald could see that the water was now up to his employer's mouth and nose.

"Hang on, Mr. O., I'm coming!" Archibald made another tremendous effort to move his chair, closer.

"I told you not pfft to!" Josiah attempted to snap.

"Yeah, well…" Archibald grunted, as he finally managed to get his chair next to Josiah's.

"Look, pfft [glug], thith ith it pfft [glug] I can't…hang on, much longer. I jutht want to thay pfft, pffble, thank you, Archie!" Josiah's head disappeared beneath the water.

"No, you bloody don't!" Archibald shrieked.

* * * *

"Where's it coming from?" Samantha looked around, anxiously.

"I don't know" D.S. Stone shook his head, "hold on! There's a sort of window down there, at ground level" D.S. Stone crouched down to look, Samantha joined him and peered over his shoulder.

"Can you see anything?" She asked.

"No, not really" D.S. Stone frowned and attempted to rub the ancient bullseye glass, clear, "it's very dirty, you can't see a thing, but I'm sure the water noise is louder down here"

Samantha cocked her ear and concentrated.

"You're right! Are you sure you can't see anything?"

"No, it's...oh, hold on, I think I can see water!" D.S. Stone virtually had his nose to the glass.

"I've got a bad feeling about this" Samantha said, darkly.

* * * *

Archibald took a very deep breath indeed and plunged his head beneath the icy water. Here it was very murky, but he could just make out Josiah's figure to his right. Using all of his strength, he forced his head underneath the crook of Josiah's left arm, then, gathering all of his remaining strength, he forced himself upwards. Moments later, both Josiah and Archibald's heads were above the water, just!

"Aagh, pfft, oosh" Josiah gasped for breath, unexpectedly finding himself again above water, "wha...wha'th happenin'? Arch pfft, wha' are you doin'?"

"Pfft, getting us another couple of minutes" Archibald spluttered, "now, SHOUT!"

"Thowt what?

"One...two ..three HELP!!" They both yelled.

* * * *

"Did you hear that?" Samantha took a step back, in surprise.

"I certainly did, miss" D.S. Stone nodded.

"Is that your 'probable cause'?" She raised an eyebrow.

"Yes, I think it is" D.S. Stone agreed, glumly, eyeing the definitely robust nature of the kitchen door.

"There's a window?" Samantha suggested, noting his reluctance.

"So there is!" D.S. Stone grinned and went in search of a suitable stone.

* * * *

"'s not gout!" Jeannie pronounced, prodding D.I. Wood's reluctant foot.

"That's what they said it was, down at the hospital" D.I. Wood winced.

"Nah, infection…or summat like that, you mark my words" Jeannie marched off to a shelf at the back of the kitchen and rooted around amongst some jars, "Ah, here y'are!"

She returned, clutching a jar containing something grey and dubious.

"Slap some of that on, couple times a day" She shoved the jar into D.I. Wood's hands. He looked at it, suspiciously. There was the sound of smashing glass.

"Oh my god! What's he doing?" D.I. Wood leapt up, and immediately regretted it, "The Chief Constable'll have my bits for cufflinks!"

"Getting' inter the 'all, are they? Good on 'em!" Jeannie chuckled.

* * * *

"HELP!!" Josiah and Archibald yelled, between splutterings.

Above the rushing water, there was the distinct sound of smashing glass.

"Did you pfft, hear that, Mr. O.?"

"Wath it pfft, wath it glath?" Josiah managed as he struggled to keep above the water.

"Reckon…so" Archibald was finding talking and holding Josiah up, a bit more than he could manage.

"We thould pfft try again. Ready 1 – 2- 3" Josiah prompted.

Dead Reckoning

"HELP!!" They yelled in unison.

"Hang on pfft can you hear that? Archibald asked.

"Hear...what?"

"The water pfft, it's stopped!"

"Tho it hath!" Josiah said, with a faint trace of hope, "mutht pfft be thome thort of thtopcock! Good old Thepherd!"

"That's great...Mr. O." Archibald grunted, "only, there's one pfft problem"

"What'th that?"

"I don't think I can keep holding you pfft..." Archibald gasped for breath and pushed up as hard as he could, "...up, much longer!"

Chapter Twenty-Six
Drowning Not Waving

"You don't look so good, Sergeant" Samantha observed when he opened the kitchen door of the Hall.

"Crawling through broken glass will do that to you" D.S. Stone agreed, ruefully, examining the state of his shredded trousers.

"Come on, we need to find the cellar" Samantha strode past him, through the large kitchen and into the dark entrance hall, beyond. "I can't hear the running water, anymore"

"No, me neither" D.S. Stone shook his head and followed her.

"There's a door here, I wonder if that could be for the cellar?" Samantha tried the door, "It's locked" She announced.

"Would be!" D.S. Stone said, miserably.

"Can you erm?..." Samantha nodded toward the door.

"I'll have a go, but I'm not promising anything" D.S. Stone grunted. He took a couple of steps back, braced himself and lunged at the door. Much to his surprise, it gave way immediately and he found himself teetering above a set of brick-built steps leading down to, what appeared to be, an indoor lake. Samantha managed to grab him before he plunged headlong into the water.

"Are you alright?" She asked, dragging him back.

"Yeah" D.S. Stone rubbed his aching shoulder and looked dubiously at the dark water spreading out before him. "I think so"

Dead Reckoning

"HELP!" They heard, in the distance.

"They *are* down there!" Samantha yelled, starting down the stairs.

"Wait a minute, miss!" D.S. Stone pulled her back, "It's dangerous, we don't know how deep that water is"

"Well, it can't be *that* deep, it's a cellar, not the Irish Sea!" Samantha glared at her companion.

"Ok, fair point, but let me go first and see what's happening" D.S. Stone pushed in front of her and set off, tentatively, down the stairs.

Ducking under the arch of the door leading into the cellar, he peered out, over the dark and forbidding water. At first, he couldn't see anything in the gloom, but then spotted, in the distance, two panic-stricken faces, just on the surface.

"I think I can see them!" D.S. Stone said, over his shoulder, to Samantha, "Mr. Oakshott!" He cried out, and his voice echoed around the cellar.

"HELP US!" Archibald responded.

"Oh god!" D.S. Stone murmured, removing his jacket and shoes, "I'm going to have to swim over to them, they're only just above the water"

"Take care, but hurry, please!" Samantha pleaded.

* * * *

"I'll kill him!" D.I. Wood staggered, stiff-legged and supported by one of Jeannie's walking sticks, up the Hall drive. "What the hell does he think he's playing at? Breaking into Evanley Hall, give me strength!"

"Must 'ave found summat?" Jeannie suggested, ambling behind him.

"He'll find the end of my boot if he can't justify this" D.I. Wood fumed, "I'll bet he's let that Samantha sweet-talk him into it!"

"Never know what you might find, up 'ere" Jeannie mused, looked up at the Hall as if seeing it for the first time.

"Hmm, well we'll see" D.I. Wood growled.

* * * *

After a fair bit of splashing and gasping, D.S. Stone finally arrived where two fearful faces could, just about, be seen above the water.

"Are you pfft, are you alright?" D.S. Stone managed.

"Just...just about" Archibald spluttered, "can you get Mr....Mr. Oaksh...Mr. Oakshott here out, 'cause I'm pfft...I'm holding him up, I've got me hea...me head under his arm...and I can't do it for much lon...much longer" Archibald kept disappearing below the water.

"I'll see pfft, what I can do" D.S. Stone took a very deep breath and dived down. He surfaced a moment later. "He's...he's tied to a chair!"

"We...we ain't here 'cause we want to be!" Archibald gulped.

"Right!" D.S. Stone nodded, "I'll try and get hold of him"

"Whe'...when you've got him, give me a tug or summat and I'll try...try an' get me 'ead out"

"Ok, wait for my signal" D.S. Stone dived down once more. A few moments later, Josiah was suddenly raised up. Archibald, gasping and spluttering, took a deep breath and ducked down. Moments later, he reappeared, shaking his head.

"I can't...can't get me 'ead free!" He choked.

D.S. Stone surfaced, coughing and snorting.

Dead Reckoning

"Wha'...what happened?" He gasped.

"I can't get me 'ead out" Archibald managed, "'e keeps pinnin' me with his elbow!"

"Mr. Oakshott...Mr. Oakshott!" D.S. Stone yelled.

"I reck...I reckon he's out of it, again pfft" Archibald struggled to get his face above water, "'e keeps doin' that"

"Must be a... a reflex action, then" D.S. Stone thought for a moment, wiping water from his face, "Right! Let me see if I can...get behind him. If I can push his arm forward, I should...I should be able to get you free"

"Soon'd be good!" Archibald gasped.

D.S. Stone took as deep a breath as he could manage and dived down, again. Swimming down and behind the two men, he could just see, through the murk, Josiah's arm wrapped around Archibald's neck. With an enormous effort, he pushed Josiah's arm up and forward. Archibald's head popped out like a cork, as he ducked down and freed himself. D.S. Stone grabbed Josiah's chair and pushed it upward. All three surfaced simultaneously.

"Bloody 'ell!" Archibald gasped.

"I've got him" D.S. Stone gulped, and looked over at Josiah, "you're right, he's out of it"

"Keeps 'appenin'" Archibald spluttered, "can you get 'im out of here, somehow?"

"I'll try and get...get him and this chair...over to the steps, there" D.S. Stone grabbed Josiah's chair and began to push it across the room. "Are...are you going to be ok?" He yelled back at Archibald.

"Jus'...jus' get 'im some help!" Archibald gasped.

* * * *

"Look! Just look at that! He's only gone and done one of the windows in!" D.I. Wood yelled.

"Improvement, if'n yer asks me" Jeannie chuckled.

"Chief Constable'll go nuts!" D.I. Wood shook his head and pushed open the half-open door. He attempted to stride in, with an authoritative manner, as best he could, with Jeannie trailing, a little reluctantly, behind him. "Sergeant! Where are you?" He shouted.

There were some clattering sounds coming from the Entrance Hall.

"Inspector! We're here!" Samantha shouted, sounding as if she was in some giant cavern.

"What the hell are they doing?" D.I. Wood tramped on.

"Cellar, shouldn't wonder" Jeannie muttered.

D.I. Wood marched into the Entrance Hall and saw the broken door.

"God! Is he trying to get me the sack? Look at all this!" He pointed at the door with his stick.

"Tole yer it'd be the cellar" Jeannie smirked.

"Inspector! We need your help!" Samantha shouted from behind the door. D.I. Wood pulled it open and saw her, at the bottom of a flight of stairs, attempting to drag a chair with an unconscious man tied to it, out of some very dark water. Behind the chair, he could see the bedraggled and wringing wet head and shoulders of D.S. Stone.

"Stoney!" D.I. Wood yelled, "What the hell are you doing?"

Dead Reckoning

"'Ere, gerrout the way!" Jeannie pushed him aside and stomped down the stairs, joining Samantha and helping her to drag the chair out of the water. "We ain't got time for no rabbit, this bloke needs 'elp, quick!"

"I'll call the paramedics" D.I. Wood pulled his 'phone from his pocket.

"He needs a blanket, or something," Samantha looked at Josiah with concern, "he's terribly cold!"

"Cupboard, top of the stairs, should be summat in there. Get to it!" Jeannie snapped. Samantha rushed off to check.

"Well done, Stoney!" D.I. Wood nodded to his wringing wet colleague, still bobbing in the water, "any sign of the other one?"

"Yeah, he's back there, I'll just go and get him, now I've got my breath back" D.S. Stone turned to look at where he had just come from, "OH NO! WHERE IS HE?"

The dark and silent water gave no answer.

Chapter Twenty-Seven
Bring Him Home

"Remind me, what's his name?" D.S. Stone asked, treading water.

"It's Archibald...Archibald Thurble!" Samantha said, stifling a sob, "Please help him!"

"Mr. Thurble!" D.S. Stone shouted, but there was no answer. "Archibald?" Still nothing. "I'll go and look for him, don't worry" He nodded to Samantha and swam back through the cold, dark water.

When he was reasonably sure that he was, more or less, in the same place where he had rescued Josiah Oakshott, D.S. Stone took a deep breath and plunged underwater. Surfacing, moments later, he shouted,

"I can't..pfft, I can't see him!"

"He's got to be there!" Samantha shouted back, frantically, "You've got to help him!"

"Hang on" D.S. Stone made another dive. The surface of the water smoothed over where he had been and remained calm, dark and forbidding. Some time passed and Samantha was getting more and more concerned, when the surface broke again, in a shower of droplets, and two heads poked out.

"I've...I've got him pfft" D.S. Stone managed to splutter, "but he's not ...he's not in a good way"

With considerable effort, the Detective guided the chair-bound body of Archibald back to the cellar steps, and a waiting Samantha.

"Oh my God, Archie!" She cried, "Are you alright?"

Dead Reckoning

"I don't think he's breathing" D.S. Stone managed to say, as he pushed the chair, and Archibald, out of the water.

"I've called the paramedics, Stoney, but as to how long they'll be..." D.I. Wood grabbed hold of Archibald and tugged.

"Paramedics my arse" Jeannie muttered, "'ere, let me see 'im" She stomped down to Archibald.

"The leg of his chair must have broken, after I left him" D.S. Stone explained, "he must have gone straight under. I don't know how long he's been like that?"

"There's a pulse, it don't amount to much, but it's there" Jeannie announced, "we need to get him off this chair and get working on 'im. Get me a knife or summat from the kitchen!"

Samantha scampered off at her command. Entering the kitchen, she saw two paramedics hovering by the door.

"Oh, thank God you're here!" She cried, flinging the door open.

"Strewth, that was quick!" D.I. Wood said, approvingly, as he limped into the kitchen after her, "I've only just rung for you!"

"We were called to attend an elderly woman" The lead paramedic pointed out, "at the cottage down the lane? Only, there doesn't seem to be anyone there"

"There isn't anyone when she *is* there!" D.I. Wood sniggered.

"I bloody 'eard that!" Jeannie yelled from the cellar steps.

"Anyway, sorry about that" D.I. Wood said to the paramedics, looking sheepish, "she seems to be doing fine, but we do have a couple of patients here who could use your help"

They all trooped back into the entrance hall, where Josiah was sitting on the chair he was tied to, unconscious, dripping wet, but covered with a blanket. Jeannie stomped up the stairs, grabbed the knife from Samantha, nodded to the paramedics, and hurried back down to Archibald.

"You'll need to look at 'im up there," She yelled back up to the paramedics, as she busied herself sawing Archibald's ties off , "keeps losing consciousness 'parently, may have taken on a bit of water too, but there's a couple of nasty 'ead wounds I'm not 'appy about" There was the sound of frantic sawing, "but this is the one I'm really worried about, not breathing, weak pulse, not sure 'ow long 'e's been underwater but it don't look good"

There was a snap as the last of the bindings holding Archibald to the chair, came free and Archibald's body slumped forward onto Jeannie, who grunted and attempted to drag him up the stairs. The two paramedics rushed forward to help her get him onto the entrance hall floor.

"Have you had medical training, ma'am?" The lead paramedic asked.

"Did a bit with Queen Alexandra's, didn't I?" Jeannie said, curtly.

"Leave him to us now, please" The other paramedic suggested, "we can take it from here"

They began working on Archibald, whilst Jeannie set to work releasing Josiah's bindings. A sloshing sound indicated that the bedraggled figure of a wringing wet, D.S. Stone, was making its way up the cellar stairs.

"Bloody well done, Stoney!" D.I. Wood went to congratulate his colleague.

"Get 'im one of them blankets!" Jeannie commanded. Samantha dragged one from the pile she had brought down earlier, and wrapped a shivering D.S. Stone in it.

"You played a blinder there, Stoney!" D.I. Wood grinned as he helped his colleague to sit down on the grand staircase. "There'll be a medal in this, you mark my words!"

"I don't want any medal" D.S. Stone shook his head, "I just want those two to be alright…after all this" D.S. Stone looked across at the scene where both Archibald and Josiah were being worked on by the technicians. "You know, it was really strange" D.S. Stone shook his head, "when I found him, under all that water, he was like…smiling. Not a proper grin, I mean, just a faint smile. Isn't that weird?"

"I guess he was glad he'd managed to get his boss out" D.I. Wood suggested.

"It'll be a…" D.S. Stone stifled a sob, "it won't be fair if he doesn't make it!"

"If I've learnt anything in this game, Stoney," D.I. Wood patted his colleague on the back, sympathetically, "it's that life ain't fair"

* * * *

Samantha sat in the Relatives Room of the hospital, absently sipping tea from a plastic cup and blankly viewing the various crisis support helpline posters and outdated covid advice, on the opposite wall.

There was a tentative knock on the door, which made Samantha jump. The door opened and D.I. Wood sidled in.

"Any news yet?" He asked.

"No, nothing so far" Samantha shook her head, "I thought that…when there was a knock on the door, I thought that it would be the Doctor"

"Sorry!" D.I. Wood said, and sat down beside her.

"How's your Sergeant, is he ok?"

"They're checking him over, now, but I think he's come out of it alright" D.I. Wood said, "thanks for asking"

"He was very brave" Samantha said, in a choking voice.

"Yeah, he did us proud!" D.I. Wood nodded, "I tried to get that bloody madwoman checked over but she wouldn't have any of it!"

"Jeannie? She's not mad, it was a good job she was there" Samantha pointed out.

"Yeah, well" D.I. Wood shrugged, "she nearly bit one of the medical staff! All she could bind on about was who was going to feed her cats if they kept her in! I've had her taken home by one of our drivers"

"That was…kind of you"

"Anything to get her out of my hair" D.I. Wood went to light a cigarette, then thought better of it. "I reckon she knows more about them three that have done a bunk, than she's letting on"

"Is there any sign of them?"

"Nah! Gone completely off the radar" D.I. Wood said, bitterly, "they know what they're about, that lot"

"I wish…I wish I could get my hands on them" Samantha said, grimly.

"You leave them to us" D.I. Wood assured her, "they'll slip up, eventually, and then we'll have them"

Dead Reckoning

"How could they..." Samantha began, crushing her empty cup in her hands, "how could they leave people to die like that? Why would anyone do that, eh?"

"I don't know" D.I. Wood sadly put his prospective cigarette back in the packet, "it's a fair jump up from distraction robberies in jeweller's shops, and no mistake"

There was a tap on the door and a doctor, in blue scrubs, entered, closely followed by a nurse.

"Miss Knight?" She asked.

"Mrs." D.I. Wood supplied, automatically, but withered under Samantha's glare.

"I'm sorry, I have to ask, are you a relative?" The doctor continued, ignoring the Detective.

"Well...I'm...I'm engaged to be married to Josiah, Mr. Oakshott" Samantha said, with a slight blush, noticing D.I. Wood's eyebrows shooting up.

"And the other gentleman, Mr. erm" The Doctor consulted her notes, "Ah yes, Mr. Thurble, is he connected to you?"

"Not as such" Samantha shook her head, "he's a colleague of mine, and Josiah...Mr. Oakshott's. How is Archie?"

"I'm sure you'll understand that I can't discuss a patient with you, unless you are related to them?"

The nurse whispered urgently in the Doctor's ear.

"Ah, yes, I see" The Doctor nodded, "apparently, it is the case that Mr. Thurble's mother and grandmother are on their way in to the hospital. Are there no close relatives of Mr. Oakshott, other than yourself?"

"Not to my knowledge" Samantha said, glumly.

"Well," The doctor nodded and sat down opposite her, "in that case, I need to give you an update…"

Chapter Twenty-Eight
Tears on My Pillow

"Where's he gone now?" D.I. Wood was holding two plastic cups of tea and looking around for his Sergeant, D.S. Stone.

"I don't know" The nurse at the nursing station shook her head, "I told him he was ok to leave and I think he went off that way" She pointed down a corridor.

"Typical! You try and do a nice thing and..." D.I. Wood fumed and stomped off in the last known direction of his colleague. He found him, shortly after, staring through the window into a small ward.

"Stoney! Where the hell have you been? I've got this for you"

"Ta" D.S. Stone accepted the luke-warm tea, absent-mindedly.

"What are you doing here?"

"The doctors said I was good to go, so..." D.S. Stone shrugged and continued to stare through the window.

"You could have waited for me!" D.I. Wood moaned, "I've been traipsing all around the hospital, looking for you!"

"Sorry, sir, I just..." D.S. Stone took a deep breath, "I just wanted a few moments to myself"

"Fair enough, Stoney, no problem" D.I. Wood nodded, and raised an eyebrow, "what's taken your fancy in there then, pretty nurse, is it"

"It's the ICU, sir" D.S. Stone explained, "it's where they've got him, Mr. Thurble. He's in an induced coma."

"Oh, I see" D.I. Wood looked thoughtful, "best thing for him, I suppose"

"You know...I couldn't even remember his name" D.S. Stone shook his head, sadly.

"Whose name?"

"Mr. Thurble" Through the window could be seen the figure of Archibald Thurble, entwined in pipes and leads trailing from him and with machines beeping at regular intervals. Two women, one very elderly, were sat at his bedside.

"We meet a lot of people, Stoney, you can't be expected to remember everyone's name"

"Yes, but..." D.S. Stone took a sip of his tea, "we've had so much to do with him, over the past few months, The least I could have done would have been to remember his proper name"

"I've always called him..." D.I. Wood began.

"Lurch! Yes, I know, and that's why I couldn't think of his real name. Just when I needed to shout out to him, to see if he was alright, all I could think of was 'Lurch'"

"He was underwater" D.I. Wood patted him on his shoulder, "he wouldn't have been able to hear you, anyhow"

"Even so" D.S. Stone finished his tea and hurled the cup into a nearby waste bin, viciously, "I should have known!"

* * * *

"It's good to have you back, Josiah" Samantha said, warmly.

"It's good...it's good to be back" Josiah managed, hoarsely, "I'm finding it diff...difficult to speak"

"It's the water, that and the tubes you've had helping you to breathe" Samantha explained, "don't feel the need to talk! I'm just glad you're back with us" She beamed at the frail frame propped up on pillows in the hospital bed.

"Me...too" Josiah nodded, with difficulty.

"They're going to be keeping you in, just for a day or two" Samantha went on, "they're concerned about the head injuries you've sustained"

"Yes...yes...not sure how I got them" Josiah frowned with the effort of trying to recall, "I'm...I'm not sure what's been happening at all, if I'm honest"

"Don't worry about it" Samantha patted his hand, "the important thing, right now, is for you to get better"

"And...and Archibald? How is he? I haven't seen him" Josiah tried to look around the ward but the effort was too much and he slumped back onto his pillows.

"He's erm..." Samantha began, but was relieved when the ward door opened and Detectives Wood and Stone walked in.

"Ah, Mr. Oakshott, glad to see you're back in the land of the living!" D.I. Wood grinned.

"Sir!" D.S. Stone admonished.

"What?" D.I. Wood looked put out, "it's just an expression!"

"It is good... to see you too, officers" Josiah made an effort to pull himself up, in the bed, but found the effort too much.

"We'll need to be taking statements from you, and from Mrs...Ms. Knight, of course" D.I. Wood corrected himself, taking note of the glare from Samantha, "but I can see that won't be possible just yet"

"I'm happy to help, however I can, Insp...Inspector" Josiah managed, with difficulty.

"As you can see, Inspector, he's having a few problems speaking," Samantha smiled, warmly, at Josiah, "I'm also not too sure that he can remember very much, at least, not at the moment"

"Yes, well, no rush" D.I. Wood fidgeted, awkwardly.

"I'm so glad to see that you're...you're doing ok, Mr. Oakshott" D.S. Stone said, quietly.

"Thank you, Sergeant. I understand, it is in no small part, due to your...your valiant efforts" Josiah coughed and slumped back in his pillows, struggling for breath.

"It was nothing, sir" D.S. Stone shook his head and blushed.

"And...Archibald?" Josiah asked.

"He's in the ICU" D.I. Wood said, matter-of-factly.

"What?" Josiah tried to sit upright, only to start another violent coughing bout.

"It's alright, Josiah" Samantha tried to ease him back onto his pillows, "I was going to tell you later" She glared at D.I. Wood, who raised his eyebrows and backed away, so that he was now behind his Sergeant, "Archibald was submerged for a while and took on quite a bit of water, they're keeping him in an induced coma..."

"Don't know how they can tell the difference" D.I. Wood muttered.

"Inspector!" Samantha snapped.

"Just trying to lighten the mood, that's all!" D.I. Wood attempted to explain, conscious of the thunderous looks of both Samantha and D.S. Stone.

"As I was saying, Josiah, I haven't heard much about Archibald because I'm not a relative. I guess they'll know more when they bring him round" Samantha went on.

"Poor, poor Archibald" Josiah said, weakly, a tear making its way down his face.

"You're not to worry" Samantha patted his hand, "he's in the best place and his mum and his nan are with him"

"He's...he's only in there because of me!" Josiah sobbed.

"Well, yes, he wanted to know what had happened to you, of course he did" Samantha nodded, "but he also wanted to see Precious"

"Ha! Precious indeed!" Josiah snorted, "although...now I think about it...water, I remember water"

"Well, you would sir" D.I. Wood chuckled, "you were up to your chin in it!"

"No, not that!" Josiah shook his head, "I mean...she brought us... water"

"Who did?" Samantha asked.

"Precious" Josiah coughed again, "she was doing that when...when ...when that man hit me!"

"Man, what man?" D.I. Wood asked.

"The...the...driver" Josiah managed, before closing his eyes and sighing.

"This would be the man known to us as Hames, sir" D.S. Stone pointed out.

"I think that he's had more than enough for one day, don't you, gentlemen?" Samantha said, sharply.

"Yes, of course, ma'am" D.S. Stone nodded, "we'll catch up with you both, later"

"Ma'am?" D.I. Wood hissed at his Sergeant, "Since when has she been a 'ma'am'?"

"I think it's the least she deserves, at the moment, sir, don't you?" D.S. Stone snapped, before marching out of the ward.

"I'll erm, I'll speak with you both in due course!" D.I. Wood muttered to Samantha and Josiah before scampering after his colleague.

"I'm worried, Samantha" Josiah said, after they had gone, "I'm worried about Archibald"

"There's no need, Josiah, he's in good hands" Samantha said, hoping against hope that this was the case.

"And…the business" Josiah lurched upright, again, "I have no right to ask this of you, particularly after…" He coughed, violently and struggled to get his breath, for a moment, "after how I've been lately, but…"

"That's enough, Josiah, you need to rest" Samantha eased him back onto his pillows, "there's no need to worry about the business, Mr. Strine and I have it all under control"

"You need…Archibald!" Josiah said, weakly.

"That's true, Josiah" Samantha smiled at him, "but, for now, I'm happy to settle for you!"

Chapter Twenty-Nine
Walking on Sunshine

"Grab your jacket, Stoney, we've got an 'unexplained'" D.I. Wood bellowed from his office.

D.S. Stone dutifully grabbed his jacket and wandered into his superior's lair.

"Where are we heading to, sir?"

"Merkin Reservoir. It's either some fool swimming where he shouldn't, or another of the terminally depressed finally getting their own way" D.I. Wood grabbed a few papers from his desk, shoved an unlit cigarette between his lips and hauled his jacket from the back of the chair.

"The reservoir?" D.S. Stone asked, warily.

"Yep" D.I. Wood nodded, "should make a nice trip out, now the sun's trying to shine" He added, cheerily.

"I erm, I've got a lot of paperwork to catch up on, sir" D.S. Stone put his jacket back on his chair, "can you do without me?"

"Stoney!" D.I. Wood sighed, "This is because it's the reservoir, isn't it?"

"No!" D.S. Stone insisted, but the blush said otherwise.

"Oh, come on Sergeant! I know it was a trauma but it's been a month since that business at Evanley Hall"

"It's nothing to do with that" D.S. Stone shook his head, vehemently, "I'm just snowed under here. Can't you find someone else? One of the D.C.s perhaps?"

"Stoney, I'm not having this" D.I. Wood sat, heavily, on the edge of D.S. Stone's desk, "we've spoken about all that business, haven't we?" D.I. Wood said, not unkindly, "You could have had counselling, you know?"

"I don't want counselling, I'm fine!"

"Oh yeah? You turn white every time the cistern fills up in the Gents!" D.I. Wood rubbed his forehead, "Look, Stoney, you're coming with, whether you like it or not, so grab your jacket"

The two officers marched out of the main office, one noticeably further behind in the procession.

* * * *

"I'm not saying it's not good to have you back, Josiah..." Samantha Knight began.

"Good!" Josiah nodded, from his place on the reinstated sofa

"I just think it's too soon, that's all" Samantha looked at him, with concern. There was no mistaking the toll that recent events had taken. Josiah Oakshott was clearly a shadow of his former self, and he had never been too robust in the first place. Half lying on the sofa, he looked pale, weak and frail.

"I'm absolutely fine, Samantha" Josiah began, before descending into a bout of coughing.

"Hmmm" Samantha said, dubiously.

"I just...I just want to get back to some form of normality" Josiah explained, struggling for breath a little.

"The doctor said you weren't to overtax yourself"

"I hardly think that sprawling on this sofa could realistically be described as overtaxing oneself, do you?"

"I'm talking about the effort involved in just getting here!" Samantha frowned.

"You drove!" Josiah pointed out.

"Yes, and I shouldn't have let you talk me into it! Just remember what we agreed, you're not to do anything whilst you're here, yes?"

"If you insist" Josiah agreed, sulkily.

* * * *

The atmosphere in the police car was icy. D.S. Stone was driving, D.I. Wood was watching the countryside zip past.

"There's no point in sulking, Sergeant" D.I. Wood commented.

"I'm not sulking, sir!" D.S. Stone insisted.

"Hmm, could have fooled me! You haven't said a word since we left the Station"

"Nothing to say, sir" D.S. Stone replied, curtly.

"Hmph!" D.I. Wood shook his head, and folded his arms, "you ever watch that Detective series, that one set in the Caribbean?"

"Erm, no, I don't think so, sir"

"That'd do me, Stoney" D.I. Wood put his hands behind his head and leant back in his seat, "blue skies, sun glinting on the ocean, rum punch, yeah, that's the life"

"I don't see why you would be in the Caribbean, sir" D.S. Stone frowned.

"They always send out some British D.I. to run the show, that's why" D.I. Wood explained, "and you know what? He's always got some drop-dead gorgeous local Sergeant carrying his bags for him."

"Sorry if I don't fill the bill, sir!" D.S. Stone sniffed.

"Horses for courses, Stoney" D.I. Wood closed his eyes and dreamed of white beaches and reggae music, "you're suited to miserable wet days heading toward reservoirs, it'd be a waste to have some beauty-contest lookalike hiding her delights under a gaberdine mac and a scarf"

"I'm not wearing a gaberdine mac, or a scarf!" D.S. Stone protested.

"Yeah, fair enough, but you ain't got any delights to hide either" D.I. Wood chuckled, "I reckon I could do that Caribbean lark. I ought to look into it, see about getting a transfer"

"I'm not sure it's a possibility, sir"

"I wouldn't have to be a D.I." D.I. Wood said, generously, "I'd be happy to do traffic duty what with all that sunshine and sandy beaches"

"You wouldn't get your drop-dead gorgeous Sergeant, not on traffic duty, sir!"

"Good point, well made, Stoney" D.I. Wood agreed, "Still, a man can dream, eh?"

"I think I know the series," D.S. Stone mused, "hasn't it got him out of The Royle Family in it?"

"Yeah, he's about the fourth one so far" D.I. Wood nodded. "Jammy buggers!" He said, with feeling.

"They're not really police officers, you know, sir" D.S. Stone suggested, tentatively.

Dead Reckoning

"I know that! I'm well aware of that, Sergeant!" D.I. Wood snapped, "But it's not a bad number, even if you're only acting the part, is it?"

"No, I suppose not, sir" D.S. Stone agreed. Silence descended, once more.

"These detectives, aren't they brilliantly deductive?" D.S. Stone risked.

"Yeah!" D.I. Wood nodded, thoughtfully, and then, "Here, what are you saying?" He rounded on his Sergeant.

"Nothing, sir" D.S. Stone smirked.

"I can do deduction!" D.I. Wood insisted.

"Of course you can, sir" D.S. Stone reassured.

"I can!"

"I don't disagree, sir"

"Hmph!" D.I. Wood's good mood disappeared, along with the imaginary Caribbean sunshine.

Silence descended again.

"You seem to be getting around a lot better now, sir" D.S. Stone observed, in an attempt to break the stalemate.

"What do you mean by that?"

"Nothing at all, sir!" D.S. Stone protested, "I was just saying, you seem to be walking more easily, which is a good thing, isn't it?"

"Yeah, yeah, I suppose so" D.I. Wood conceded.

"Those pills from the hospital doing the trick?"

"Well, no, not exactly" D.I. Wood squirmed in his seat, a little, "I packed them up a few weeks back"

"Were they not working, sir?"

"No, not really" D.I. Wood admitted, "It didn't seem to be getting no better, so I tried something else, and it's pretty much cleared up!"

"That's brilliant, sir! What did the trick?"

"Erm, well, just between you and me, Sergeant…"

"Yes, sir?"

"It was that ointment I got from that mad old biddy back in Cheshire" D.I. Wood admitted, guiltily.

"Jeannie?"

"Yeah, her" D.I. Wood nodded, "I'm on my second jar of the stuff. I don't know what's in it, and I don't want to know, but I can walk again and the swelling's gone right down"

"Fancy that!" D.S. Stone exclaimed, "At least there's some good come out of that Evanley Hall business, then?"

"Yeah, yeah, you're right there" D.I. Wood leaned back and scratched his head, "I just wish we could get our hands on that mad mob that nearly killed you and the others"

"Thanks for reminding me, sir" D.S. Stone sighed, "I think the reservoir's just up here"

* * * *

In the relative silence of Josiah Oakshott's office, only the ticking of the grandfather clock and the clicking of the laptop keyboard could be heard. Josiah was dozing on the sofa and Samantha was busily typing up the details of a recent commission. The peace was shattered by a crash against the door, followed by some furious knocking. Josiah jerked awake and looked around in a state of some confusion.

"Wha...What's that?" He asked, sleepily.

"Someone at the door, Josiah" Samantha observed, fully focused on her screen.

"Oh, Mr. Strine, I suppose" Josiah rubbed his eyes.

"Could be?" Samantha nodded, "you'd better tell them to come in"

"Me? Oh, yes, well, erm...come!" He intoned, although somewhat out of practice.

There was another almighty crash, and then the door sprang open. A trolley lurched through, leaning perilously to one side. A cup slid, inevitably, to the floor.

"Bugger!" A familiar voice exclaimed.

"Archibald!" Josiah sprang up from the sofa.

"'Lo, Mr. O." Archibald nodded, and grinned.

"Oh, Archibald, you are certainly a sight for sore eyes!" Josiah looked amazed.

"I told him he could come back, on a very limited basis, for a start at least" Samantha grinned.

"Your trolley seems to be somewhat askew" Josiah observed.

"Yeah," Archibald nodded, ruefully, "only, Mrs...Miss...oh, to hell with it, Ms. Knight told me I weren't to carry nowt"

"You were not to carry anything" Josiah clarified.

"Yeah, that's right" Archibald agreed, "so I got this from that antiques place, down the road. It was dead cheap an' all" He looked pleased with himself. A saucer followed the cup on a dive to the floor.

"It does seem to be a bit erm, on the slant" Samantha pointed out.

"Yeah, well, you see, it were cheap, 'cause it only had three wheels…" Archibald explained.

"It appears to have four now, Archibald" Josiah observed.

"Right!" Archibald nodded, "'cause I borrowed a spare from our Stores, them what we use on our trolleys for the coffins, you know? Only, they ain't the same size, which is why…" Another cup bounced on the office carpet.

"Resourceful as ever!" Josiah chuckled, "It's good to have you back, Archibald" Josiah advanced toward him, holding out his hand.

"D'you reckon a hug'd be alright?" Archibald asked, shyly.

"A hug?" Josiah was clearly panic-stricken and looked to Samantha for support. She raised an eyebrow, rested her chin on her hand and glared at him. Josiah took a deep breath, smiled and said,

"Yes, Archibald, you're quite right, a hug *would* be in order"

Chapter Thirty
There's a Guy Works Down the Chip Shop Swears He's Elvis

"Off for lunch, Archie?" Samantha asked, brightly, as they both headed toward the exit door.

"Yeah, I erm," Archibald looked a little sheepish, "I'm heading for the chippy, to be honest"

"Ah yes, why not?" Samantha beamed at him.

"Well, to be honest, me mam's had me on all this healthy stuff ever since I came out of hospital, and there's only so much of that sort of thing you can take" Archibald explained, "so, seeing as how it's the first time *I* get to choose what I'm going to eat…"

"Hence the chips shop, I quite understand Archie" Samantha nodded, "but don't overdo the 'unhealthy' stuff, your mum's just trying to take care of you, you know?"

"Yeah, I know, she's been pretty good, to be fair" Archibald agreed, "even me Nan's tried to help! She keeps bringing me bottles of stout to build me up, reckons it's got iron in it"

"Really? Well, she may have a point" Samantha chuckled, "I hope you're sticking with what we agreed about your return to work, here?"

"Oh yeah, I ain't been out of the Stores all morning"

"Good, make sure you keep it that way! No heavy lifting and no exerting yourself, not until we're sure you're fully fit again" Samantha wagged an admonitory finger.

"Yeah, yeah, I know" Archibald held the door open for her as they exited the premises.

"Enjoy your chips, Archie" Samantha winked at him, "I'm off to the Health Food store to get Josiah one of those nutrition shakes for lunch"

"Is that what he wanted?" Archibald asked, astounded.

"Oh no, but it's not about what he wants, it's about what he gets, and what's good for him!" Samantha grinned, and marched off, breezily, in the direction of town.

* * * *

"Anything on our 'sudden' up at the reservoir?" D.I. Wood asked as D.S. Stone entered his office.

"No sir, nothing yet" D.S. Stone consulted a manilla folder, "he's not on the system, so he's not known to us. Nothing in our Mispers matches, so we're asking the neighbouring forces"

D.I. Wood nodded, vaguely, and continued flicking through the brochure before him. D.S. Stone couldn't help but notice that it appeared to be something to do with the Caribbean.

"How about the PM?" D.I. Wood enquired, eventually.

"Again, nothing yet. They're backed up down there...that bus crash, you know?"

"Yeah, of course" D.I. Wood nodded and continued browsing his brochure, "it'd be good to put that one to bed though, Stoney, that's all. Got more than enough paperwork as it is!"

"Yes, so I see, sir" D.S. Stone remarked, pointedly.

Dead Reckoning

"What's that supposed to mean, Sergeant?" D.I. Wood snapped, noticing the tone.

"Nothing sir" D.S. Stone shook his head, "it would be good to get an identity, so we can inform his next of kin"

"Hmm," D.I. Wood glared at him, suspiciously, "well, keep at it. Let me know when you've got anything"

"There was one odd thing about it" D.S. Stone added.

"Oh yeah?" D.I. Wood didn't seem overly interested, "What was that then?"

"He was all dressed up, as if he had been for an interview or something"

"Well, perhaps he had!" D.I. Wood flicked a page over.

"Possibly" D.S. Stone looked dubious, "but the pathologist said, at first glance, it looked like he had probably been living on the streets for some time. Just seems odd"

"Life's odd, Sergeant" D.I. Wood commented, with a sigh.

D.S. Stone left his superior with his dreams of white sand and endless sunshine and went back to trawl the records for their drowned man.

* * * *

Archibald stood outside 'Angelo's Chippery' and took a deep and satisfying breath of hot fat and vinegar with a tinge of fish. With a happy heart, he stepped inside.

"Hey, itsa the 'ero of the 'our, innit!" The eponymous Angelo (nee Colin) announced, when he looked up from his fryers to see who the new customer was, "Welcome back, Archie!"

"Thanks Angelo" Archibald blushed.

"You alright, mate?" Angelo studied him, closely, "You had a bit of a time, eh? And you lost a bit a weight, innit? That's 'cause we ain't seen you in weeks"

"I've been on a diet" Archibald nodded.

"You don't want no diet!" Angelo shook his head, fiercely, "itsa plate of chips, that's what you want, boy!"

"Yeah, well, I've started back to work today, so…"

"That's good news!" Angelo reached over and patted him on the shoulder. Archibald had noticed how, since his brush with death, everyone seemed to think it was ok to hug and pat him! It wasn't that he objected, particularly, but he wondered how Mr. O. was managing if the same thing was happening to him? "Fishcake, chips and peas onna tray, is it?" Angelo enquired.

"Please!""

"I'lla get the younga lady to serve you" Angelo nodded, "Hey, Gemma!" He shouted over his shoulder, "we gotta customer, get yourself out 'ere"

A young girl appeared from the store room at the back. It was difficult to see much of her because, as well as the mandatory full length overall and head covering, she was also sporting a full-face mask, the sort Archibald had last seen at the height of the pandemic.

"Is fishcake, chips anda peas he wants" Angelo explained to the girl, who nodded and set to work preparing the order.

"Gemma?" Archibald looked at Angleo quizzically and mimed the face mask.

"Yeah, she'sa new innit?" Angelo busied himself with his fryers, but whispered "it's some immune thing or other, that'sa why she has to

Dead Reckoning

wear that mask, so she reckons" And then, for the benefit of the shop as a whole, "now you keepa your 'ands to yourself, young Archie, I already lost two good assistants on account of you" He winked and wagged a finger at him.

"I'm a reformed character, Angelo" Archibald grinned, "I'm off women for the foreseeable"

"Oh yeah? I 'eard it all before, Arch" Angelo smirked, "you justa wait, some other pretty face'll give you the eye an' then, whoosh! You watch 'im, Gemma, 'e's got quitea the reputation 'round 'ere"

Gemma appeared to blush and giggled a little. Archibald noticed her eyes, which were both striking and, somehow, familiar.

"Here we are, fishcake, chips and peas, on a tray" She announced, somewhat muffled because of the mask, handing him the warm parcel of white paper.

"I chucked on a few batter bits, an' all, 'cause you 'eros as got to keep your strength up, innit?" Angelo grinned.

"Thanks Angelo, ta Gemma" Archibald tucked the parcel under his arm, paid the bill and turned to go.

"I hope you enjoy them, Archibald!" Gemma said, as he marched out.

Samantha was just passing, as he came out, clutching his prized parcel of stodgy lunch. She was holding a large plastic container with some violently green liquid inside it.

"Hey, Archie! Mission accomplished?" Samantha grinned.

"Yeah, I'm really looking forward to these" Archibald nodded, "hey, they've got a new assistant at Angelo's, calls herself Gemma"

"Well, you've been responsible for a lot of their labour turnover" Samantha pointed out.

"Yeah, that's what Angelo said, an' all" Archibald smiled, "this one wears a face mask, on account of she's got some immune thingy or other, so I don't know what she looks like"

"That's a pity for her" Samantha said, "but it's good of Angelo to give her a job"

"Yeah, he's not a bad bloke" Archibald agreed, "although why he has to put on that fake accent, I don't know! He went to school with me, you know, he's no more from Cyprus than I am"

"I guess it adds to the ambience" Samantha chuckled.

"Yeah, I s'pose" Archibald snuck a chip from the parcel as he walked along, then stopped dead, with a perturbed look on his face.

"What's the matter, Archie? Are you alright? There's nothing hurting, is there?" Samantha looked extremely concerned.

"Archibald!" Archibald said, vacantly.

"I'm sorry? Are you sure you're ok?"

"She called me Archibald!"

"Who did?"

"That Gemma, the one with the face mask I was telling you about."

"Well, what's wrong with that? That's your name!"

"Nothing, 'cept nobody calls me that, other than Mr. O." Archibald shook his head, "Angelo don't, never has done, so how did she know to call me 'Archibald'?"

Chapter Thirty-One
She's Not There

"You know, Archie," Samantha said, looking at her companion with some concern, "It's perfectly understandable that you should be a bit 'on edge' after everything that you've been through"

"I just think it's bloody odd, that's all" Archibald grumbled.

"Look, I suspect you and Josiah have been the talk of the town for weeks now," Samantha pointed out, "You were headline news, you know? So, it's hardly surprising if your name is on everyone's lips, now is it?"

Archibald clutched his chip shop parcel closer to him, hunched over and mumbled to himself as they made their way back to Oakshott and Underwood.

"There's no point in being grumpy about it" Samantha chuckled, "you're famous around here, just at the moment. Not for a good reason, I'll give you, but you're still famous!"

Archibald took himself off to his workbench, still grumbling, to enjoy his fishcake, chips and peas, whilst Samantha made her way back to Josiah's office, to deliver his healthy nutritional shake.

"Ah yes, thank you" Josiah said, dubiously, when Samantha nudged him awake from his doze on the sofa, "Lunch, eh?"

"It will do you a world of good" Samantha insisted, seating herself at the desk.

Josiah held the green liquid up to the light and frowned.

"It looks like a stagnant pond" He observed.

"It's full of nutrients designed to build you up and return you to full strength"

"I would imagine that is also the case you could make for a stagnant pond" Josiah had removed the lid and was sniffing the liquid with distaste. "I don't imagine that Archibald is partaking of anything similar to this?"

"No, he's treated himself to fishcake, chips and peas" Samantha smiled, "he's on a bit of a line, actually"

"Why is that?" Josiah asked, attempting to put off the evil moment when he would have to drink the concoction.

"There's a new girl in the chip shop…" Samantha began.

"Oh no! He's not going down that road again?" Josiah looked concerned.

"No, he tells me he's foresworn romantic entanglements" Samantha grinned, "no, he was put out because she called him Archibald, not Archie, he thinks it's suspicious"

"Suspicious? Why should that be the case?"

"I think he's just a bit jumpy at the moment, and who can blame him?" Samantha shrugged, "This girl was wearing a face mask, because of some immune-problem she had, so he's convinced she's up to no good"

"Hmm, do you mean he thinks she might be one of that gang that tried to kill us?" Josiah frowned.

"I guess so" Samantha nodded, "I suppose he's bound to be wary, you would be too, I would imagine, but it seems pretty unlikely"

"What was this girl's name?"

Dead Reckoning

"Erm, Gemma I think" Samantha opened a file on her desk and perused some paperwork. Josiah looked thoughtful, eased himself up from the sofa, gratefully put the nutritious shake down on a side table, and pottered over to a bookcase. After a few moments browsing, he prised a book from the shelf and proceeded to consult it.

"Gemma, you said?" He flicked through some pages, "With a 'G'?"

"I guess so" Samantha replied, distractedly, engaged in her paperwork.

"Oh!" Josiah cried out, suddenly, sitting back down on the sofa with a thud, "I think our young friend may have a point"

"Hmm? What do you mean?"

"I've had this book for ages, it concerns the meaning of names. It's sometimes useful when composing eulogies" Josiah explained, "take a look at this page" He held the book out, weakly, to her.

Samantha sighed, closed the file she was working on, and strode over to the sofa.

"Where am I looking? Ah, yes" Samantha peered at the page, "Oh!"

There was a one-word definition for the name 'Gemma'. It read, quite simply:

'Precious'

* * * *

"I've got the results back from that 'Suspicious' at the reservoir, sir" D.S. Stone proffered a manilla folder to his superior, who now seemed to have a collection of Caribbean holiday brochures to peruse.

"Just give me the edited highlights, Stoney" D.I. Wood said, from whichever sandy beach he was currently lying on, in his imagination.

"Well, like we surmised before, the victim had definitely been living on the streets but was very well dressed, 'as if he was attending an interview', it says here" D.S. Stone began.

"That's possible" D.I. Wood nodded, "some of these homeless charities set 'em up with decent clobber if they're going for a job"

"True, sir, but why then would he finish up in our reservoir?"

D.I. Wood shrugged his shoulders.

"But there's something else, and you're not going to be happy about it" D.S. Stone tentatively turned a page over, anticipating his boss's reaction.

"If it's anything that implies this wasn't an accident, you're damn right!" D.I. Wood snarled.

"Yes sir, I'm afraid there is. It seems that the water in the deceased's lungs is not the same as the water in the reservoir" D.S. Stone started counting under his breath, waiting for the reaction.

"What? What the hell's that supposed to mean?" D.I. Wood threw his holiday brochure down onto his desk.

"It means, sir, that he drowned somewhere else and then his body was dumped in the reservoir"

"Murdered then?" D.I. Wood glared at his sergeant.

"It looks that way, sir, yes"

* * * *

"Oh heck!" Samantha dropped onto the sofa, beside Josiah, and put her head in her hands.

"I suppose it might be a coincidence" Josiah suggested, weakly.

Dead Reckoning

"That a girl, with a name that means 'Precious', turns up in the same Chip Shop that Archibald always uses, with her face covered by a mask, and then calls Archie 'Archibald', which is something that no-one other than you and Precious DeVille have ever done? Yes, I suppose it might just be a coincidence!"

"Well, now you put it like that" Josiah nodded, miserably, "so, what do we do? I suppose the police should be informed?"

"Do you seriously think that shower are going to take this seriously?" Samantha stood up, smartly, "*They'll* say it's just a coincidence! I'm going to have to go down there and see what she's got to say for herself"

"Really? Is that wise? What about Archibald?"

"I think he needs to come with me, if he's up to it" Samantha bit her bottom lip in concentration, "I'll need him to identify her"

* * * *

"There's something else, sir" D.S. Stone continued, reluctantly.

"What?" D.I. Wood asked, wearily, from behind the hands that were currently covering his face.

"Well, I expanded the mispers search to neighbouring forces, like you said"

"Yes?"

"Seems he matches the description of a lad they had living rough on the streets of Chester. Our lot had dealings with him a few times, nothing serious, they were just concerned for his welfare. Anyway, they haven't seen him for a few days, possibly a week or so"

"Don't suppose we've got any DNA, fingerprints or anything to match him up with?"

"No sir, nothing like that. Like I said, he's never been in any trouble, so there was no need"

"Bugger!" D.I. Wood said, with feeling, "So we've got some unknown lad, possibly off the streets of Chester, finishes up in our reservoir after some sod's drowned him somewhere else? Is that about the size of it, Sergeant?"

"Yep, that's how it could be, sir" D.S. Stone confirmed, with trepidation.

"Bloody marvellous!" D.I. Wood swept his holiday brochures from the desk, onto the floor, "this is all I'm short of. I was just thinking about putting in for some extended leave, get a bit of sun, sand and…stuff, you know? And now, this"

"They reckon they might be able to narrow down the source of the water in his lungs, but it may take a few days, sir"

"I don't suppose there's any faint hope that it might be a mistake, eh?" D.I. Wood asked, hopefully.

"I'm afraid not, sir. They've run multiple tests"

"Right" D.I. Wood sighed, "you'd better see if you can find anyone from the Chester lot who thinks they might be able to formally identify him. That would be a start, I suppose"

"Will do, sir" D.S. Stone made good his escape from the office.

* * * *

Samantha Knight strode down the street like an avenging angel, with Archibald Thurble stumbling along in her wake.

Dead Reckoning

"I hope you're not right" He mumbled, trying to keep up with her.

"Me too, Archie, but we've got to find out"

As they approached Angelo's Chippery, they could see the eponymous owner standing on the street outside, looking this way and that.

"Hah! 'ere 'e is" Angelo announced, "I dunno 'ow 'e does it! I can't keep any girls in my shop, 'cept 'e chases 'em away"

"What seems to be the problem?" Samantha asked.

"Problem? It's me girl assistant, innit?" Angelo flapped his arms, hopelessly, "'e's only driven 'er off, ain't 'e? 'E comes in, all fishcake, chips and mushy peas innit, she serves 'im, next thing, she's out the back, I call 'er to come serve the next customer, she's only gone ain't she? Took 'er coat, 'er bag, everything!"

"Did you know her name?"

"Gemma, innit?" Angelo said, still looking up and down the street.

"Gemma what?" Samantha persisted.

"I don'ta ruddy know, do I?"

"Do you have an address for her?"

"Address? Address? Course I don'ta 'ave no address, I ain'ta plannin' on shackin' up with 'er, I just need 'er to serve chips, is thata too much to ask, eh?"

"I'm sorry, Colin" Archibald said, miserably.

"You don'ta call me that, not outa 'ere, alright?" Angelo hissed.

"We're going to have to inform the police" Samantha said, firmly.

"You what? Is just some girl, cleared off from 'er job, innit?" Angelo said, looking astonished, "is not crime ofa the century or nowt, issit?"

"You might be surprised, Mr. Angelo" Samantha said, dialling the familiar number on her mobile 'phone, "You might be surprised!"

Chapter Thirty-Two
Photograph

D.S. Stone strode out of 'Angelo's Chippery' looking less than pleased. He snapped his notebook shut and made his way over to his boss, who was leaning against a squad car, stabbing ineffectually, with his wooden fork, at something on the cardboard tray he was clutching. All around, blue lights were flashing and police officers were milling about.

"How the hell are you supposed to eat mushy peas with one of these, eh? Tell me that, Sergeant?" D.I. Wood seethed.

"I don't really know, sir, I can't say that I've ever tried!"

"Waste of bloody time, if you ask me" D.I. Wood tore a piece of battered fish from the morass of chips and peas and munched it, thoughtfully, "Speaking of wastes of time, you found anything in there?"

"No sir, nothing" D.S. Stone shook his head, miserably. "There's no sign she was ever in there. Do you want me to get the Forensics boys in?"

"You're having a laugh, aren't you Stoney?" D.I. Wood looked at his colleague in astonishment, "How the hell do you think I could justify the cost of that to the powers that be, eh?"

D.S. Stone looked around at the squad cars and police officers wandering here and there.

"Well, if we're talking about cost, sir..." He gestured at the scene.

"Ah, well" D.I. Wood dragged a reluctant chip from its hiding place and devoured it, "you've got to put on a bit of a show, haven't you? People like to see we're making an effort"

"I don't think Mr. Angelo is too impressed. You're the only one to have had any fish and chips this lunchtime, and he's moaning that you didn't pay for them!"

"Miserable bugger!" D.I. Wood snarled, "He should be grateful. He'll be snived out with customers once we clear off, they'll all want to know what's been going on"

"So, we do nothing?"

"Not much we can do" D.I. Wood continued munching, happily, "I mean, look at what we've got. Some bird wearing a face mask gets herself a job serving chips, big deal!" D.I. Wood tapped a finger to indicate one point made, "Then, after serving Lurch…"

D.S. Stone gave him a hard stare.

"Alright, alright, after serving…what's his name?" D.I. Wood queried.

"It's Mr. Thurble, sir, Archibald Thurble"

"Yeah, him" D.I. Wood nodded, chasing a pea around the tray, "well, any road, after serving him, she clears off. Again, big deal! The only other evidence we've got is that she's called 'Gemma' and that her name may, or may not, mean 'Precious'. I'd like to see you take that lot to the CPS and get a conviction"

"Suspicious though, isn't it, sir?"

"Look, I'm not saying there's nowt in it" D.i. Wood shrugged, "maybe it was her, maybe it wasn't, who knows? I'm just saying, no-one's going to thank us for wasting any more resources than we already have done, on this"

"Ms. Knight wanted a word with you" D.S. Stone pointed out.

"Who?" D.I. Wood looked puzzled, then realised, "Oh God, not her again! Can't you deal, Sergeant?"

"She specifically asked for you, sir"

"Bugger!" D.I. Wood said, with feeling, hurling the empty tray and chip papers into the nearby bin.

D.S. Stone made a gesture and Samantha Knight came bustling over.

"Have you got anything, Inspector?" She asked.

"Bloody indigestion, I shouldn't wonder" D.I. Wood patted his chest and emitted a resounding burp, "Better out than in" He grinned.

"I meant about Precious" Samantha snapped, "Archie's very concerned"

"Well, if it *was* her, and there's no way of telling if it was or not, she's long gone" D.I. Wood wiped his hands on a handkerchief and dabbed at his lips. "Bit of a wild goose chase, really"

"So, now what?" Samantha folded her arms and gave him a hard stare.

"Well, nothing, to be honest" D.I. Wood shrugged, "if this 'Gemma' puts in another appearance, give us a shout and we'll have a word, otherwise, we're done here"

"Aren't you going to search for her?"

"Where?" D.I. Wood looked around him, "Any ideas? 'Cause I certainly wouldn't know where to start! If people kept decent records…" He nodded toward the chip shop, "or any bloody records, for that matter, we might have a chance, but, without any evidence, there's nothing we can do!"

"So, what do I tell Archie?"

"I'd tell him to give fish and chips a miss, for a start" D.I. Wood smirked, climbing into his car, "Come along Sergeant, we haven't got all day"

"No sir," D.S. Stone walked around the car, "Sorry miss!" He smiled, weakly, at Samantha, who turned on her heel and marched off.

* * * *

Back at the Merkin-under-Heathwood Police Station, D.S. Stone was talking animatedly, with another police officer, in the open-plan outer office. He patted the other man's shoulder, nodded and, with a manilla folder and his tablet under his arm, made his way into D.I. Wood's inner sanctum, where the man himself was engrossed in his Caribbean holiday brochures.

"We've got something more on that 'suspicious' in the reservoir, sir" He announced on entry.

"Please tell me that it's all a cock-up, he died of natural causes, and we can all go home" D.I. Wood suggested, without looking up from his brochure.

"'Fraid not, sir" D.S. Stone shook his head, sadly, "I've just been talking to one of the Chester lads, he's kindly been down and identified the body…"

"So, we know who he is?"

"Well, not really sir, no" D.S. Stone admitted, reluctantly, "All we do know is that he called himself 'Jimmy' and he lived on the streets, mostly. Fetched up in Chester about a year ago" D.S. Stone consulted his file, "never caused any trouble, they spoke to him once or twice, tried to get him into a hostel, but he wasn't having any of it…"

"Fat lot of bloody use that is, then" D.I. Wood said, moodily.

Dead Reckoning

"At least we know, for sure, where he came from." D.S. Stone pointed out, "but it gets better" He grinned.

"Go on, tell me we know who did him in"

"Not exactly, sir, but there's a possible connection I thought you might find interesting"

"Go on!" D.I. Wood put his chin on his hand and looked at his Sergeant with studied disinterest.

"The lad from Chester brought us a bit of CCTV footage he thought we might like to see" D.S. Stone flipped open his tablet, pressed a key or two, and spun the screen around to show his boss.

"What am I looking at?"

"As far as they know, this is the last recorded sighting of 'Jimmy' in Chester before he rocked up here" D.S. Stone explained, "now, watch this" D.S. Stone pressed another key and the CCTV footage began to play.

In the grainy picture, it was possible to see the hunched-up figure of, what could be, a young man, sitting with his back against a wall, outside a shop. He was dressed in a tatty, rather ripped, bomber jacket and jeans. A baseball cap with, what appeared to be, a few coins, was placed in front of him. Shoppers were walking past him, most making a careful detour around the cap.

"He's going to struggle to get a pint out of that lot, tight-fisted bastards!" D.I. Wood observed.

"Yes, but watch what happens next, sir"

A girl, wearing a cloak and a shawl around her head, walked along but, instead of avoiding the begging man, made a bee-line for him. She bent over and seemed to be in earnest conversation with him. At no time could you see her face.

"So? Could be anyone!" D.I. Wood commented, "Could be Little Red Riding Hood for all I know!"

"Yes, she seems to have a good idea where the CCTV cameras are" D.S. Stone nodded, "but, just wait a minute"

The conversation seemed to have ended. The girl in the cloak and shawl appeared to be helping 'Jimmy' to his feet, and then she looked to her left, and it was just possible to see her face in profile.

"Ring any bells, sir?" D.S. Stone raised an eyebrow.

"Not to be honest, no" D.I. Wood shook his head.

D.S. Stone tapped a few more keys. Now the frozen still from the Chester video was side-by-side with a still from Merkin High Street.

"I reckon it looks like her from that jewellery job. The one that Mrs. Knight identified as Precious DeVille, from this very photo. If it is her, then it means…"

"Oh God!" D.I. Wood covered his face with his hands and sighed, deeply, "it means that this 'Jimmy's' death and the attempted murder of Lurch and his boss, are probably linked, doesn't it?"

"I'm afraid so, sir" D.S. Stone nodded, with a satisfied smile on his face.

Chapter Thirty-Three
Strange Brew

Samantha strode into the storeroom of Oakshott and Underwood to find Archibald morosely leafing through the local newspaper. She gave a quick 'ahem' to warn him of her impending arrival and he jumped up and attempted to hide the newspaper behind him. Then, realising that he wasn't supposed to be doing anything, anyway, he returned the paper to his makeshift desk.

"'Lo Ms. Knight" He muttered.

"I wish you would call me Samantha" She chided, "How are you feeling?"

"I'm alright" He shuffled his feet, "It's just...I'm just a bit..."

"Jumpy?"

"Yeah, that's about the size of it" Archibald nodded, "Did they find owt, at the Chippy, the police that is?"

"No, I don't think so" Samantha shook her head, sadly, and sat down beside him, "I didn't get the impression that they were going to look all that hard"

"She's too bright for them" Archibald mused.

"Yes, well, there may be something in that" Samantha nodded, "But we can't just leave it like that, can we?"

"Can't we?" Archibald looked surprised, "What else can we do?"

"We need to ask some questions. I think we need to go back to Evanley Hall"

"Go back? Why would you want to go back there?" Archibald yelped.

"Well, not the Hall itself, more the cottage. I think Jeannie knows more than she's been telling us" Samantha looked at him, hopefully.

"Well, good luck!" Archibald turned back to his paper.

"I was hoping you could take me?"

"WHAT? Why?" Archibald spluttered, "Why would I want to do that?"

"Well, it would help me a great deal" Samantha explained, "For one thing, I don't think Josiah's put me back on the Company Car Insurance yet and, of course, you know the way"

"I want to FORGET the way!" Archibald folded his arms and tried to look resolute, "I don't want to go there ever again!"

"Yes, yes, I know Archie" Samantha soothed, "But, the sooner we get to the bottom of all this, the sooner you can stop feeling..."

"Jumpy?"

"Yes, amongst other things" Samantha smiled warmly at him, "Shall we go?"

There was a series of muttered expletives but Archibald eased himself from his stool.

"And this'll be the end of it?" He fixed Samantha with a 'look'.

"Well, I think it might be the beginning of the end, eh?"

* * * *

Dead Reckoning

"Right!" D.I. Wood announced as he entered the open-plan office, "I've been and seen the Governor. As expected, he's doing his fruit about all this. Buggered up his budget forecast for this month and no mistake! Any road, what you lot need to do now is find out anything and everything you can about these three" He pinned the CCTV still images of Jeanette, Hames and Precious to the central whiteboard.

There was a collective groan from the seated officers. In an effort to look focused, however, many of them started to instantly tap on keyboards or pull files from cabinets, without any real hope of achieving anything constructive. D.S. Stone, looking somewhat thoughtful, began to access the National Police Database.

* * * *

Archibald pulled the limousine into the dark and rutted lane, leading to Evanley Hall, and stopped almost immediately.

"Why are we stopping here?" Samantha asked.

"This is as far as I'm going!" Archibald said, grimly, taking his hands off the steering wheel and folding his arms.

"Really? Ok, no problem" Samantha sighed, "we'll just have to walk up to the cottage"

"WE??" Archibald looked startled.

"Well, yes, of course" Samantha smiled at him, sweetly, "you'll have to come with me"

"WHY??"

"Because you've had dealings with all three of them, haven't you? There's that Nenette, the chauffeur cum butler, Hames and this daughter of Nenette's, Precious"

"I still don't see why I've got to come" Archibald grumbled.

"Come on, Archie" Samantha said, encouragingly, "you can play with the kittens!"

"Humph!" Archibald looked less than happy but climbed out of the car, anyway.

Samantha made her way, gingerly, up the rutted track, cursing her decision to wear high heels. Archibald trailed some way after her, muttering all the time. When she finally reached the dilapidated gate of the cottage, Samantha managed to drag it to one side, walked up to the cottage door and knocked smartly.

"WHO IS IT? A voice shrieked.

"It's Samantha Knight, Jeannie." Samantha yelled through the letterbox, ignoring the potent smell of cats and ancient cooking that emanated from within, "We met some weeks ago, when there was all that business up at the Hall?"

"BUGGER OFF!"

"Now, don't be like that, Jeannie" Samantha pleaded, "we just want a quick word"

"WE? WHO'S 'WE'?"

"It's me and Archibald. You remember Archibald? You helped him when we dragged him out of the water"

"I don't need reminding" Archibald chuntered, scuffing his shoes.

There was the sound of heavy furniture being moved about and doors being dragged open, before the front door opened a crack and an eye peered out.

Dead Reckoning

"Ah, right, so it is" Jeannie said, "yer'd better come in, but mind the cats, yer hear?"

"Thank you, Jeannie" Samantha smiled at her less than cheery host and led the way into the dark recesses of the cottage.

"'Ow are ye doin', son?" Jeannie asked as Archibald squeezed past her, through the door.

"Oh, you know…" Archibald flapped his arms, at a loss for words.

"He's not himself" Samantha said, with some concern, as they made their way into the kitchen.

"'Ow's that then?" Jeannie frowned.

"He's …how would you put it, Archie?" Samantha asked.

"Jumpy, I guess" Archibald admitted, reluctantly.

Jeannie looked him up and down and frowned.

"Not surprisin', considerin' what went on up there" Jeannie nodded, "sit yersen down, I'll fix yer summat"

Samantha and Archibald cleared a couple of dining chairs of cats and assorted towels and blankets and sat down at the table. Jeannie put a kettle on to boil and began grinding something up in a bowl, using a pestle and mortar.

"Ow's the other one?" She called over her shoulder.

"Josiah? Not too great" Samantha admitted, "He's very tired, always. He comes to work with me but he hasn't got any energy and sleeps most of the time."

"Yeah, sounds about right. They both on 'em 'ad a bad time of it" Jeannie pondered, still grinding and pummelling whatever was in the bowl, "were lucky to come out of it at all, that's what yer 'ave to tell yersen." More ferocious pounding, "Yer've got to give 'em time to convalesce! Yer can't just jump back inter life after some bugger's tried to drag yer out of it, can yer, eh?"

"Shall I make the tea?" Samantha suggested, now that the kettle had boiled.

"It's not fer tea, it's fer 'im" Jeannie emptied the bowl's contents into a mug and then added the boiling water, "but yer can make a pot with what's left, if yer've a mind to" She conceded.

She stirred the mug, vigorously, and brought it over to Archibald. He looked at the greenish/brown concoction, with bits of leaf and twig swirling about on the surface, with definite suspicion.

"Now, get that dahn yer, while it's 'ot" Jeannie instructed.

Archibald looked to Samantha for moral support, but she was busy making a pot of tea. Under the intense glare of Jeannie, he took a deep breath, and had a go at drinking the evil brew.

* * * *

"If you've got a moment, sir, I think I might have something" D.S. Stone said, tapping on the door of D.I. Wood's office.

"Good work, Stoney! Come on in and tell me all about it!" D.I. Wood said, without enthusiasm and without looking up from his Caribbean brochure.

"Well, sir, it struck me that no-one can go through life without leaving some sort of bureaucratic trace..." D.S. Stone began.

"A paper trail, that sort of thing?" D.I. Wood flicked a sun-drenched page, over.

Dead Reckoning

"Yes, sir. So, I've had a look at the police database to see what I could find out about Evanley Hall. After all, that's the one thing we can be sure of, with this lot, that all of them have a connection to the Hall..."

"Yeah, good point" D.I. Wood nodded, still studying the brochure.

"Well, as far as I can see, sir, there's been no-one registered as living there for years. Thirty years ago, there was just the two girls, Jeanette and..."

"Nenette, stupid bloody name" D.I. Wood snarled.

"Yes, Nenette. Both the same age, so I think we can surmise they were probably twins. I'm waiting on their birth certificates to confirm. The only other person there was their grandfather, Shepherd Mountjoy. Now, he died about five years later..." D.S. Stone produced a copy Death Certificate.

"Leaving them two with a wodge of cash and the Hall, I suppose?" D.I. Wood suggested.

"You would have thought so, yes sir" D.S. Stone nodded, "But, according to his Will, he left a few grand to various Navy and Service charities, a couple of grand to Nenette and everything else to Jeanette"

"That would have gone down like a lead balloon!" D.I. Wood put down his brochure, picked up the Will and perused it.

"I would have thought so, sir" D.S. Stone grinned, "Not long after that, the Hall appears to fall empty and stays that way, right up to the present day"

"So, we've no idea where they went, once the Hall fell empty?"

"Not Nenette, no" D.S. Stone shook his head, "up to press, I can't find any record of her."

"Bugger!" D.I. Wood said, with feeling.

"Jeanette, however, now that's a different story, sir" D.S. Stone said, looking somewhat smug.

"How come?"

"Take a look at who's registered as living at the Estate Cottage?"

D.I. Wood scrutinised the proffered document.

"Jeanette Mountjoy! You mean that...that Jeannie...the mad old bint with the cats, she's the heiress of Evanley Hall?" D.I. Wood looked astounded.

"Looks that way, sir" D.S. Stone beamed.

"So, she's the one old Oakshott was sniffing around, all those years ago?"

"Seems so. Takes all sorts, sir, eh?"

"Well, I'll go to the foot of our stairs!" D.I. Wood shook his head in wonder, "Get your coat, Stoney, I think we need to go and have another chat with our Jeannie"

Chapter Thirty-Four
Who's That Girl?

"'Ow yer feelin' now, son?" Jeannie asked, studying Archibald carefully.

"I'm erm…" Archibald considered and grinned, "pretty bloody good, ack…actoo…acshually!" He started to giggle, uncontrollably.

"Seems to 'ave got the jumpiness sorted" Jeannie said, prising the empty mug from Archibald's hand.

"Was it alcoholic?" Samantha looked at Archibald with some concern.

"Not alcoholic, no" Jeannie shook her head, vigorously, "narcotic…werl, mebbes"

"Narcotic!" Samantha looked shocked.

"Yer didn't want 'im jumpy, didjer?"

"Well, no, but…"

"I'm a little teapot…" Archibald contributed to the discussion.

"There y'are then" Jeannie shrugged and took a sip of tea, frowned and said, "This is like gnat's water"

"Don't mention it!" Samantha sniffed.

"…short and st…" Archibald slumped back in his chair and started to snore.

"Won't 'urt 'im to sleep" Jeannie nodded.

"I guess not," Samantha agreed, "Jeannie, there's a reason why we came to see you, today"

"Dint think it were for me tea" Jeannie grinned.

"We need to find out a bit more about the people who did this to Archie" Samantha explained.

"'Ow should I know?" Jeannie went to refill her tea mug, after giving the pot a vigorous stir.

"You seemed to know a bit about them, when we were here last"

"Werl, yer 'ear stuff, dontcher?" Jeannie shrugged and settled herself by the fire. A cacophonous snore from Archibald scared off the cat that was just about to settle on her lap.

"I don't know, do you?" Samantha looked at her hostess, quizzically, "Such as?"

Jeannie squirmed in her seat, much to the cat's annoyance.

"Werl, she's supposed to be the Lady of the Manor, ain't she?" Jeannie raised an eyebrow, "But that ain't right. Then there's that chit of a girl what she reckons is her daughter, but she ain't no daughter of her'n and she weren't 'ere when they first turned up. Then there's 'im what's supposed to be 'er servant..."

"This 'Hames' person?"

"Yeah, 'im. Git!" Jeannie rubbed her wrists, remembering where she'd previously been tied. "Werl, I seen 'em carryin' on an' doin', so I don't reckon 'e's no servant" Jeannie chuckled, "Less'n she's got a thing for 'er servants, o' course"

"So, they're not a family?"

Dead Reckoning

"Nah!" Jeannie spat into the fire, "fer a family, yer'd 'ave to 'ave a babby, an' she's too posh to push"

There was a loud knocking on the cottage door.

"Bugger!" Jeannie snarled, "'oozat nah?"

She evicted the cat from her lap and tottered toward the door, which she opened a crack and peered out. Samantha could hear the familiar, if unwelcome, voice of D.I. Wood, saying;

"Jeannette Mountjoy, I presume?"

"Who?" Jeannie replied, still not opening the door fully.

"Jeanette..." D.I. Wood sighed, deprived of his amusing opening line, "You are Jeannette Mountjoy!"

"No, I ain't" Jeannie replied, flatly, opening the door and staggering back to her chair.

"With respect, ma'am" D.I. Wood said, with as much patience as he could muster, "there is only one person listed as occupying these premises, and that person is Jeanette Mountjoy. Oh, Mrs. Knight!"

The Detectives were surprised to find Samantha seated by the fire.

"Inspector, Sergeant" She nodded to each, in turn.

"I dunno wot yer on with" Jeannie muttered, sipping from her mug, "if'n yer want tea, there's some in the pot"

D.S. Stone went to investigate the tea pot whilst D.I. Wood pulled up a dining chair, reversed it and straddled the result, glaring all the time at Jeannie.

"Are you denying that you are Jeanette Mountjoy?"

"I'm Jeannie" Jeannie said, matter-of-factly, "'ave been fer years"

"Hang on!" Samantha looked puzzled, "Wasn't Jeanette the old flame of Josiah's that he was supposed to be meeting for dinner on the night he went missing?"

"Nowt ter do with me" Jeannie shook her head, "I were tied up, remember?"

"CAN WE JUST ESTABLISH, ONCE AND FOR ALL, THAT YOU ARE JEANETTE MOUNTJOY?" D.I. Wood yelled, all patience gone, scattering cats in all directions.

"Alright, keep yer 'air on" Jeannie sipped her drink, noisily, "Ow's yer foot?"

"Much better, thank you!" D.I. Wood admitted, reluctantly.

"Toldjer!" Jeannie replied, with a smirk.

"Will you *please* just answer the question" D.I. Wood implored.

"Oh, werl…" Jeannie sighed, deeply, "I s'pose I might 'ave been…once"

"Gosh!" Samantha looked shocked.

"Dunner look so surprised!" Jeannie snapped, "I 'ad a lot of suitors in me day"

"Including Josiah?"

"That 'im what were in the watter, with 'im?" Jeannie nodded toward the sleeping Archibald.

"Yes" Samantha nodded.

"Huh!" Jeannie shrugged and shook her head, "Dint reckernise 'im! E's changed"

Dead Reckoning

"So, that's why you knew your way around the Hall? You knew where there might be blankets!" Samantha went on.

"Werl, I grew up there" Jeannie nodded, "Oughter know a bit"

"What can you tell me about your sister, Nenette?" D.I. Wood asked.

"Nuffin!" Jeannie folded her arms and stared at the fire.

"She *is* your sister?" D.S. Stone insisted.

"Twin sister, yeah" Jeannie looked troubled, "Nowt terdo with me though, nah" She poked at the fire, violently.

"Do you know where she is?" D.I. Wood asked.

Jeannie shrugged and continued to stare at the fire.

"How about her daughter, Precious?"

Jeannie spluttered and chuckled.

"Precious?" She giggled, "She ain't got no daughter, 'Precious', it's like I was tellin' this'n, she's too posh to push"

"You don't believe she has children?" D.I. Wood frowned.

"Nah, never in a rain of pig's puddin'" Jeannie shook her head, "I dunner know where the girl came from, just turned up one day, I think"

"How about this man" D.I. Wood held up a CCTV image, "Hames?"

"Jeannie told me that she thinks he and Nenette might be…in a romantic liaison" Samantha supplied.

"Thank you, Mrs. Knight, but I would be grateful if you would allow Miss Mountjoy here, to answer the questions" D.I. Wood snapped.

"Romantic lee-ay-zon?" Jeannie giggled, "ain't 'eard it called that fer a while" She wheezed.

"Do you know who he is?" D.S. Stone enquired.

"Nope" Jeannie shook her head.

"Do you know his full name?"

"Nope" She shook her head, again.

"Do you know what his relationship is to either Nenette Mountjoy, or the woman known as Precious?" D.I. Wood asked.

"Dunno!" Jeannie shrugged, "Dunno if they've got any! 'E turned up with 'er, a while back. Prob'ly 'ad a few lee-ay-zons, mindjer!" She chuckled.

"We're not getting anywhere, sir" D.S. Stone sighed.

"No, Sergeant" D.I. Wood frowned, "I suppose finding out what they are *not*, is something. Not much, but something. What's the problem with Mr. erm...Thurble?"

"Archie? Jeannie's given him something to erm...make him feel better" Samantha looked at her sleeping colleague with concern.

"E'll be alright" Jeannie rubbed her hands in front of the fire, "E's 'ad a bad time of it, is all"

"So, we know Nenette *is* Jeannie's twin sister, Hames *may* be her boyfriend..." D.S. Stone ticked each off on his hand.

"*Boyfriend*!" Jeannie laughed, heartily, at the idea.

"...and Precious is not the daughter of either of them" D.S. Stone continued.

"There might 'ave been a babby once, though" Jeannie mused, staring at the fire and oblivious to her guests.

"Yes, that's about the size of it, Sergeant" D.I. Wood nodded, gloomily, ignoring Jeannie's remark.

"Doesn't help a lot, does it sir?"

"No, Stoney, it doesn't!"

"Looks like we've all had a wasted journey, apart from Archie!" Samantha said.

Another loud snore indicated that Archibald was enjoying his rest.

Chapter Thirty-Five
Reunited

"How are you feeling this morning, Josiah?" Samantha asked as they both made their way from the car to the offices of Oakshott and Underwood.

"Well, whilst I would not say that I was invigorated," Josiah began, thoughtfully, "I think it would be fair to say that I have considerably more energy than was the case before"

"That's good to hear!" Samantha grinned, "The potion Jeannie sent did the trick then?"

"It would be a surprising coincidence if the potion was not the cause of my improvement" Josiah agreed, opening a door for her, "although the two facts may not, of course, be causatively linked"

"It certainly seemed to do the trick for Archibald" Samantha nodded toward the beaming bulk of Archibald Thurble, currently ambling down the corridor in their direction.

"Yes, I'm delighted that we both seem to be returning to something akin to normal health" Josiah smiled at his young colleague.

"Morning Mr. O., Ms. Knight" Archibald grinned.

"Hi Archie" Samantha responded, "anything to report?"

"There's a note here from Mr. Strine for you" Archibald produced a piece of paper.

"Thanks Archie" Samantha grasped the paper and headed for the office, "Do you want to put the kettle on?"

Dead Reckoning

"Yep! Will do!" Archie strode off to the kitchenette, whistling.

"It's fantastic, the difference that potion of Jeannie's has made to both of you" Samantha said, putting her bags down on Josiah's desk.

"She's a remarkable woman" Josiah agreed.

"Well, you should know" Samantha said, slyly.

"Ah, I fear not" Josiah shook his head, "the Jeanette that I knew, so many years ago, was a very different person from Jeannie. It was quite a shock to find that they are one and the same person"

"Yes, it was a surprise" Samantha agreed, peering at the bit of paper Archibald had given her.

"We were most fortunate that she was on hand after that business in the cellar" Josiah observed, "I doubt that either Archibald or I would have survived had it not been for her ministrations"

"Yes, that's true" Samantha said, frowning at the message on Mr. Strine's note, "Josiah, do you think you might be up to taking on a small project?"

"Hmm?" Josiah said, still lost in his memories of Jeanette.

"I wondered if you were up to a little bit of work?"

"Oh, well, I suppose I might be able to manage something," Josiah said, dubiously, "what did you have in mind?"

"Well, Mr. Strine seems to have taken on a bit of a commission," Samantha said, waving the paper, "at least, if I've read this correctly"

There was a thumping on the door which preceded Archibald crashing through, bearing the tea things.

"Ah, your partner in crime!" Samantha grinned.

"I don't think it was us what was the criminals, Ms. Knight" Archibald said in a hurt tone.

"That's not what I meant, Archie" Samantha chuckled. "I was thinking that you and Josiah might do a little job together, today. What do you say?"

"Oh, right! Yeah, why not?" Archibald looked relieved.

"What, exactly, would our 'mission' be?" Josiah asked.

"Well, that is something of a conundrum" Samantha frowned, "all I have on this piece of paper is an address and a note that 'they is looking to talk about their funerals'. Do you know anything more, Archibald?"

"Nah, sorry Ms. Knight" Archibald shook his head, "Mr. Strine just said he'd had a phone call from some woman what wanted to talk to someone about their funeral arrangements"

"And he didn't take a name, or even a telephone number?" Samantha frowned.

"Sorry!" Archibald looked glum.

"You see, Josiah, as I've said before, whilst there's no-one to beat Mr. Strine when it comes to the nuts and bolts of funerals, his administrative skills leave a lot to be desired" Samantha said, tapping the piece of paper.

"We don't use no nuts and bolts, miss" Archibald interrupted, "it's not like we've got no Frankensteins" He chuckled.

"Frankenstein's monster" Josiah couldn't stop himself automatically correcting.

Dead Reckoning

"No, Archibald, that isn't what I meant" Samantha sighed, "I was referring to Mr. Strine's undoubted expertise at the actual mechanics of delivering a funeral on a day-to-day basis"

"And his shortfalls when it comes to taking a simple telephone message" Josiah added.

"Ah well, be fair" Archibald said, stoutly, "it ain't always that easy. They don't always tell you everything"

"That's why we have to make sure we get the information we need, Archie" Samantha pointed out, with a smile.

"Where are we needed, Samantha?" Josiah asked.

"It's Wigton-under-Heathwood, so not far at all"

"A nice run out in the countryside then, Archibald" Josiah said, encouragingly.

"I'll get the car sorted out then" Archibald said, cheerfully.

* * * *

"Anything, Stoney?" D.I. Wood asked, hopefully, standing beside his Sergeant's desk.

"No sir, nothing at all" D.S. Stone replied, glumly, "we've been trawling through hours of CCTV from here and Chester but there's no sign of any of them"

"That Precious must be pretty smart at avoiding our cameras, that's all I can say" D.I. Wood seethed, "the gaffer's doing his fruit, you know? He wants something to show the powers that be to justify all the time and money we've spent"

"We can't *make* something happen, sir" D.S. Stone pointed out, "They'll have to surface, sooner or later, though"

"It's the 'later' bit that worries me, Sergeant"

"They'll have to do something, they'll need money. I just wish we knew when and where" D.S. Stone stared blankly at the computer screen, on which a street scene flowed past in real time.

"Let me know as soon as you find anything, Stoney" D.I. Wood sighed, heading for his office, "We need a break on this"

"I just need a break" D.S. Stone muttered, yawning as he returned to his street scene.

* * * *

"This is somewhat like old times!" Josiah eased himself back in the passenger seat of the limousine and smiled.

"Yeah, innit?" Archibald grinned, "It's been ages since I last drove one of these. I'm a bit out of practice" He admitted.

"I had noticed" Josiah frowned, "however, I am sure that we are both a little rusty, in our respective ways"

"Must 'ave been all that water" Archibald chuckled.

"I think that remark may be in somewhat questionable taste, Archibald" Josiah shuddered, silently.

"Well, you've got to laugh, haven't you?" Archibald mused.

"I beg leave to doubt that particular premise, Archibald"

"Nice day for it though" Archibald looked at the passing countryside, approvingly.

Dead Reckoning

"It is nice to have a change of scene, I must concur" Josiah thought for a moment, "It occurs to me, Archibald, that I have not properly thanked you for your efforts at Evanley Hall"

"You what?" Archibald asked.

"You saved my life, in that cellar"

"Nah, I just did what anyone would 'ave done" Archibald shook his head, vigorously, "Any road, I don't like remembering all that. I 'ave nightmares" He said, in a small voice.

"PTSD" Josiah nodded.

"Putsed?" Archibald looked at him, quizzically, "Is that like 'drunk' or summat?"

"Not at all, Archibald. It is an abbreviation for Post Traumatic Stress Disorder, a condition in which the mind and body continue to react to a major trauma that one has experienced, long after that trauma has passed."

"Oh, right!" Archibald nodded, "me Nan's got summat like that."

"Is that so?" Josiah asked, dubiously.

"Yeah, someone nicked a bottle of Mackeson from her 'and when she dozed off in this pub and now she flinches if you go anywhere near her when she's sleeping"

"Ah, yes, well I think it would be somewhat disingenuous to attribute that reaction to PTSD" Josiah observed, "Whereas your nightmares, resulting from your near-death experience, are a classic symptom"

"Don't you get 'em, then?"

"I have had occasions when I have woken in a state of panic, I must admit" Josiah nodded, "Whether these were prefaced by bad dreams, I could not say with certainty. I rather hope that Ms. Mountjoy's concoction may serve to lessen my...apprehension, shall we say?"

"Oh yeah, me too. I've been as jumpy as hell since all that. Egbert jumped out from behind a coffin and shouted 'Boo!' and I nearly had an 'eart attack!"

"Egbert should have better things to do with his time" Josiah said, sternly, "I will speak to him on our return"

"Oh, well, he was just messing about" Archibald shrugged, "like you do, you know?"

"I do not *know*, Archibald, as I have never 'messed about' at my labours!"

"Ey up, we're here!" Archibald announced, as they pulled into a quiet cul-de-sac, "now, what number was it?"

Josiah perused the scrappy bit of paper.

"Number 13, according to this" He announced.

Number 13 proved to be a pleasant, albeit somewhat old-fashioned, small bungalow tucked away at the very end of the cul-de-sac. Archibald eased the limousine onto the drive.

"Well, here we go then, Archibald, once more into the breach!" Josiah said, taking a deep breath and opening the passenger door.

"Not much chance of sandcastles 'ere, I don't reckon" Archibald chuckled as Josiah gave him one of his 'looks'.

Josiah marched briskly to the front door and pressed the doorbell. There was the faint sound of chiming, beyond. The two men fidgeted

Dead Reckoning

on the doorstep as the minutes ticked past, but no-one appeared. Josiah made several more attempts with the doorbell, to no avail, and then resorted to knocking with increasing intensity.

"I do hope Mr. Strine has taken down the right address!" Josiah muttered.

"Doesn't look like there's anyone home" Archibald observed, looking around the property.

"This really isn't good enough" Josiah snapped.

"These things 'appen!" Archibald shrugged, philosophically, "Hang about, can you hear a noise?"

"No, what noise?" Josiah strained to hear, without success.

"I thought it sounded like a…car engine, but there's no-one around" Archibald looked around the empty cul-de-sac. "I reckon…" He hesitated and listened carefully, "I reckon it's coming from the garage"

"The garage? You mean the garage to this property?"

"Yeah, that's what it sounds like" Archibald nodded.

"Oh!" Josiah looked extremely troubled, "Do you know, Archibald, I have a rather bad feeling about this"

Chapter Thirty-Six
Drive

The small cul-de-sac was illuminated from all angles by the flashing blue lights of the vehicles parked all around. Curtains were twitching spasmodically and a few of the braver residents had ventured onto their front lawns for a better view, albeit close enough to the front door to be able to scamper back, if approached.

On a low wall, at the front of the bungalow that seemed to be the centre of attention, two men sat, despondently, sporting silvery blankets around their shoulders.

"Feeling a bit nippy, are we?" D.I. Wood asked, as he strolled up to them.

"I believe the paramedics were concerned that they might be suffering from shock, sir, hence the insulating blankets" D.S. Stone whispered to his superior.

"Right? Well, anyway, can one of you tell me exactly what's been going on?" D.I. Wood looked from one to the other of the two men on the wall.

"Nice to see you again, Inspector" Josiah said, without a great deal of enthusiasm.

"I wish I could say the same" D.I. Wood said, ungraciously, "So, what's going on?"

"We did explain this to one of your colleagues" Josiah pointed out.

Dead Reckoning

"Well, I'm just a bit picky in that regard" D.I. Wood said, sitting down on the wall beside Josiah, "I like to hear it for myself" He drew a pack of cigarettes from his coat pocket and affixed one to his lip, "Don't mind if I smoke, do you?"

"Not at all, Inspector" Josiah smiled, thinly, "I get most of my customers that way"

D.I. Wood considered this, for a moment, and returned the cigarette to its packet.

"How do you come to be here, Mr. Oakshott?" He asked, with a sigh.

"We were answering a call for our assistance, Inspector" Josiah explained, producing the note taken by Mr. Strine, "This note, in point of fact"

D.I. Wood scrutinised the note and then passed it to his Sergeant.

"We'll need to keep that as evidence, Stoney" He remarked, "Not that it tells us a lot! Just an address - this address, and '*wants to talk about funerals*'"

"The note was taken by my employee, Mr. Strine, who has, to his credit, been partly managing the business during my enforced absence. Mr. Strine has certain erm, administrative deficiencies" Josiah began.

"He's crap with people" Archibald commented, conversationally.

"Well, yes, indeed" Josiah shuffled, uncomfortably, "He does lack people skills, that is true. However, he is second to none when it comes to dealing with the deceased."

"Must be a fun guy to have around" D.I. Wood sniggered.

"He has been invaluable during this difficult period" Josiah said, stoutly.

"Anyway, you've got this bit of a note, why did you both come out?"

"Samantha...Ms. Knight, that is, thought it would be good for both of us to be engaged on a small project. A form of rehabilitation, if you will" Josiah explained.

"Doesn't seem to have worked out too well, that idea" D.I. Wood looked around at the assembled emergency services.

"No, indeed Inspector, I doubt this was her preferred outcome" Josiah nodded, gloomily.

"So, what happened when you arrived here?"

"We rang the door-bell of the bungalow in question, repeatedly, but there was no response. I tried knocking but to no avail. It was whilst my colleague..."

"That's me!" Archibald added, proudly, pointing to his chest.

"Indeed...it was whilst my colleague, Archibald, was searching around the vicinity of the property for the occupants, that he noticed the sound of a car engine running"

"You hadn't noticed that, then?" D.I. Wood asked.

"I fear not, my advancing age means that my hearing does not have the acuity it once had"

"Then what?"

"We determined, well, Archibald determined, that the sound was emanating from the garage of the property to which we had been summoned. We, therefore, opened the garage door but were beaten back by the accumulation of fumes. Accordingly, we telephoned for the emergency services, to whit, the ambulance and your good selves."

Dead Reckoning

"Is there an owl 'round here?" Archibald asked, looking around the surrounding trees.

"You didn't attempt to gain access to the car?" D.I. Wood pressed on, ignoring him.

"I don't like owls" Archibald frowned.

Josiah, despite his best efforts to remain focused on his conversation with the Inspector, felt compelled to respond.

"You don't like owls?" Josiah said, with surprise, "There is nothing to NOT like about owls, Archibald"

"You wouldn't say that if you were a mouse!" Archibald said, folding his arms.

"Do you think we might return to the matter in hand?" D.I. Wood tapped his pen on his notebook, D.S. Stone attempted to stifle a laugh in the background, "I was enquiring, if you can spare a moment, of course, from your woodland meanderings, whether you attempted to gain access to the car?"

"Regrettably not, Inspector" Josiah looked downcast, "I fear that neither of us were, either physically or mentally, prepared for such an eventuality. You must understand, Inspector, that, following recent events, this has been a considerable shock for us both"

"I was scared sh...quite a bit" Archibald mentioned.

"Yeah, yeah, I understand" D.I. Wood nodded, "Did you recognise the car or the occupants"

"Occupants?" Josiah and Archibald said in unison.

"Yeah, more than one" D.I. Wood confirmed, "Presumably not then, how about the car? That should have meant something to you"

"I regret that my glimpse of the vehicle was fleeting, what with the smoke and everything" Josiah admitted.

"I *thought* it rang a bell" Archibald mused.

"It should do" D.I. Wood agreed, "if our records are correct, we think it's probably the vehicle that transported you, Mr. Oakshott, to your assignation at Evanley Hall a few weeks back"

* * * *

"Ah, Mr. Strine! Thank you for popping by the office" Samantha said, far more brightly than she felt.

"Not a problem, Mrs." Mr. Strine beamed at her, "'Ow can I 'elp?"

"I wondered if there had been any sign of Josiah…Mr. Oakshott that is, or Archibald?"

"Nah, not that I've seen, Mrs." Mr. Strine removed his ubiquitous bowler hat, scratched his head and stroked his chin, "'Ave they gone missin' then?"

"They were responding to that message you took, about someone wanting to discuss their funeral arrangements, do you remember?"

"Oh ar, yeah, I remember" Mr. Strine grinned, "she sounded too young for all that"

"I'm sorry, who sounded too young?"

"The girl, on the phone" Mr. Strine explained.

"You took the message from a young girl?"

"Yeah, that's right" Mr. Strine nodded, proud of a job well done, "Well, that's what she sounded like"

Dead Reckoning

"But you didn't make a note of her name?"

"Ah, now, I see where you're goin' with that" Mr. Strine conceded, "But, I've only got one pair of 'ands, and I've been run off me feet just lately as it is!"

Samantha considered the anatomical complexities of this reply and decided to ignore them.

"Any road, they got the address" Mr. Strine added, by way of compensation.

"We must thank heaven for small mercies"

"P'raps they've gone down the pub?" Mr. Strine mused, "I would if I were them"

"I think that is unlikely, Mr. Strine" Samantha bit her lip and wondered what to do next.

"You tried their phones?"

"Oddly enough, Mr. Strine, I have. I can only assume that they are somewhere where there is little, or no, signal" Samantha couldn't help wondering if that was entirely a coincidence.

* * * *

"If that was the car that took me to the Hall, then..." Josiah began, thoughtfully.

"I know what you're going to say, Mr. Oakshott" D.I. Wood grinned, "but, until we can get some formal identification arranged, we can't say, for sure, who the occupants are"

"But, you must know something about them?"

"We do, indeed" D.I. Wood nodded, "we found a male and a female in the vehicle. Both had been overcome by the fumes and had clearly been there for some time"

"A male...and a female? Then it must be..." Josiah looked shocked.

"We can't be any more specific, sir" D.S. Stone intervened, "but you should know that, based upon their apparent age and gender profile, we are working on the assumption that the deceased may well be Nenette DeVille and the man known as Hames"

Chapter Thirty-Seven
I Fought the Law

D.I. Wood looked up from careful study of his Caribbean holiday brochure to see D.S. Stone hovering in the doorway to his office, clutching a file. He looked like someone who was awaiting a particularly daunting dental procedure.

"Come on in, Stoney!" D.I. Wood bellowed, cheerfully, "You can make my day if you tell me that those two in the car are definite suicides"

"I'm sorry, sir" D.S. Stone said, mournfully, "it doesn't look like it. Both were very heavily sedated, meaning they would have been unlikely to be able to even get into the car without help, let alone restrain themselves..." D.S. Stone consulted the file before him.

"This is the official S.P. from the Pathologist, right?"

"Yes, sir. On top of which, they had both been restrained in an identical manner and whilst it would be possible for one to have restrained the other..."

"...It's just not possible that the second occupant could have tied their own bonds in the exact same way" D.I. Wood completed, dismally.

"Yes, sir, it's just...well, a non-starter. I'm sorry, sir, that's what it says in the report" D.S. Stone closed the file and looked a picture of misery.

"Oh, bugger!" D.I. Wood sighed, "I'll have to tell the gaffer"

"There's also the possibility that we may be looking at a serial killer, sir" D.S. Stone ventured, timidly, edging back out toward the door.

"WHAT?" D.I. Wood looked at him open-mouthed, "How the heck do you come to that conclusion, and for God's sake don't let the gaffer hear you say that?"

"Well, look at it this way, we think the murder of the lad in the reservoir, Jimmy, might have been connected to that Precious DeVille, the one who went missing from the chip shop…"

"Yes" D.I. Wood agreed, slowly.

"And *she's* a known associate of Nenette DeVille and that bloke, Hames…"

"Go on, Sergeant" D.I. Wood frowned.

"Well, if she *did* do for 'Jimmy' and now these two (if it is them) turn up dead…"

"Oh God!" D.I. Wood put his head in his hands, "I can't tell the boss that, he'll have a seizure"

"It's just a possibility, sir" D.S. Stone attempted to soften the impact of the news.

"Yeah, well, it's one I don't want to think about, not just at the moment, thank you very much, Sergeant!" D.I. Wood snapped.

D.S. Stone edged out of the office, gratefully.

Sometime later, as he was happily absorbed in checking off the few items they had recovered from the bungalow on his spreadsheet, he became aware of his boss looming over his desk.

"You're not going to like this, Stoney" D.I. Wood began.

"What's the problem, sir?" D.S. Stone responded, with trepidation.

Dead Reckoning

"The boss wants us to bring our friend Josiah Oakshott and his oppo in for questioning"

"But, we've got their statements, sir, I don't see what else they could add" D.S. Stone pointed out.

"No, Stoney, not as witnesses, as 'persons of interest'" D.I. Wood looked thoroughly miserable.

"You're having a laugh, sir! On what basis?"

"On the grounds that they've got motive and opportunity" D.I. Wood shrugged, "Look, I'm no happier about it than you are, Stoney, but the gaffer says we should always look hard at whoever makes the discovery, and that applies even more to these two. Plus, he says the public will expect to see someone brought in for questioning."

"I'll do it, sir" D.I. Stone snapped, dragging his jacket from the chair and struggling into it, "but I want it noted that I disagree, strongly"

"Duly noted, Sergeant"

* * * *

Josiah Oakshott sat on one of the hard chairs, in the sparse Interview Room, and gazed around at the blank walls. There had to be a good reason as to why he was here, but, at the moment, he was at a loss to think what it might be. At that moment, D.I. Wood stalked into the room, accompanied by a younger, female colleague. He sat down heavily on the chair opposite Josiah, threw a file on the table between them and nodded to his colleague to start the tape recorder.

"The time is 15.02, this is an Interview with Josiah Oakshott" He intoned, "Present: Myself, Detective Inspector Wood, my colleague..." He nodded to the companion,

"Detective Constable Ryecroft" She supplied, leaning slightly toward the tape recorder.

"And..." D.I. Wood looked at Josiah, expectantly,

"Oh, erm, Josiah Oakshott" Josiah said, looking thoroughly confused.

"Thank you. Now the purpose of this interview is..." D.I. Wood began, but was interrupted by a knock on the door, "Yes, what is it?" He snapped.

"Sorry to interrupt, sir, but Mr. Oakshott's legal representative is here" D.S. Stone grinned and nodded amiably to Josiah.

"Legal rep...you never told me you had asked for a brief!" D.I. Wood said, "I wouldn't have started this, if I'd known"

"In all honesty, Inspector, it is news to me, too" Josiah said, "but, I must say, I was somewhat surprised at the formality of this interview for what is, surely, simply an evidence-gathering exercise"

"Ah no" D.I. Wood shifted in his seat, uncomfortably, "I thought you had been informed. Your position in our inquiry has changed somewhat. You are no longer just a witness; we are now treating you as a 'person of interest'"

"I'm a *what*?" Josiah looked shocked.

"Your brief will explain" D.I. Wood got up from the desk and gathered his papers, "shut the recorder off, Constable, we'll resume when Mr. Oakshott has had chance to catch up with his legal bod"

The door opened to admit an elderly man who, Josiah thought, looked remarkably like the actor Alistair Sim, only an Alistair Sim who was suffering from a severe hangover. He tiptoed into the room as if afraid to make the slightest noise.

Dead Reckoning

"Detective Inspector, I am Arnold Threadready, I will be acting for Mr. Oakshott in this matter" Mr. Threadready held out his hand and managed a thin smile.

"I don't think we've had the pleasure, Mr. Threadready" D.I. Wood said, shaking the proffered hand.

"Ah no, this is not my preferred area of expertise, but needs must, Inspector, needs must" He produced a business card, "should you ever need assistance with any matter of conveyancing or probate, Threadready & Partners would stand ready to assist"

D.i. Wood took the card, shook his head and, with D.C. Ryecroft, filed out of the door.

"Now, Mr. Oakshott..." Mr. Threadready began, taking a seat beside Josiah and neatly placing a large A4 notepad and pen, on the table.

"Forgive me, Mr. Threadready, but I was unaware that I *had* a legal representative"

"Ah yes, indeed" Mr. Threadready nodded, "I too was surprised. I was contacted by a colleague of yours, a, erm..." He consulted his notepad, "...a Ms. Knight. She informed me that she had found our card in your address book"

"Threadready?" Josiah frowned, "Threadready? Oh, was it your firm that dealt with my late father's probate"

"That was, indeed, the case sir. Your late father and mine went back a very long way" Mr. Threadready nodded and smiled.

"And now you're dealing with criminal law?" Josiah looked surprised.

"Well, no, not exactly" Mr. Threadready squirmed in his seat, "to be entirely honest, Mr. Oakshott, probate and conveyancing are my 'bread and butter' as it were. I have precious little experience of criminal matters but, we shall prevail, sir, we shall prevail. Now then, with what have they charged you?" He sat with his pen poised over the notepad.

"Charged me? They haven't 'charged' me with anything" Josiah replied, indignantly, "I have, however, been informed that I am considered to be a 'person of interest'"

"Ah, is that so?" Mr. Threadready nodded and made a note.

"What would your advice be?" Josiah asked.

"Why sir, I would say…nothing"

"Nothing?"

"Nothing at all, sir. You see, they will seek to lure you into saying something that might incriminate you"

"But, I *can't* incriminate myself." Josiah shook his head, "I've done nothing wrong!"

"Ah, indeed, sir" Mr. Threadready gave Josiah an exaggerated wink, chuckled slightly and made a further note.

"I haven't!" Josiah protested, "Just a minute, Archibald was brought in at the same time as me, does he have legal representation?"

"Ah, that would be Mr. erm," Mr. Threadready consulted his notes, "Thurble, yes, that's it. Yes, I can confirm that he has the good offices of my nephew, Jasper"

"Oh really? Well, that's all right then" Josiah groaned, with his head in his hands.

* * * *

Dead Reckoning

In an adjoining Interview Room, Archibald was staring in wonderment at the young man sitting beside him. He had, so far, covered most of the table with ring folders and books, periodically knocking some onto the floor as he repositioned others.

"You're my legal wotsit then, are you?" Archibald asked.

"Yes, yes, indeed" The young man nodded, vigorously, "Threadready & Partners, Jasper Threadready at your service" He held out a somewhat worn-looking business card.

"It says 'ere, probate and conveyancing, what's all that when it's at home?"

"Erm, well, probate is Wills, in short, and conveyancing is dealing with property sales and purchases" Jasper explained.

"What about murders?"

"To be absolutely honest, I have had little experience of criminal law since I qualified..." Jasper began.

"When was that, then?" Archibald asked, studying the business card.

"March of this year" Jasper admitted, "but, actually, you are in luck! As I have only *just* finished my studies, the topic will be so much fresher in my mind than, say, that of my Uncle, for example, who is representing the interests of your Mr. Oakshott"

"Oh, right" Archibald cheered up a bit.

"All I've got to do is find my Course Notes" Jasper said, scrabbling through his collection of ring folders, "Ah, here we are!" He announced, turning a section divider over, "Oh!"

"Problem?" Archibald asked, with foreboding.

"Yes, a little" Jasper nodded, "it would seem that Criminal Procedure was dealt with in the term when I was hospitalised with appendicitis" Jasper indicated the ring folder with a paltry single sheet of paper in that section. "However, nil desperandum, as they say!"

"Was it? Who were they playing?" Archibald asked, now thoroughly confused.

"By which I mean, Mr. erm" Jasper managed to sneak a look at his notes, "Mr. erm Furball, that there's bound to be something in one of these text books" He began rooting through the pile of books, causing a partial landslide.

"Would it be easier to just plead 'guilty'?" Archibald asked, looking very concerned.

"Good heavens, no!" Jasper shook his head, vigorously, "Wherever would the legal profession be if we all took that attitude, eh, Mr. Furball?"

Chapter Thirty-Eight
Another Cup Of Coffee

"Where the heck have you been?" Samantha shouted as Josiah, closely followed by the tiptoeing figure of Arnold Threadready, made his way through the door into the Waiting Area of the Police Station. "I've been so worried!" She added, rushing up to Josiah and enveloping him in a hug.

"My, my!" Mr. Threadready observed, enviously, "I wish I could engender the same degree of loyalty within *my* staff"

"There are certain erm, mitigating factors at play here, as you might say" Josiah explained, somewhat muffled by the enthusiastic hug.

"I wondered what was going on" Samantha explained, stepping back and looking him up and down, "particularly when Archie came out after no time at all" She nodded towards Archibald and his legal counsel who were perched on a bench behind her. Archibald gave a little wave of recognition; his legal associate, too preoccupied with keeping his collection of folders and textbooks within his grasp declined to make any sudden movement.

"I can only imagine that my interview was somewhat more in depth" Josiah shrugged.

"I think it might be prudent to continue this discussion somewhere other than in the confines of this Police Station" Mr. Threadready suggested, diplomatically, "Perhaps we might repair to somewhere where we could partake of some refreshment and compare notes? I believe there is a coffee emporium not many yards away?"

A few moments later, the party filed into the warmth and relative comfort of the local coffee shop, 'Sacred Grounds".

"In view of your kind efforts on my behalf, please allow me to purchase some refreshments for you all" Josiah announced as they entered.

"Well, that would be most kind of you" Mr. Threadready beamed and wasted no time in settling down in a convenient booth. Josiah took note of the various requests, without problem, until it came to Archibald.

"What would you require, Archibald?"

"Oh, I dunno!" Archibald looked blankly at the board behind the counter, listing the various options on offer and tugging his jacket sleeve in a clear sign of agitation, "I never know what to 'ave in these places"

"Well, perhaps when you have made up your mind, you would be kind enough to order for yourself and Mr. erm?"

"Oh, he's another Threadready" Archibald explained, "calls hisself, Jasper"

"Right, well, if you could order for both of you, you can claim the cost back from Petty Cash when we return" Josiah suggested.

"Oh brilliant!" Archibald grinned, "Expenses!"

"Do *not* feel the need to throw caution to the winds" Josiah said, sternly.

Having placed the order, Josiah joined the party in the booth, leaving Archibald hopping from one foot to the other as he tried to make up his mind.

"So, what happened?" Samantha asked.

Dead Reckoning

"Well, Ms. erm, Knight" Mr. Threadready Senior began, "the most notable outcome of the interview was that my client, Mr. Oakshott, is apparently now considered to be a 'person of interest'"

"What?" Samantha looked shocked, "What is that supposed to mean?"

"Erm, well, in short, rather than having been called in as a witness to the recent, rather tragic, events concerning the apparent suicide of the lady and gentleman concerned…"

"Which was my natural assumption" Josiah interjected.

"Indeed, Mr. Oakshott" Mr. Threadready nodded, "Instead, the police seem to have shifted their stance to one in which Mr. Oakshott and, I assume, his colleague…?" He looked to his nephew for acknowledgement, who nodded despite being preoccupied with arranging the books and folders on the bench beside him. "Yes, indeed, his colleague, as being 'persons of interest', which is to say that the police purport to believe that they may have been, to some extent or other, *involved* in the incident rather than simply a witness to events"

"Which is cobblers, 'cause we didn't do nothin'" Archibald contributed, returning to his seat. "This place is alright, innit?" He grinned, bouncing up and down on the leather bench seat, which did nothing for Jasper Threadready's carefully piled books and folders, "It used to be full of goths, back in the day" Archibald continued.

"Goths?" Josiah asked.

"Yeah, 'cause they had that Arthur Dimwoody do the shop sign, didn't they?" Archibald explained.

"I fail to see the connection. Ah, do you mean the Mr. Dimwoody who was later diagnosed with dyslexia?"

"Yeah, 'im" Archibald nodded, "So, for months, the sign said 'Scared Gourds', nobody could figure out what it was supposed to be for"

"JOSHUA?" The man behind the counter yelled out.

"I suspect that might be you, Josiah" Samantha suggested.

"JOSHUA!" The man yelled again.

"Surely not?" Josiah frowned, "I gave my name quite clearly to the young person taking the order"

"JOSHUA!" This time with a degree of impatience.

"Ah yeah, but 'im doing the drinks and stuff, he's that Dimwoody's lad, innit" Archibald observed.

"Ah, I see" Josiah nodded, "I will go and retrieve our order, then"

He returned, a few minutes later, bearing a tray of fancy coffees.

"What did you order, Archie?" Samantha asked, taking delivery of her mochaccino.

"I dunno" Archibald admitted, reluctantly, "I get that confused in these sort of places. I just, sort of, had stab at it, sort of thing"

"ARCHIE…BLAD?"

"What?" Archibald frowned.

"I think it's you" Samantha giggled.

"Oh, right" Archibald nodded, "It's BALD!" He yelled back at the assistant.

"You what?"

"BALD!" Archibald yelled, insistently.

Dead Reckoning

"No, I ain't" The assistant said, in a hurt tone, "it's just a wide parting"

"This sort of nonsense seems to follow us around" Josiah groaned.

"I wonder why that might be?" Arnold Threadready mused.

Archibald returned a few moments later, bearing an Americano for Jasper and some sort of frothy concoction for himself.

"Any idea what it is?" Samantha asked.

"Not really" Archibald said, glumly, "I think it might have nutmeg in it, on account of how its seasonal but it could be owt, really. I just panicked"

"Leaving Archibald's esoteric choices to one side" Josiah suggested, watching his employee suspiciously sip his drink, leaving a wide 'moustache' of froth on his upper lip, "what, exactly, in your opinion, Mr. Threadready, has been the outcome of our interviews today?"

"Difficult to say, Mr. Oakshott" Mr. Threadready Senior said, sipping his Flat White ruminatively, "On the one hand, they gained nothing from the interview that could possibly confirm their suspicions but, on the other, they gave no assurance that your status would be changed, either. Would you agree, Jasper?"

Jasper Threadbody jumped slightly, as he had been day-dreaming about defending Archibald on a murder charge in Crown Court.

"Erm, no Uncle, indeed not"

"Indeed not, what?" Mr. Threadready Senior asked.

"Erm, whatever you said" Jasper replied, desperately.

"Jasper, you must pay attention, we have spoken about the need for attentiveness and focus before, have we not?"

"I reckon we was lucky not to get done for wasting police time" Archibald said.

"What? Why ever would you say that, Mr. erm…"

"Furball" Jasper suggested.

"It's not, it's bloody THURBLE!" Archibald said, vehemently.

"If you insist" Jasper said, tetchily.

"What did you mean, exactly, Mr. *Thurble*?" Arnold Threadready asked, wearily.

"Well, what with 'im covering the desk with books and stuff, there weren't nowhere for the Sergeant to put his papers" Archibald gestured toward Jasper's tottering literature collection.

"Sneak!" Jasper hissed at Archibald.

"I have counselled you against the widespread, and, if I may say so, somewhat indiscriminate use of reference materials, Jasper"

"Yes, Uncle" Jasper blushed.

"Not to mention 'im not knowing what 'e was talking about!" Archibald said, "Any road, it didn't make any odds in the finish, on account of 'e didn't believe we was 'interesting persons' anyhow"

"'Persons of Interest'" Jasper snapped.

"Yeah, them" Archibald conceded.

"That would explain why you were out, long before Josiah?" Samantha suggested.

"Mr. erm…Thurble, is correct that the Detective Sergeant seemed to give little credence to the notion that he, that is to say, Mr. …Thurble, could possibly be a 'person of interest' Jasper nodded, "he did, however, seem to be markedly interested in a girl, possibly wearing a cloak and hood?"

"Precious!" Josiah and Archibald said, in unison.

Chapter Thirty-Nine
Santa Baby

"I must say, it does seem such a shame that the place has to be quite so...austere, particularly at this time of the year" Samantha complained, looking around Josiah's office with her hands on her hips.

"I have, regrettably, had to converse with Archibald on this topic in previous years" Josiah observed, looking up from the papers on his desk.

"Why, did Archibald fancy some Christmas decorations?" Samantha chuckled at the thought.

"More than that, he took it upon himself to fashion a seasonal display for our window, which I unfortunately had to remove, thus causing a little... friction" Josiah explained (see 'Brightest and Best of the Sons of the Mourning')

"A window display?"

"Yes," Josiah nodded, gloomily, "he had noted that other businesses have such things and he failed to see why it could not be the case, here. To be fair, he had shown considerable ingenuity in devising it"

"Oh, I'm intrigued now" Samantha dropped onto the chaise longue and grinned, "what was in it?"

"As I recall, it was a form of nativity scene" Josiah shuddered at the thought, "made somewhat macabre by the fact that the infant, in this instance, was contained in a miniature coffin"

"What?"

Dead Reckoning

"I know!" Josiah shook his head, "he had the usual accoutrement of animals crowding around the scene, too. As I pointed out, it rather made it seem as if they were attending a doll's funeral"

Samantha giggled uncontrollably.

"There were, as I'm sure you can imagine, complaints" Josiah went on, "A *lot* of complaints! I had to explain to him that we are not as other shops. We do not tout for trade, nor is Christmas different, in our profession, from any other time of the year, except that our clients may well need more support and understanding at such a poignant time"

"Oh dear, good old Archibald!" Samantha said, wiping the tears from her eyes. "Is that really what you said to him?"

"I believe those were my very words" Josiah nodded.

"You really can be a bit pompous sometimes, Josiah" Samantha shook her head.

"That was not, however, the end of it" Josiah added, miserably, "as an alternative, he proposed putting Santa on a cross! Can you imagine?"

"Oh my word! I would have paid good money to see how that went down amongst the good folk of Merkin-under-Heathwood"

"As I had no desire to find out the customer reaction to such a tableau, I stamped on that idea fairly quickly

"Well, I'm not suggesting anything of that sort, but I did wonder if we might find somewhere to at least display the Christmas Cards we receive from our suppliers, here in your office?" Samantha looked at him, hopefully.

"Well, I'm not at all sure…" Josiah looked dubious.

"Somewhere here, on the back wall, out of the line of sight of any client that might be visiting?" Samantha suggested.

"I suppose that might be just about acceptable" Josiah squirmed, "but there would be nowhere to put them"

"I was thinking about a little shelf?"

"I suppose I could ask Archibald, if he had a few spare moments..." Josiah began.

There was a knock on the door, immediately followed by Archibald staggering in, with difficulty because of the heavy toolbox he was carrying, as well as the two planks of wood.

"Where do you want this shelf, then?" He asked, crashing his tools and materials on the ground.

"I erm, I had already had a quiet word with Archie" Samantha admitted, with a blush.

"So I see!" Josiah noted, with a raised eyebrow, "Oh well, why not!" He shrugged.

"Excellent! Come on, Archie, I'll show you what I have in mind" Samantha grinned.

* * * *

"Jeannie's been in" D.S. Stone announced as he entered his superior's office.

"Hmm?" D.I. Wood continued to leaf through his Caribbean brochure.

"You know, Jeanette DeVille? The mad cat-woman of Evanley Hall?"

"Oh, right, what did she want?"

Dead Reckoning

"Well, *she* didn't want anything, apart from to bring you this" D.S. Stone produced a jar of some green ointment, which he placed on the desk.

"Oh, brilliant!" D.I. Wood grinned, "I was getting low on that. I'll have to settle up with her"

"As I said, sir, she didn't come in because she wanted something from us. If you recall, we asked her to come in to see if she could identify our two bodies"

"Oh yes" D.I. Wood nodded, inspecting the newly acquired ointment, "Go on, make my day, tell me she's never seen them before"

"I wish that were the case, sir" D.S. Stone looked glum, "but I'm afraid she could. She confirmed that the female was her twin sister, Nenette DeVille"

"Bugger! And the bloke?"

"The bloke is the person known to her as 'Hames'" D.S. Stone nodded, "She said she was sure because she…" He consulted his notes, "…*had a really good look at the bugger when he tied me up, in me own home, an' all!*'"

"Yeah, well you would, wouldn't you" D.I. Wood agreed.

"So, we're back to these two being linked to Jimmy the homeless guy's murder, wouldn't you say, sir?"

"Not in the boss's hearing I wouldn't, no" D.I. Wood shook his head, firmly.

"But, surely you've got to fancy Precious for all three of them, now?"

"Why though?" D.I. Wood shook his head, "That's what I can't figure? Why off some vagrant, then do your pretend parents in, as well? Just doesn't make sense!"

"All three *were* dressed up as apparent suicides" D.S. Stone pointed out.

"Yeah, there's that" D.I. Wood sighed, "I suppose we need to get her in and have a bit of a chat, don't we?"

"Always provided we can find her, sir, that's the very least we should be doing!"

"There is that, Stoney," D.I. Wood agreed, returning to his brochure, "There is that"

* * * *

"How are you progressing with your endeavours, Archibald?" Josiah asked, aware that the sawing and banging of the last half-hour had abated.

"I'm er, I'm not too sure" Archibald admitted, scratching his head, "I can't find me bubble!"

"Is that some form of slang term of which I'm unaware?"

"Slang? Oh, no, it's this spirit level, I can't find me bubble"

"And this is a problem because...?" Josiah raised an eyebrow.

"Well, without me bubble I can't be sure if this shelf is level, sort of thing" Archibald shrugged.

"Have you tried to see if things slide off?"

"Like what?"

"Well, you could place a coin on the shelf, for example" Josiah suggested.

Archibald ferreted around in his pocket, extracted a coin and slapped it onto the putative shelf. Nothing happened.

Dead Reckoning

"I couldn't see as how that was going to work" He announced.

"Clearly I should have made my meaning plainer" Josiah said with a sigh, "What I had in mind was that the coin should be on its edge, its rim if you will, thus affording it the opportunity to roll, should it wish to do so"

"Oh, right!" Archibald made the required adjustment, the coin remained in place.

"Again, I should have been more explicit" Josiah removed his glasses and pinched the bridge of his nose, "In this instance, a 50p coin is not optimal, you really require a round coin of some nature, perhaps a 10p would suffice?"

"Fair enough, I'll give that a go" Archibald agreed.

He replaced the 50p with a 10p coin and they both watched it roll relentlessly off the shelf and drop to the ground with a metallic thud.

"You see, that's why I wanted to check with me level" Archibald said, feeling vindicated.

"Yes, I do perceive your problem" Josiah sighed, "Look, if you've reached a hiatus, perhaps this might be an opportune moment to break for lunch?"

"Reached a what? I don't think I've reached anything, other than that cable what I drilled through, just now"

"Yes, I think we were all aware of that" Josiah said, sternly, "However, by 'hiatus' my meaning was that you had reached a natural break, or pause, in your endeavours"

"Oh right, got you!" Archibald nodded, but looked despondent, "But, I've forgotten me pack-up"

"Really? In that case, and given your efforts, albeit somewhat mixed, on our behalf, perhaps you might agree to join Ms. Knight and myself. We could pop down to the tea room for a light bite?"

"Oh, that would be smashing, Mr. O.!" Archibald bounced up and down, looking, for all the world, like a puppy with a new bone.

"I'll just call Samantha, Ms. Knight, and let her know" Josiah picked up his mobile phone, "Samantha? We're just about to break for lunch and I've invited Archibald to join us. Could you ask Mr. Strine to 'mind the shop' as it were, in our absence? Thank you"

A few moments later, Samantha burst into the office, carrying something behind her back. She slipped her coat on and grasped Archibald by the arm.

"Come on, Archie" She beamed, "Lunch is on Mr. Oakshott. By the way, Josiah, I've had another seasonal idea" Samantha beamed.

"Really?" Josiah said, dubiously, putting on his coat and hat.

"Yep! Secret Santa"

"What's one of them, then?" Archibald looked puzzled.

"It's very simple. I've put everyone's names in a bag" She produced a hessian bag from behind her back, "Each person pulls a name out of the bag, all you have to do is buy them a gift of not more than £10, put the gift in the Santa Sack I've placed in the kitchenette, and then we'll give them out at the Christmas Party."

"I'm really not sure that's appropriate, Samantha..." Josiah began.

"Oh, now don't be such a wet blanket, Josiah" Samantha scolded, "It won't impact on the clients, or the general public at large, and it will be good for staff morale."

"It'd make the Party more like it an' all" Archibald muttered, "there's only so much fun you can get out of a glass of sherry and a mince pie"

Josiah glared at him.

"So, I've been around the workshop and everyone has taken a name now, bar you two" She jiggled the bag in front of Josiah, "Dip in"

Josiah glumly extracted a piece of paper from the bag.

"I seem to have…"

"No, don't say anything!" Samantha admonished, waving a finger, "It's a secret! The clue's in the name"

Archibald removed the last piece of paper from the bag, studied it, raised his eyebrows but said nothing.

"Good!" Samantha grinned, and grabbed Josiah by the arm, so that she was now holding both of them, "Now, time for a slap-up meal, I think"

"Well, I had something slightly more modest in mind…" Josiah complained.

"Josiah!" Samantha snapped, shoving both of them out of the door.

Chapter Forty
It's My Party

"I think it's gone rather well, don't you?" Samantha said, beaming as the assembled employees of Oakshott & Underwood stood around, chatting and joking, in the Workshop, enjoying the Company Christmas Party.

"I have to admit that the atmosphere has been markedly more convivial this year, than in years past" Josiah nodded, sipping his glass of British Cream Sherry. "It has to be said that your Secret Santa innovation, despite my concerns regarding the appropriateness of such a scheme, has made a real difference"

"Yes, it seems to have gone down well" Samantha grinned.

"In previous years, once they had consumed the obligatory sherry and mince pie, and, of course, heard my summary of the year's events, they couldn't wait to go home but, this year, they seem much happier to stay and chat"

"I think they've been busy comparing and contrasting what they've each had as a present. Speaking of which, next year we're going to have to do a bit better than a bottle of British Sherry as their present from the Company" Samantha said firmly.

"But, it's traditional" Josiah pleaded.

"I don't care! It's old-fashioned and parsimonious and does nothing for morale. We need to find something that they'll actually want and value.

Dead Reckoning

We can start thinking about that in the New Year" Samantha flipped open a notebook and made a quick note.

"We're erm, planning for next year then, are we?" Josiah mused.

"Well, yes, if you're happy for me to continue to be involved?" Samantha blushed a little.

"As a matter of fact, I've been meaning to have a word with you on that topic…" Josiah began but was interrupted by Archibald.

"I just wanted to say thank you, Mr. O." Archibald winked broadly, "I know as 'ow I shouldn't, like you said, but I just wanted you to know 'ow grateful I am, sort of thing" He winked again, beamed and then hurried away.

"How very odd!" Josiah looked puzzled.

"I take it you were his Secret Santa?" Samantha asked, with a grin.

"Well, yes, there was a certain inevitability about that, I thought" Josiah nodded.

"I presume you bought him something a bit special then, did you?"

"Well, no, not really" Josiah confessed, "I managed to pick up a pair of cufflinks from that Antiques & Curios place in town"

"Cufflinks? Does Archie wear cufflinks?"

"Not to my knowledge, no"

"Then, why cufflinks?"

"Oh, I see, well they had upon them a motif showing a drum and drumsticks, I thought they were rather appropriate. They were only £10" Josiah explained.

"I'm surprised he was quite so grateful" Samantha frowned, "I mean, yes, it was a thoughtful present in one respect, but hardly the stuff of undying gratitude, would you say?"

"Well, clearly they have been better received than either you or I could possibly have imagined" Josiah shrugged.

"I jusht wanna shay, Mister Oaksh...Mistrah Oaksh...Shir" Mr. Strine was swaying before Josiah, "Jusht wanna shay, thanks" He held out his hand to shake and then stared at it, owlishly, as if surprised to find it there.

"Not at all, Mr. Strine" Josiah smiled weakly and perfunctorily shook the proffered hand, "Thank you for your invaluable help and expertise this year"

"You're welcome Mistrah...Mistrah...you're welcome" Mr. Strine stemmed a burp in mid-flow and grinned, vacantly. "I'll see yer after Chrish...Chrish...I'll see yer" He waved vaguely and began to stagger away.

"How the dickens did he manage to get like that?" Josiah asked

"I rather think he's been drinking the sherries that people didn't want. There must have been quite a few" Samantha giggled.

"Hey! I know worrimeant to shay" Mr. Strine had turned around in mid-stride and lurched back to them, "what did that girl want?"

"Girl? What girl, Mr. Strine?" Josiah asked.

Dead Reckoning

"'Er what come in when you wash all at lunch, t'other day" Mr. Strine attempted to explain, whilst also attempting to keep a considerable quantity of Cream Sherry, gastrically at bay.

"I was not aware of any girl, Mr. Strine"

"Musht of bugg...gone then!" Mr. Strine shrugged, turned and lurched off again.

"I hope you're going home now, Mr. Strine" Samantha suggested.

"Nah, goin' dahn the pub with the lads, enni?" He grinned, broadly, hiccoughed and made his unsteady way to the door.

"I really do think Christmas has a lot to answer for" Josiah said, sternly.

"Oh, he's alright. Just had several too many" Samantha grinned, "What was that he was saying about a girl?"

"I have no idea" Josiah shook his head, "Why, what are you thinking?"

"Well, we can't be paranoid about any and every reference to a girl," Samantha sighed, "It can't always mean that Precious has been about, *but* we can't dismiss it, either" Samantha frowned, "I wonder...?"

Amidst the flurry of people laughing, joking and saying their goodbyes, she strode over to the Secret Santa sack, now apparently empty and deposited on the floor. She picked it up and held it upside down. A solitary small, wrapped gift, dropped to the floor. She retrieved it and took it back to Josiah.

"This wouldn't be your cufflinks, would it. This minute parcel without a tag?"

"Ah yes," Josiah examined the small parcel, guiltily, "I do believe so! In that case, what was it that Archibald was so pleased about?"

"I'm not at all sure" Samantha turned the small gift over and over in her hands, "but I've got to admit, Josiah, I'm worried"

* * * *

A little while later, Archibald was bouncing up the steps of The Merkin Country Club, Spa & Restaurant, brimming with excitement. He stopped, open-mouthed, in the Reception Hall, admiring the huge Christmas Tree that stretched up to the distant ceiling and dominated the whole area.

"Wow, that's quite summat, innit?" He said, still staring upward, to the well-dressed young man behind the Reception Desk.

"It has been commented upon, favourably sir" The man nodded, "Do you have a reservation, sir?"

"A reser…oh, right, I've got this" Archibald handed over a printed voucher.

"Ah yes, I see sir" The man inspected the voucher and then tapped some information into his computer. "Mr. erm, Throughball, is it?"

"Thurble" Archibald corrected.

"Indeed?" The man nodded, without looking up from his screen, "You have a reservation for one night in one of our luxury suites, sir"

"Luxury eh?" Archibald bounced from one foot to the other, with anticipation.

Dead Reckoning

"Indeed, sir" The man smiled, "Will sir be dining with us tonight?"

"Is it included?" Archibald looked worried.

"It is indeed, sir"

"Oh well then, yeah, definitely!" Archibald grinned.

"Excellent, sir, I will reserve a table. Would eight-o-clock be acceptable?"

"What, for dinner? Oh yeah, bring it on!" Archibald made a thumbs-up sign.

"Fine, that table is booked for you, sir. Here is your key, you are on the fourth floor. Now, in your suite you will find a comprehensive list of all of the facilities available in our Spa. Should you wish to avail yourself of any of these treatments and services, you will need to telephone the Spa Reception Desk on the number provided"

"Is that included an' all?"

"It is, indeed, sir, as is your choice of breakfast in the morning"

"Smashing!" Archibald rubbed his hands, "I'm definitely going to book meself one of them full body massages, I've always wanted one of them"

"A very popular choice, I am led to believe, sir" The man nodded, solemnly handing over the key. "Does sir have any luggage?"

"Oh no, just me overnight bag" Archibald held up a sports bag.

"The lift is to your left, sir. I do hope that you enjoy your stay, but do let me know if you require anything further" The man bowed slightly.

"Oh yeah, not half" Archibald grabbed the key and bounded toward the lift.

The lift whisked him swiftly and silently to the Fourth Floor. Archibald peered at the sign displaying the room numbers, consulted his key card and then marched off, over thick and luxurious carpet, toward his room.

He managed to get the door-lock light to turn to green on his third attempt with the key card and shoved the heavy door open with his shoulder. It was pitch-black inside and flicking the light switches didn't seem to make any difference. The door sighed shut, behind him. He scrabbled in his pocket and retrieved his 'phone. With a couple of shakes, he managed to activate the flashlight function so that he could finally see what he was doing. More flicking of the switches had no effect and he was muttering darkly to himself, when he turned around to see where he could find the room telephone.

He gasped with horror when he saw a body lying on one of the beds.

He emitted a shrill yelp when the body then eased itself up onto its elbows, looked at him and said,

"Hello, Archibald!" In a silky voice.

Chapter Forty-One
The Party's Over

"Did I startle you, Archibald?" Precious DeVille swivelled her feet to the floor in one smooth movement and sashayed toward Archibald, through the gloom of the hotel room.

"Well, erm, yeah, you did!" Archibald admitted.

"There's no need to be nervous, now is there?" Precious said in soothing tones, getting ever closer to Archibald, who was becoming increasingly aware that she was only wearing, very skimpy, lingerie.

"No, no, it's not that.." Archibald began, spluttering somewhat, "it's just…well, I wasn't expecting nobody, was I?"

"No, of course not" Precious grinned, "otherwise, it wouldn't have been a surprise now, would it?"

Archibald was aware that she was pressed close to him. He could smell the heady scent of her perfume and feel her breath upon his neck.

"Yeah, but how did you…" Archibald tried, again.

"Shhh, now" Precious placed a beautifully manicured finger to his lips, "no more questions"

He realised that she had snaked one of her legs around his. It wasn't an altogether unpleasant experience. However, in one slick move, she spun him around and caused him to fall backwards onto the bed, with her on top.

"There now, that's more comfortable, isn't it?" She smiled.

Archibald had somewhat mixed emotions. On the one hand, being pinned to a bed by a partially dressed, very attractive, girl was decidedly 'comfortable' but, on the other hand, the fact that she had left him to drown and might well be a serial killer, rather took the edge off any burgeoning passion he might be feeling.

"Erm?" Was the best he could manage, under the circumstances.

"You know, it's a dreadful shame, Archibald" Precious said, pouting a little, "I think, under any other circumstances, you and I could have got along *really* well"

"Erm?"

"But, as it is…" She sighed and retrieved something from under the pillow.

"'Ere, what're you doing?" Archibald asked, panic beginning to edge into his voice.

"Oh, hush now" Precious shook her head, "You know your problem, Archibald? You're convinced that you're the prey, aren't you?"

"Eh? I don't…" Archibald felt a sharp pain in his left thigh.

"You're not the prey, sweetie" Precious reassured him, leaning forward to whisper in his ear, "You're the bait!"

And, with that, the night closed in on Archibald completely.

* * * *

Dead Reckoning

Josiah and Samantha were shuffling around the Workshop, retrieving the detritus left from the previous afternoon's 'Christmas Party'.

"Seems really quiet, with just us here, doesn't it?" Samantha said, consigning a mince pie container to the black bin bag she was holding.

"Yes, it's always a little unsettling to be somewhere which one normally associates with the hustle and bustle of a busy commercial enterprise, when it is, to all intents and purposes, closed" Josiah agreed.

"Who is 'minding the store' over Christmas and New Year>"

"We have a 'skeleton staff' arrangement, a term that Archibald finds somewhat risible..." Josiah began.

"I can see his point!" Samantha giggled.

"Well, yes, it is somewhat ironic" Josiah nodded, "However, the arrangement, such as it is, largely consists of myself and one other member of staff, from a rota I drew up a while ago. For example, today should consist of myself and Mr. Strine"

"Ah! Is he here?" Samantha looked around the premises, curiously.

"No, he is not. In all honesty, I am not surprised" Josiah shook his head, "Given the condition he was in when he left the party, yesterday evening. I heard, from the milkman, that he, Mr. Strine that is, then proceeded to The Frog & Crumpet, with the other employees, and was thrown out, not long after, for being loud, argumentative and, as the landlord put it, 'rascally drunk'!"

"Oh dear!" Samantha stifled a titter.

"Normally, I would have hoped to have been able to avail myself of Archibald's services, in his place, at least on a 'stand-by' basis" Josiah sighed.

"Did you try his home?"

"I spoke to his mother, my cousin Ophelia, which was not a pleasant experience for either of us, but it is fair to say that she is somewhat concerned"

"Why, what's happened?"

"Apparently, he returned from work, yesterday, in a state of high excitement, whereupon he packed an overnight bag for himself and went straight out again, only saying, on leaving that (and I quote) 'Old Mr. O.'s done me proud, Mam. I'll see you tomorrow!' She, therefore, holds me personally responsible should anything have happened to him"

"And, she doesn't know where he went, or with whom?" Samantha frowned.

"No, she does not. As of 9am this morning, there was still no sign of him"

"Should we go to the police, do you think?"

"And tell them what?"

"Yes, you have a point there" Samantha nodded, glumly.

In the distance, the office telephone could be heard ringing.

"Ah well, duty calls" Josiah said, with a sigh, and hurried off to answer it.

Dead Reckoning

Samantha returned to her litter-picking duties. A few moments later, Josiah returned looking bemused.

"Problem, Josiah?" Samantha asked.

"Possibly" Josiah nodded, "It is most odd. That was Ezekiel Cadwallader on the telephone…"

"The chap who runs the other Undertakers' in town?"

"Yes, him. Apparently, there was a fatality reported at The Merkin Country Club in the early hours of this morning. A couple of his chaps went out to deal with it, and they have not been seen since. He admitted that he was clutching at straws, but he wondered if they had returned here, for any bizarre reason" Josiah shook his head.

"How strange!" Samantha frowned, "I presume they would have a van?"

"Yes, of course, in which to transport the deceased"

"And that's missing too, I take it?"

"Apparently so" Josiah nodded, "I counselled him to advise the police, without further delay"

"Yes, that makes sense" Samantha looked thoughtful, "The Merkin Country Club…" She mused, "might be the sort of place you would go to if you had an overnight bag, don't you think?"

"Well, one of many such places, I suppose" Josiah agreed, "I take it you are wondering if there might be some sort of connection between the disappearance of Ezekiel's two employees and the absence of Archibald?"

"When odd stuff like this happens, I worry about Precious"

"I think the tendency to ascribe anything strange, or potentially criminal, to the machinations of that young lady, has all the characteristics of conspiracy theorising! I would strongly counsel against going down that particular rabbit hole" Josiah said, with a kindly smile.

The office telephone rang again.

"Duty calls, once more" Josiah sighed and disappeared. When he returned, a few minutes later, he looked ashen.

"Is everything alright, Josiah?"

"Erm, yes, everything is fine" Josiah said, tersely, "I have to attend to a client"

"Do you want me to come with you?"

"NO, no, that will not be necessary" Josiah looked about him, distractedly.

"Would you like me to call one of the other members of staff to assist, Egbert perhaps?"

"No, there's no need. I can manage perfectly well on my own" Josiah said, firmly, slipping on his overcoat and gloves, "However, when you have concluded clearing up in here, perhaps you might like to assuage your curiosity by popping out to The Merkin Country Club"

"Really? You think there might be something in it, then?" Samantha sounded surprised.

Dead Reckoning

"Indeed, I think that might be a potential line of enquiry" Josiah nodded, and then, much to Samantha's surprise, he came over and kissed her tenderly on the forehead. "You must take great care of yourself, Samantha" He hesitated, and stared at her for a few moments. "You may remember, yesterday, I mentioned that we might have a discussion about the future, by which I meant *our* future?"

"Yes, I wondered at the time…" Samantha began.

"Just remember that I had hoped to have that conversation, will you?" Josiah said, before turning on his heel and striding out to his car.

'What in the world was that all about?' Samantha thought, as she waved him on his way.

Chapter Forty-Two
Nowhere Man

"His name is Archibald Thurble…" Samantha said, firmly.

"I am really sorry, madam, but…" The Reception Clerk responded.

"That's T-H-U-R-B-L-E, if you want to check your records"

"With respect, madam, the spelling is irrelevant. I cannot share the private details of any of our guests with you"

"I don't want to know his intimate details, I just want to know if he's staying with you, is that too much to ask!" Samantha glared at the unfortunate Clerk.

"I'm rather afraid that it is, madam" The Clerk shook his head, sadly, "I am bound by the Data Protection Act"

"I don't care if you're bound by leather thongs every weekend, I just want to know if he stayed here last night!" Samantha said, her voice rising in volume with each word.

"Once more, madam…" The Clerk began, with a sigh.

"Bloody hell! Have you got a thing about Undertakers or something?"

Samantha swivelled around from her confrontation with the Clerk, to see D.I. Wood and D.S. Stone standing behind her in the Reception area.

Dead Reckoning

"Ah, Inspector, just the person I need...hang on, what do you mean about my having a thing about Undertakers?"

"I mean, Mrs. Knight, that we've been called to look into the possible disappearance of two gentlemen from the business of" He checked his notebook, "Cadwallader and Carruthers and who do we find has beaten us to it...?"

"I'm not here about them"

"And yet here you are" D.I. Wood folded his arms and looked at her, sternly.

"I'm not!" Samantha protested, "I've heard about them, I'll admit that, because Ezekiel Cadwallader telephoned Josiah earlier..."

"It's like a morticians' mafia in this town, I've never known anything like it!" D.I. Wood rubbed his forehead, distractedly.

"It was because Ezekiel said that they had been despatched to here, that I thought I would..."

"Come along and hope to pick one of them up on the rebound?" D.I. Wood suggested, sarcastically.

"No, not at all, look I'm trying to find Archibald..." Samantha began.

"Mr. Thurble. The one you call 'Lurch', sir" D.S. Stone supplied, in an effort to be helpful, but received a withering look from his superior.

"I think I know who 'Archibald' is, in this context, Sergeant. Our paths have crossed, you may recall?"

"...only this *gentleman*" Samantha clearly used the term, loosely, "won't provide me with the simple information of whether he was here last night, or not"

"As I have tried to explain to this *lady*..." The Reception Clerk began, again, with a certain emphasis.

"Hush!" D.I. Wood held a hand up, "Do you think there's some sort of connection between the two we're looking for and your Mr. Thurble then?" D.I. Wood frowned.

"I don't know, to be honest" Samantha shook her head, "but I suspect that Josiah did"

"I'm sorry?" D.I. Wood looked puzzled.

"This morning, Josiah had two 'phone calls in quick succession" Samantha explained, "The first was from Ezekiel Cadwallader. Ezekiel said that he knew it was a long shot, but he wondered if the two guys he had sent out to pick up a body, that had been reported for collection from *here*, had somehow turned up at Josiah's, for whatever reason. Josiah told him to call you"

"Very sensible of him" D.I. Wood nodded, "and the other call?"

"I don't know who that was from, but he seemed pretty shaken up by it. It was supposed to be a call-out to a client. I offered to go with him to help, but he wouldn't hear of it"

"Wasn't there anyone else on duty who could have gone with him?" D.S. Stone asked.

Dead Reckoning

"No, it should have been Mr. Strine but we think he may have overdone it with his pre-Christmas celebrations. One too many Emva Creams, if you know what I mean?"

"I can see why Mr. Oakshott would be reluctant to involve you." D.S. Stone nodded, "I shouldn't think that collecting the deceased is exactly a load of fun?"

"No, probably not" Samantha conceded, "He went out more or less straight after the second 'phone call but, before he went, he did suggest that I might start looking for Archibald, here"

"Hmm, did he indeed? D.I. Wood looked at his Sergeant, who was making notes, "Stoney, have a word with chummy there on the desk, see if you can get anywhere. Mrs. Knight, come with me, I need to ask a few more questions" He guided Samantha away from the Reception desk, to the side of the foyer.

"I must admit, I'm worried. What with Archie going missing..." Samantha said. "And Josiah was behaving really oddly just before he left"

"When you say that Mr. Thurble has gone missing, what do you mean exactly?"

"We had our Christmas Staff Party yesterday..." Samantha began.

"The Undertakers have a Christmas party?"

"Yes, I know it seems unlikely" Samantha nodded, "It's hardly an occasion of wild abandon, I can tell you! Anyway, this year I persuaded Josiah to allow a 'Secret Santa' arrangement, and it seemed to go down well. Archie was due to get a present from Josiah, and he seemed to think that he *had* received one..."

"But he hadn't?"

"Well, not the gift he should have had, no" Samantha explained, "Josiah had bought him a set of cufflinks and we found those at the bottom of the sack. However, he seemed to think he'd been given something, because he was really pleased with it."

"He never mentioned what it was?"

"Sadly, no" Samantha bit her lip, "but Josiah rang Archie's mother this morning and she said he'd bounced out yesterday evening, looking pretty pleased with himself, with an overnight bag"

"Ah, I see where you're going with this, now" D.I. Wood nodded.

"And then, just after Josiah had received that second 'phone call, he suggested to me that I should start looking for Archie, here"

"And do you think the second 'phone call was connected, somehow, with Mr. Thurble's disappearance?"

"I don't know! As I said before, Josiah said he had to 'attend to a client'" Samantha shrugged, miserably. "But when he left, he told me to take great care of myself and to remember that he had hoped to have a conversation about our future. It was almost as if he was saying goodbye!" She sobbed.

"I do sympathise and I can see why you're worried but it's very early days." D.I. Wood shook his head, "Both Mr. Thurble and Mr. Oakshott may not be missing at all, there may be some perfectly innocent explanation. In the meantime, we're here to try and find out what's happened to Mr. Cadwallader's employees and we're no further forward with that!" D.I. Wood ran his fingers through his remaining hair but looked happier when he saw D.S. Stone approaching.

"Stoney, what have you got?" D.I. Wood looked at his colleague, expectantly.

"Well, I've managed to prise him away from the Data Protection Act, a bit" D.S. Stone grinned, "He's confirmed that Archibald *was* here last night"

"Oh!" Samantha gasped.

"There's a bit more, sir" D.S. Stone looked at his boss for permission to continue.

"Yeah, go ahead" D.I. Wood shrugged, "Mrs. Knight here seems to know more about it than we do, anyway"

"Well, apparently, the Reception bloke thinks there may have been a girl waiting for him in his room. He said he didn't enquire too closely because he assumed it was some sort of 'clandestine arrangement'" D.S. Stone made the quotation marks with his fingers and raised his eyebrows.

"There was a girl?" Samantha looked shocked.

"It doesn't necessarily mean anything" D.I. Wood reassured her, "Perhaps it was something he cooked up, and that was why he was so excited about it?"

"I don't think Archibald has anyone in his life, presently" Samantha mused, "but I suppose I could be wrong"

"Hmm, well, I'd like to know how she got into his room, for a kick-off" D.I. Wood turned to his Sergeant, "Did he say if they *had* reported a fatality to Cadwallader and Carruthers?"

"There's nothing in the Night Porter's records apparently, and there would definitely be extensive documentation if that was the case."

"If they did have a fatality, how would they deal with it, do you know?" D.I. Wood rummaged in his pocket for a cigarette, more out of habit than anything else.

"He said they would be as discreet as possible. A van would be brought to the Goods Entrance, and the deceased would be transported down in the Goods Lift" D.S. Stone reported.

"Ok, let's get Mr. Reception in for a bit of a chat, Stoney and I want any and all CCTV from last night covering Reception, the floor Mr. Thurble was on and the Goods Lift and Entrance. Got it?"

"Will do, sir" D.S. Stone marched away, purposefully.

"What about Josiah, and Archibald?" Samantha looked worried.

"It's like I said, there could be a perfectly innocent explanation for all of this, such as Archibald being on a promise with some random girl and Josiah actually going to collect a client! We're up a gum tree anyway there because we don't know where he was going, do we?" D.I. Wood shrugged, "Did you check the number that called?"

"Yes, it was withheld"

Dead Reckoning

"Pity! Huh, we might make a copper out of you, at this rate" D.I. Wood grinned, "Is he coming quietly, Stoney?"

"He has volunteered to help us with our enquiries and he's arranged for the CCTV footage to be transferred to us asap" D.S. Stone nodded and winked, "I think he's wetting himself, if I'm honest" He whispered.

"Right then, Mrs. Knight, we'll get Sonny Jim here back to the nick and have a chat with menaces. See what we can find out but you have to remember, our focus has to be on the men who have gone missing from Cadwallader and Carruthers. We can be reasonably confident that something has gone amiss there, whereas we don't know that there's a problem at all with Josiah and Archibald."

"Is there anything I can do?" Samantha asked.

"I would go back to the office and wait. If you hear from them, let us know immediately. And if you can try and figure out where Messrs. Thurble and Oakshott have gone, that would be two less things for us to worry about"

"I wish I knew, Inspector" Samantha looked glum, "I wish I knew!"

Chapter Forty-Three
Don't Blame It on That Girl

"We've got the CCTV footage, sir" D.S. Stone said as his superior ambled into the open-plan office.

"Good! We need to go through that with a fine-tooth comb, Stoney. I reckon it could be quite revealing, particularly after the chat I've just had with Sunny Jim off Reception"

"What did he have to say, sir?"

"Well, for a kick-off, it seems that he's been supplementing his income by taking backhanders from...what are we supposed to call them these days?"

"Call what, sir?" D.S. Stone frowned.

"Tarts"

"Ah, you mean 'sex workers', sir"

"Yeah, them. Well, anyway, the way it works is they bung him a few quid and he coughs up a spare key. That's what happened in the case of our Archibald, he reckons. Money changed hands and this mysterious girl went up to the room to give Archie-boy a big surprise"

"I've got the CCTV from his floor here. I'll just fast-forward and see if I can spot her" D.S. Stone peered at the screen and tapped a few times on the keyboard. "Oh, hang on. Is that her, do you think?"

"That's definitely his room" D.I. Wood confirmed, consulting the piece of paper he was holding.

"She's wearing a cloak with a hood, so we can't see much of her" D.S. Stone pointed out, "Hang on, isn't that the same outfit that the woman who abducted our vagrant, Jimmy, was wearing?"

"It could be" D.I. Wood nodded, peering at the screen, "It's bloody annoying, I know that much. Perhaps Lurch has got a thing about Red Riding Hood?"

The 'phone rang on D.S. Stone's desk and he answered.

"You won't like this, sir" He said, turning to his boss.

"Now what?"

"Ms. Knight's in Reception"

"Oh, flaming hell! I told her to wait and see if either Oakshott or Thurble got in touch. What's she doing here?"

"Perhaps she has some news, sir?"

"Bring her up but she's going to get short shrift from me if she's here to waste our time"

A few minutes later, Samantha walked into the office.

"I'm really sorry, Inspector, but I couldn't just sit there waiting for the telephone to ring" She saw the screen with the frozen CCTV image, "Oh, is that the girl who was supposed to be meeting Archibald?"

"As a matter of fact, it is" D.I. Wood said, with a degree of hostility, "I don't suppose you might recognise her?"

"No, but there's not much to go on, is there?" Samantha peered at the screen.

"Well, I'm sorry about that, Mrs. Knight! We'll obviously have to try harder" D.I. Wood snarled.

"Let me run the footage on. We should see Mr. Thurble, eventually" D.S. Stone suggested.

The images flickered across the screen. Mostly, the floor corridor was empty, with occasional intervals where a resident headed to and from the lifts.

"Hang on! That's him" Samantha yelled as the familiar bulk of Archibald Thurble stumbled out of the lift and consulted his key card. "How was the room booked, Sergeant?"

"Online, apparently. Nothing on record as to who made the booking, yet, but we're working on it. Likewise. the credit card used" D.S. Stone supplied.

"Alright, Stoney! It's me you report to, remember?" D.I. Wood seethed.

"Yes sir, sorry sir" D.S. Stone moved the footage on, frame by frame. They saw Archibald fumble with his key card and eventually shoulder the room door open. "Well, that's confirmed that they're both, now, in the same room"

"Why didn't he notice her straight away?" Samantha wondered.

Dead Reckoning

"Perhaps he did. Perhaps he was expecting her to be there" D.I. Wood suggested.

"I wish we knew what was going on in there" Samantha looked worried.

"I think I'm happier *not* knowing" D.I. Wood said.

"I'll fast forward a bit more" D.S. Stone tapped a few keys. The corridor remained remarkably free of both Archibald and his mystery woman, for some time.

"What hour are we up to now, Stoney?" D.I. Wood asked.

"Gone midnight, sir"

"Well, you can't blame him for making a night of it, can you?" D.I. Wood leered.

"I've told you, Inspector, I don't think there is anyone in Archibald's life, at the moment" Samantha snapped.

"Ah well, if what the Reception bloke has told me is true, then this one's affection is somewhat negotiable. In other words, she's a t…"

"Sex worker, sir" D.S. Stone interrupted.

"Whatever" D.I. Wood shrugged.

"Hang on, someone's coming out of the room" D.S. Stone slowed down the recording, "It's a woman, but this one seems to be wearing some sort of uniform"

"I would say, from the tabard she's got on, that she's supposed to be part of the Housekeeping staff" Samantha got closer to the screen, "You know, I'd swear that's Precious"

"She seems to know where the CCTV camera is, sir" D.S. Stone pointed out, "She's looking directly at it"

"Cheeky beggar!" D.I. Wood fumed, "She's rubbing our nose in it! Where's she off to?"

"She's not heading for the customer lifts. She must be going to the stairs or the Goods Lift, but we can't see from here" D.S. Stone said.

"How about the Goods Entrance, can you get us to that?" D.I. Wood asked.

"Hang on, I should be able to" D.S. Stone hammered away at the keyboard, until, finally, "Yes, here it is. Now, it was just after midnight, wasn't it? Let's see..."

The loading dock remained obstinately empty for ages but then, a dark van could be seen backing up to it. D.S. Stone slowed the recording.

"This'll be the lads from Cadwallader and Carruthers" D.I. Wood rubbed his hands together, "Do you know them, Mrs. Knight?"

"No, I'm sorry, I don't"

Two besuited men climbed out of the van and were met, on the loading dock, by the uniformed woman they had just seen exit Archibald's room. The group conversed, briefly. The two men opened rear of the van and removed a trolley, which they wheeled after the woman and off screen.

Dead Reckoning

"Ok, so if what we suspect *is* the case, they should reappear on the Fourth Floor, in a few minutes" D.S. Stone tapped a key and the screen view switched back to the hotel floor.

"There they are!" Samantha pointed at the screen, "Oh my god! They're going to Archibald's room" She stifled a sob.

They watched the trio enter the room and close the door. A few minutes elapsed and then the door opened, again. The uniformed woman poked her head out of the doorway, looked left and right, then said something over her shoulder. She went back into the room and then the trolley appeared, but this time, bearing a body bag.

"Oh no! She's killed him!" Samantha shrieked.

D.I. Wood and D.S. Stone exchanged a worried glance.

"Let's just see what happens, eh?" D.I. Wood said, in a sympathetic tone.

The trolley, wheeled by the two men, disappeared from view, closely followed by the woman in the uniform who closed the hotel room door, placing a 'Do Not Disturb' sign on the handle, then looked directly at the CCTV camera, giving a broad grin, before also disappearing from view.

"Right, back to the Goods Entrance, Stoney"

The view on the screen flicked to the empty loading dock but then the trolley, with the two men, appeared. The trolley was loaded onto the van, the back doors closed and the two men went to board but were stopped by the woman in uniform.

"Now what's she doing?" D.S. Stone frowned and tried to get a close-up of the scene. The men and woman seemed to be in animated conversation. Then all three climbed on board the van and it pulled away.

"Stoney, check the ANPR and see if we can track that van" D.I. Wood ordered, "What the hell was she doing going with them?"

"I suppose she might have asked them for a lift home? Told them she was at the end of her shift, something like that?" D.S. Stone guessed.

"Yeah, that's as likely as anything" D.I. Wood nodded.

"She's killed him! She's killed Archibald!" Samantha sniffled.

"I don't know" D.I. Wood shook his head, "It just doesn't make sense!"

"What do you mean?" Samantha asked.

"Well, why go to all of this trouble? Eh?" D.I. Wood looked questioningly at them both, "If she has offed him, she could just have left the body in the room and cleared off. It wouldn't be found 'til morning at the earliest, probably a lot later given that 'Do Not Disturb' sign. By which time, she'd be long gone"

"Yes, I see what you mean, sir" D.S. Stone nodded. "Why involve another two people? It's got to complicate matters"

"That's right, Stoney! She's making it ten times more difficult and much more likely she'll get her collar felt. I don't buy it" D.I. Wood shook his head, "Stoney, I want forensics all over that room"

Dead Reckoning

"We'll have to hope they haven't serviced it yet, sir" D.S. Stone frowned, "and, you know what it's like with hotel rooms. Every man and his dog have been in there"

"Well, we'll just have to hope we'll get lucky" D.I. Wood shrugged.

"How close can you get to those images" Samantha asked.

"Well, pretty close" D.S. Stone demonstrated, "but you start to lose quite a bit of definition unless it's a very high-quality CCTV system, which this one isn't"

"Why, what do you want to look at?" D.I. Wood asked her.

"Well, I think the woman had a name tag on her uniform" Samantha speculated, "Do you think we could get a closer look at it?"

"Hang on, I'll try" D.S. Stone rewound the file until he had the image of the woman staring straight at the CCTV camera. "There, that should do it"

"What does it say, Stoney? I can't make it out from here" D.I. Wood almost had his nose to the screen.

"Erm, I think it says, 'Lorna', no, hold on, it's 'Lana...something'" D.S. Stone tapped a key a couple of times and peered at the result, "Heyvell...it's Lana Heyvell" He said, triumphantly.

"Brilliant, Stoney!" D.I. Wood patted him on the back, "Get on to the hotel and check if they've got anyone of that name on their books. Well done for spotting that, Mrs. Kn..." D.I. Wood looked behind him and realised she wasn't there anymore. "Now where the heck's she gone?"

303

Chapter Forty-Four
Hit Me with Your Rhythm Stick

"It's a bloody cheek, that's what it is!" D.I. Wood slapped a stack of papers down on his desk and fumed, "She comes swanning in here without a 'by your leave' and then just clears off without any explanation whatsoever!"

He extracted a cigarette from his pack, rolled it around his lips and then, noticing the disapproving look of his Sergeant, stuffed it back in the packet with ill temper.

"Do you think she spotted something, sir?" D.S. Stone asked, "Maybe that's why she shot off in such a hurry?"

"Spotted something? Like what?"

"Well, I don't know" D.S. Stone shook his head, shrugged and looked thoughtful, "Must have been something on that CCTV footage, I suppose"

"I didn't see anything particularly enlightening, did you?" D.I. Wood frowned.

"Not to be honest, sir"

"Better get on to the hotel and check out that girl's name. I don't think for a minute that she'll turn out to be one of the staff, but you never know your luck in a raffle"

Dead Reckoning

"Will do, sir" D.S. Stone marched back to his desk.

"Oh, and Stoney," D.I. Wood shouted after him, "While you're at it, run an ANPR check on Mrs. Knight's car. Let's see if we can figure out where she's off to, eh?"

"Right, sir"

* * * *

For Josiah Oakshott, the delights of the Cheshire countryside were not proving to be much of a distraction from the grim reality of his mission. He kept running, over and over again, the content of the 'phone call he had received:

"Oakshott and Underwood, Josiah Oakshott speaking, how may I help you?" He had said, in his best 'customer-friendly' voice. A mix, he liked to think, of both sympathy and businesslike efficiency, that he had been honing over the years.

"Hello, Josiah" said a voice that he knew only too well. A voice that sent a shiver down his spine.

"Miss DeVille, is that you?"

"You know it is, Josiah" She had snapped, "Now be quiet and just listen to me. If you want Archibald back, safely and in one piece, you'll do exactly as I tell you…"

"You…you've got Archibald!"

"You're interrupting, Josiah, don't interrupt! You will come to Evanley Hall, now. You will tell no-one where you are going. You will come alone. You will not involve the Police or anyone else, is that clear?"

"Yes, perfectly"

"If you disobey any of my instructions, ANY of them, Archibald will suffer, do you understand?"

"I...I understand"

"Good! Then I will look forward to seeing you shortly"

And that was it. The whole thing had only taken a couple of minutes, if that, but, in that time, his whole world had been turned upside down. In a daze, he had returned to Samantha, told her he had to attend to a client, put on his overcoat and gloves and set off. He had managed to point Samantha, he hoped, in the right direction to try to get some answers about Archibald's disappearance, but he also worried that that might constitute 'involving someone else', with dire consequences for Archibald, and that worried him, a lot.

He had also, as far as he possibly could, tried to say goodbye to Samantha. He hoped she would remember and understand. After all, Josiah thought, with a heavy heart, if he was going to be brutally honest with himself, this was not a trip from which he could reasonably expect to return.

* * * *

"Anything, Stoney?" D.I. Wood looked up from his Caribbean brochure at his Sergeant, who had entered the office and was looking rather thoughtful.

Dead Reckoning

"Not really, sir" D.S. Stone sucked a pencil and consulted his notebook, "As expected, the Country Club doesn't have anyone of that name on their staff"

"Quelle surprise!" D.I. Wood raised an eyebrow and tutted. "Remind me, what was her name supposed to be?"

D.S. Stone flicked through a couple of pages and said, eventually, "Erm, Heyvell, sir, Lana Heyvell"

"Hmm" D.I. Wood frowned, "Bloody funny name to make up for a name tag, isn't it? I mean, you'd think she'd go for something simple like 'Jane Smith', or something, wouldn't you?"

"Yes, you would, sir" D.S. Stone frowned as he studied his notebook.

"How about ANPR? Any luck with tracking Mrs. Knight?"

"No, not really, sir" D.S. Stone shook his head, still studying the notebook, "We clocked her leaving Merkin-under-Heathwood heading north, but then she must have gone down one of the back roads. Nothing since, sorry sir"

"North? She's shot off out of town? What the hell's she up to?"

"I don't know sir, it's…oh hell!"

"What's the matter, Sergeant?"

"It's an anagram!"

"What's an anagram?"

"That girl's name, sir. It's an anagram, at least, I think it is" D.S. Stone scribbled a few words in his notebook and started crossing letters out.

"I wish you'd tell me what the hell it is you're doing, Sergeant!" D.I. Wood snapped, "Anyone would think that I'M NOT YOUR SUPERIOR OFFICER!"

"Sorry, sir" D.S. Stone looked up from his notebook, "You're not going to like this"

"There's nothing about this case that I like, Stoney, so go on, surprise me" D.I. Wood put his chin on his hand and stared at his Sergeant.

"Lana Heyvell, sir" D.S. Stone took a deep breath, in anticipation of the coming storm, "It's an anagram of 'Evanley Hall'"

* * * *

Josiah negotiated the deeply rutted track leading up to the Hall with mounting trepidation. He noted that there were some dim lights illuminating Jeannie's dilapidated cottage. It was, he thought, somehow, comforting that someone was going about their normal everyday business just a few yards away from his destination. He sighed and drove on. He couldn't, he reflected, realistically expect any help from that quarter, even if he had been able to raise the alarm.

He drove over the cattle grid and onto the gravel drive. He winced at the memory of his excitement on the last occasion when he was driven to the Hall, a time when he had anticipated a romantic, candlelit dinner with an attractive former girlfriend, only to be knocked unconscious and left to die in a water-filled cellar.

Dead Reckoning

There were no welcoming lights on at the Hall, on this occasion. In fact, it looked deserted. He eased himself out of the limousine and closed the door as quietly as he could manage, in the hope that his arrival had not been noticed. All was quiet in the twilight of this miserable day. He looked all around him, but there was no-one to be seen. Then, a faint noise, right on the edge of his hearing, grabbed his attention. It sounded like… someone digging!

* * * *

"Evanley Hall! REALLY?" D.I. Wood had a face like thunder.

"I suppose it could be a…coincidence, perhaps?" D.S. Stone responded, unconvincingly.

"She spotted it, didn't she?" D.I. Wood put his head in his hands, "That's why she shot off like that, that's the truth of it, isn't it?"

"Well…possibly?" D.S. Stone squirmed.

"Heading north! She's heading for Cheshire, isn't she?" D.I. Wood groaned.

"It's certainly a possibility, sir" D.S. Stone nodded, miserably.

D.I. Wood took a deep breath, sighed and then squared his shoulders. Rising from his desk like an avenging angel, he grabbed his coat, patted his jacket pocket for the reassuring presence of a packet of cigarettes, and swept out of his office.

"Right, Stoney." He shouted over his shoulder, "Get a couple of Uniforms and have them follow us. We're heading back to bear country and this time; I'm taking an elephant gun!"

Philip Whiteland

* * * *

Josiah followed the sound he had heard, with considerable trepidation. It led him around the corner, past the kitchen window, and into the rear garden, beyond. In the distance, he could see some lanterns, apparently arranged on the ground. The sound of digging had now stopped. Instead, there was just an eerie silence, as if the whole house and surrounding area was holding its breath. He continued to walk, tentatively, toward the arrangement of lights. There didn't seem, he noted gratefully, to be anyone in the vicinity.

As he drew closer to the spectacle, he became aware of just what the lanterns were, apparently, illuminating. It was something he was very familiar with indeed. There was no mistaking that there was an open grave right there, in front of him. He began to quicken his pace, and started to mutter:

"Oh God no, not Archibald, please God, no!"

He found himself on the edge of the grave and forced himself to look down, dreading what he might find. To his immense relief, the grave was empty. He straightened up, sighed deeply and momentarily relaxed. Then the silence was broken. A man's voice behind him said:

"Sorry, Mr. Oakshott"

He spun around, just in time to see the flat side of a shovel hurtling straight toward him.

Chapter Forty-Five
Reach Out and Touch (Somebody's Hand)

Samantha gingerly made her way up the ramshackle path and through the overgrown garden that led to Jeannie Mountjoy's cottage. She hammered on the door and waited for the inevitable barrage of expletives.

"Who the bloody 'ell's that? Yer've made me cats run off agin, come 'ere yer little buggers!"

"JEANNIE!" Samantha shouted.

"WHO'S THAT?" The voice replied, suspiciously.

"JEANNIE, IT'S ME, SAMANTHA"

"BUGGER OFF!"

"JEANNIE, I NEED YOUR HELP"

There was a considerable amount of chuntering, the sound of furniture being scraped over the tiled floor, a shout of "GET BACK YER LITTLE SODS!" and then the door opened, just a crack. An eye peered out.

"Yeah?" The voice said.

"Jeannie, it's me, Samantha. Samantha Knight."

"Don't know no Samantha" The door started to close but Samantha managed to get her foot in the way, first.

"I was here, before, with Archibald and the police. You remember, after that business with the flooded cellar up at the Hall?"

The eye looked at her, steadily.

"Oh ar!" The voice acknowledged, and the door creaked open a little more, "I reckon yer now. What d'yer want?"

"it's...it's about Josiah" Samantha said with a catch in her voice, "You remember Josiah?"

"Yeah, I know who yer mean" Jeannie said, cautiously.

"He's missing. Archibald too!"

"Yer best come in" The door opened a bit more and Samantha managed to edge into the gloom. Jeannie shuffled through the next door, into the kitchen, which was still the same jumble of used plates, cups and cats. "I dint 'ear yer come in no car" Jeannie said, turning to look at her.

"I left it on the road" Samantha explained, "I didn't want anyone to hear or see me" She nodded in the direction of the Hall.

"There ain't nobody there, not as I know of" Jeannie frowned, "Hang on, come to think of it, there were a van..."

"A van? When?"

"Early hours. Set the cats off. They dunner like being disturbed, yer know?"

"I think that might have been Precious, you remember her? I believe she's got Archibald. I don't know if he's alive or dead. She...she took him away in a body bag" Samantha choked back a sob.

Dead Reckoning

"Body bag?" Jeannie looked at her, quizzically, "That's a bad do, that. What meks yer think it's 'er?"

Samantha explained about the CCTV footage from the Country Club.

"It was when I saw the name badge on her uniform, 'Lana Heyvell', I thought it was an odd name to use and then, it dawned on me that it's an anagram of 'Evanley Hall'. So I came straight here. I think Josiah might be here, too. He left suddenly after a 'phone call and I haven't seen him since"

"Yeah, there might 'ave been a car, earlier, an' all" Jeannie nodded, slowly, "I dunno, there's allus summat goin' up and down this lane" Jeannie slumped down in her rocking chair, by the kitchen fire, "What d'yer want with me, then?"

"I thought you might help me?" Samantha looked pleadingly at Jeannie, "I need to get up to the Hall and see what's going on"

"I ain't goin' up there" Jeannie shook her head, furiously, "I 'ates it up there!"

"If not for me, then for Josiah? You used to mean something to each other, didn't you?"

"That...that were a long time ago" Jeannie stared, moodily, at the fire.

"I'm worried, Jeannie" Samantha sat down, unbidden, on the chair opposite to Jeannie, "For all I know, Archie might already be dead, and if she's got Josiah too..." A tear rolled down her cheek, "You know what she's capable of, you had to identify your sister's body"

"Yeah" Jeannie nodded, still staring intently at the fire, "There weren't no call for 'er to do that, not to 'er. She were barmy, Nenette were, I know that, but if we all went 'round killin' everyone who was a bit barmy... well!"

"They think she might have killed a young, homeless boy, too. She's very dangerous"

"What d'yer reckon *we* can do?" Jeannie looked up from the fire and stared at Samantha.

"We could at least go up there and find out what's going on. If I'm wrong, well that's fair enough. But, if I'm right..."

Jeannie took a deep breath, and sighed.

"Right!" She said, slapping both hands on her knees, "We'll go up there. But we only tek a look, mind, right?"

"Fine" Samantha managed a weak smile, and reached out to touch Jeannie's hand, "Thank you, Jeannie. I'm very grateful"

"Werl, it's like yer said, we were summat to each other once. I owe 'im that, if nowt else"

* * * *

"I'll personally throttle her, if she's gone and put herself in danger" D.I. Wood fumed, "Not to mention buggering up our investigation"

The police cars sped along the country roads with D.S. Stone attempting to concentrate at the wheel, despite his superior's constant distractions.

"To be fair, she's been ahead of us all along, sir"

Dead Reckoning

"She shouldn't be messing with stuff she doesn't understand!" D.I. Wood snarled, "She should leave it to the professionals"

"That would be us, would it sir?" D.S. Stone looked slyly at his boss.

"Too bloody right, Stoney! Proper police work takes time, you have to follow procedure, gather evidence, eliminate suspects, you can't go off half-cocked"

"She cracked the anagram though, well, at least, we suspect she did" D.S. Stone pointed out.

"So did we!" D.I. Wood said, indignantly, "It's not like the T.V., Stoney, sudden flashes of inspiration and stuff. It's about doing the boring stuff, that's what gets the job done"

"And that's what you're good at, sir" D.S. Stone said, straight-faced and staring determinedly ahead.

"Yes, that's...hang on, what?"

"Boring stuff, that's what you're good at, sir"

"I can do inspiration if I need to, Sergeant, don't you worry!" D.I. Wood folded his arms and snorted.

"I'm sure you can, sir"

"I'm just saying, it's the procedural stuff that makes the difference"

"I'm sure it will be greatly prized in the Caribbean, sir" D.S. Stone chanced a smirk, whilst still staring pointedly forward.

"Yeah, well, we'll see Sergeant" D.I. Wood looked like someone who had taken up lemon-sucking as a hobby.

* * * *

Josiah Oakshott swam, slowly, into the shallower waters of consciousness. Unfortunately, with that, came an awareness of a sickening pain in his head. There seemed to be something collecting on his lips and in his mouth. He coughed and spluttered, causing the pain to bounce around, and realised what a vile taste he now had in his mouth. He tried to wipe his lips but found he couldn't move his arms. He risked slightly opening one eye. What he saw caused him to shut it pretty quickly and pray that this was some sort of awful hallucination.

Chapter Forty-Six
Can You Dig It?

Samantha Knight strode, purposefully, along the driveway leading to Evanley Hall. Jeannie followed, a little way behind, with considerably less enthusiasm. Light was fading fast on this winter's day and Samantha had to be careful where she trod on the uneven ground. Jeannie, at her rear, kept up a constant muttered monologue of complaints and dire warnings.

When they reached the Hall, Samantha started to edge her way around to the left, passing the kitchen windows, but stopped when she heard voices.

"Can you hear that?" She hissed at Jeannie.

"Ar, I can 'ear some bugger spoutin'" Jeanne nodded.

"It's a girl's voice. I think it might be Precious. There seem to be some lights flickering around there, too"

"If'n we go 'round that corner, we're likely to walk straight into 'em" Jeannie warned, darkly.

"We can't just stay here though. We have to do something!"

"We need to go t'other way 'round" Jeannie jerked a thumb behind her.

Samantha and Jeannie retraced their steps. At Jeannie's insistence, they bent double, in an effort to try to avoid being seen from the windows of the great house. They made their way, slowly, with Jeannie leading, past the front entrance and across the front garden, to the corner of the Hall where they could then access the rear garden.

"Right, keep schtum" Jeannie whispered, "and keep as close to the 'All as yer can. With a bit of luck, if it is 'er, she won't see us comin'"

Samantha nodded and the two women edged along, tangling with shrubs and bushes as they went.

* * * *

"Ah, Josiah, you *are* with us!" Precious said, cheerfully, leaning on her shovel.

Josiah Oakshott coughed and spluttered. Apart from some of his face, his body was buried in about a foot of soil. He was lying at the bottom of, what appeared to be, a shallow but professionally dug, grave.

"Wha...What are you doing?" Josiah managed, between coughs.

"Oh, come now, Josiah. I should have thought that was perfectly obvious" Precious chided, "Rather a good grave, wouldn't you say? Frank and Arthur here helped me to dig it"

Two men, of whom he had previously been unaware, edged into view on the left-hand side of the grave.

"'Lo Mr. Oakshott" One said, sheepishly, "Sorry about this, an' all that, only, she's got a gun, see?"

"'Lo, Mr. Oakshott" The other man edged, forward, nodded, and attempted a cheery little wave.

Dead Reckoning

"Frank does have a point" Precious nodded, "Poor chaps thought I was getting them to dig their own grave!" She laughed, a little too heartily for comfort.

"Where's Archibald?" Josiah asked.

"Oh, don't you worry about him. He's just having a little nap in the kitchen, over there" Precious grinned.

"He's all right, Mr. Oakshott, we've seen him and everything" Frank added in an apologetic tone.

"Yes, thank you Frank. That will be all." Precious snapped. "Now, Josiah, I'm glad you're awake and taking notice because it would have been such a shame to have buried you alive and have you sleep through it"

"Bury me? Alive? Why?"

"Ah, now *that's* the reason why I'm glad you're back in the land of the living" Precious nodded and chucked another couple of spadefuls of earth into the grave, "Because, you see, all of this would be a bit pointless if you didn't know why we were doing it, wouldn't it? You do follow me, don't you?"

* * * *

"What's going on, can you see?" Samantha whispered to Jeannie, as she peered around the corner of the building.

"There's some lights, like you said" Jeannie began, screwing her eyes up to focus better in the dim light, "Lanterns or summat, shoved all 'round some sort of 'ole...oh bugger!"

"What's the matter?"

"It ain't an 'ole"

"It isn't? What is it, then?"

"It's a grave!"

* * * *

"I don't know why you're doing this! What have I ever done to you?" Josiah spluttered.

"*So* glad you've asked me that, Josiah" Precious beamed and shovelled some more earth into the hole, "You see, when you and mummy were having *loads* of fun, all those years ago, you never gave a thought to the outcome, did you now?"

"Outcome, what outcome?" Josiah sneezed as the dust swirled in the hole.

"Why, me, of course!" Precious stopped shovelling and looked at him with her head to one side, "Daddy" She added, sardonically.

"Daddy? What, me?" Josiah looked astonished, as far as possible, given the limitations of only part of his face being visible.

"Don't act surprised!" Precious snapped, "You and that bitch knew exactly what you were doing. Pushing me out for adoption, so I didn't spoil your happy little lives"

"Look, listen to me," Josiah said, desperately, "firstly, we didn't have that sort of relationship..."

"Hah!" Precious shook her head and began to shovel again, enthusiastically.

"And…secondly…if you would stop that for a moment?"

Precious stopped shovelling and looked at him, quizzically.

"And secondly," Josiah continued, panting somewhat with the exertion of trying to breathe with his chest compressed, "the woman you were living with, the one you called 'Mama'? She was not my girlfriend"

"What are you talking about? Of course she was, you said so yourself when you came crawling around here trying to worm yourself back into her affections"

"Perhaps you didn't hear then, that time when we were tied up in the cellar and she came down to talk to us, just before you all left us to drown? Do you remember? She told me then, that she wasn't Jeanette…"

"You're lying to me!" Precious screamed, and started shovelling furiously.

* * * *

"What's happening?"

"I dunner no, I've 'eard some stuff but we're too far away" Jeannie muttered and looked thoughtful, "if'n we go along the wall, a bit, get to that corner by the kitchen, we'll 'ear 'em. They're in the kitchen garden"

"Ok" Samantha nodded. A few more bushes and hedges later, Jeannie cautiously peered around the corner.

"She's shovelling muck in that 'ole like nobody's business" She announced, "And I can 'ear another voice"

"Whose?"

"Could be yer bloke"

"What, Josiah?"

"Yeah, 'im. I reckon it's comin' from that 'ole"

"You mean, she's got Josiah in that hole, that GRAVE, and she's shovelling earth on him?" Samantha shrieked, as quietly as it was possible to shriek, under the circumstances.

"Looks that way to me" Jeannie nodded.

"Right!" Samantha grabbed a stout branch from a nearby bush.

"What yer gonna do with that?"

"Put a stop to her, that's what I'm going to do" Samantha said determinedly.

"What, with that? But, yer'll 'urt 'er"

"I plan on taking her head off her shoulders" Samantha weighed the branch in her hands and then started to run forward. She hadn't gone more than two steps before she fell to the floor, with Jeannie's arms wrapped around her ankles.

"What the hell are you doing?" Samantha hissed at her.

Dead Reckoning

"Yer canna do it, yer'll 'urt 'er" Jeannie said.

"Of course I'll bloody hurt her, she's trying to bury Josiah alive, what do you expect me to do? And God knows what's happened to Archibald. You do remember what she did to your sister, don't you"

"Leave 'er to me, I'll do it" Jeannie stood up, with some difficulty, and helped Samantha to get upright.

"Why the hell should I leave you to do it? Why don't you want her hurt?" Samantha was furious, and puzzled.

"I canna see 'er 'urt" Jeannie shook her head, and sighed, "I know about Nenette and everything, I know it's all wrong but...I think..." Jeannie took a deep breath and looked straight at Samantha, "I think she might be me daughter" She said in a small voice.

Chapter Forty-Seven
Mother and Child Reunion

"I'm telling you," Josiah shouted, as best he could, between coughs, as the swirls of dust rose from the soil being heaped upon his person, "it was Nenette that you were living with, not Jeanette. She only pretended to be her sister to lure me here" He coughed violently again and his dirt-imprisoned chest complained, bitterly, "She was jealous of my relationship with Jeanette, that's why she tried to kill me"

"I'm not listening" Precious snapped, put her shovel down and placed her fingers in her ears, "Da-dee-da-dee-dee-da-dee, see, I'm not listening"

"What will killing me achieve?" He tried an appeal to logic.

"It'll make me feel better, that's what!" Precious spat, and resumed her shovelling.

* * * *

"Your daughter?" Samantha looked astonished, "What do you mean 'your daughter'?"

"Worrisay" Jeannie jutted her chin out, "look, I canna explain now, can I? Yer've just gotta trust me"

"And what are you going to do?" Samantha frowned.

"Make her see some sense!" Jeannie snapped.

Dead Reckoning

* * * *

"It gives me the creeps, this place" D.S. Stone said, with a shudder, as their car slowly climbed the gravel drive up to the Hall.

"Shouldn't think you would have fond memories" D.I. Wood chuckled, "It comes to something, Stoney, when you're the only policeman to have nearly been drowned in the middle of Cheshire"

"It wasn't a laughing matter, sir" D.S. Stone said, tersely.

"No, no, course not" D.I. Wood suppressed a titter, brought the car to a halt and climbed out. D.S. Stone did likewise, nodding to the two uniformed officers sitting in the squad car behind them, who also exited their vehicle.

"I think I can hear voices, sir" D.S. Stone said.

"Right, Sergeant, approach with caution and no heroics, are you listening?"

"Sir" D.S. Stone nodded and led the way, to the left of the Hall, in the direction of the sound.

* * * *

"Look, think about it logically" Josiah implored, spluttering dreadfully, "If she thought I was your father, why didn't she say anything? Why did she try to kill me and not say a word about you, eh?"

Precious stopped her shovelling for a moment and thought.

"I don't know" She said, eventually, "But then, nothing you and her do, or did, surprises me! Anyone who could abandon a child, as you both did, without a care in the world. And don't try to deny it, you're on the birth certificate, you know? When I got my adoption papers, it was there for all the world to see"

"I know nothing about that..." Josiah began.

"Shut up, just shut up!" Precious screamed and hurled a shovelful of soil over his face.

* * * *

"There's an open grave" D.S. Stone reported, peering around the corner of the kitchen, as they all stood flush to the stone wall, "and there's a young girl shovelling soil into it"

"Precious, do you think?" D.I. Wood asked.

"Looks that way, sir" D.S. Stone nodded, "there's another couple of blokes standing to one side who could be that pair we're looking for from the other Undertaker's"

"Any sign of whatsisname, the dopy looking one?"

"Archibald Thurble, you mean, sir? No, but I suppose he could be in that grave"

"Then there's that Mr. Oakshott, where the hell is he?"

"I think I saw his car parked on the front, sir"

"God almighty! It's like a Mothers Union meeting, this place! Why can't they all steer clear and leave it to the professionals? Do you think she's armed?"

Dead Reckoning

"Only with the spade, as far as I can see, sir"

"Do you think you could rush her, safely?"

"I could give it a go, I suppose" D.S. Stone conceded, dubiously, "If the lads would back me up?" He looked at the uninformed officers, who looked less than keen.

"Right then Stoney, you two, on Stoney's count, charge at her"

"Ok then, one...two..." D.S. Stone began, "Oh, bloody hell!"

* * * *

"PACK THAT IN!" Jeannie launched herself at Precious, causing her to fall to the ground kicking and writhing.

"What the...!" Precious screamed, "Get off me you mad old bat!"

"You shut up and lie still, my girl" Jeannie ordered.

"Get off me, I'm warning you!" Precious yelled, whilst attempting to wrestle the old woman off her.

"That's enough, d'ye hear me?" Jeannie tried to force the struggling young woman down. There was a sudden 'CRACK' like the sound of a firework exploding and Jeannie gave a low moan.

"I bloody warned you!" Precious shouted.

"Oh my god! You've shot her!" Samantha rushed up to the scene, branch in hand. She realised that Precious, although still trapped under the inert body of Jeannie, was trying to point the gun in her direction.

She brought the branch down in a swinging arc across Precious's wrist and the gun went spinning away.

"You bitch!" Precious screamed, in pain.

Samantha was about to bring the branch crashing down, once again, when she suddenly saw D.S. Stone and two uniformed officers sprinting toward the scene. D.I. Wood was ambling along, a few paces behind them.

"Put that down, miss, and step back" D.S. Stone commanded. Samantha dropped the branch, breathing heavily, and stepped back, as ordered.

"She...she shot her" She said, in a choking voice, "and Josiah...he's...he's down there" She pointed to the grave and the pile of earth within it, which was ominously quiet.

"Where's the gun?" D.S. Stone asked. Samantha pointed to the edge of the grave. He marched forward briskly, picked it up, with a handkerchief around the handle, and checked if it was loaded. "One shot fired, sir" He reported.

"Good work, Stoney" D.I. Wood nodded, "Get it bagged up"

One of the uniformed officers was checking Jeannie for signs of life.

"There's a pulse, sir, but it's weak" He reported.

"Let me look" Samantha eased the body of Jeannie away from the struggling Precious. D.S. Stone leapt forward and slapped handcuffs on the girl.

"Precious DeVille, I'm arresting you for..." He looked at his superior, quizzically.

Dead Reckoning

"Erm, on suspicion of the murders of Nenette DeVille, the person known as 'Hames', the young man known as 'Jimmy', and the…" He looked down into the grave, where the other uniformed officer was clearing the soil from Josiah's face.

"He's alright, sir, well, he's breathing any road. But he's in a bad way"

"…*attempted* murders of Josiah Oakshott and Jeanette DeVille" D.I. Wood concluded, "Other charges may be brought in due course"

"Hang on! What? Who?" Precious asked.

"Josiah Oakshott and Jeanette DeVille" D.S. Wood repeated.

"Jeanette? What do you mean, 'Jeanette'?"

"The lady you just shot, allegedly" D.S. Stone advised.

"That old bat? Are you saying she's…" Precious looked stunned.

"…You do not have to say anything. But it may harm your defence if you do not mention when questioned something which you later rely on in court. Anything you do say may be given in evidence." D.S. Stone intoned.

Precious spat at him.

To one side, Samantha was checking Jeannie over.

"She's been shot in the thigh" She yelled, "She's lost a lot of blood" Samantha slipped off her jacket, wrapping it in a ball and pressing it hard against the wound.

"Get an ambulance, pronto, and some more officers" D.I. Wood shouted to one of the uniforms, "There's her, and him in the grave, at least. It's like a bloody war zone, this place" He ran his hands through his, rapidly thinning, hair, "Where the hell's Lurch, does anyone know?"

"I'll check, sir" D.S. Stone handed Precious to one of the uniformed officers.

"We're just off then" Frank said and waved a cheery goodbye, "You'll find Archibald in the kitchen, but he's out cold"

"Where the hell do you two think you're going?" D.I. Wood looked at the two Undertakers assistants, incredulously.

"Well, if it's all over, we thought we'd get back." Frank explained, apologetically, "Mr. Cadwallader will be wondering where we are"

"Get back? Are you mad? At the very least you're material witnesses and, for all I know, you might be part of a conspiracy to kidnap and murder. So, no, you are not 'just off then', you're coming back with us to answer some serious questions, alright?" D.I. Wood fumed.

"I've found Mr. Thurble, sir" D.S. Stone reported, "As the gentleman said, he's unconscious but seems to be breathing normally and, as far as I can tell, he's otherwise unharmed"

"Well, that's a blessing, of sorts" D.I. Wood rubbed a throbbing temple, "Right then, we need him checked out medically as well. We should be able to keep a few ambulance crews busy, at this rate! How's Miss DeVille doing, Mrs. Knight?"

"She keeps slipping in and out of consciousness" Samantha said, in a worried tone, "I'm really concerned about her, she's lost a lot of blood and she's not as young as she was, she needs medical attention urgently"

"How about Mr. Oakshott?" D.I. Wood shouted down to the grave.

"Breathing reasonably ok but he's not in good shape" The uninformed officer reported.

"Bloody hell!" D.I. Wood put his face in his hands, "At this rate, we're going to need some Undertakers and the ones we've got are either under arrest or unconscious!"

"That's not in very good taste, is it sir" D.S. Stone admonished.

"Probably not, Stoney, but it's bloody true, isn't it?" D.I. Wood sighed, "It's bloody true!"

Chapter Forty-Eight
Working My Way Back to You

With his bare hands Josiah Oakshott was digging, furiously, but nothing seemed to change. All he could see was the terrible blackness before him, all he could feel was the relentless pressure on his chest. There was a vague impression of light, somewhere in the distance, but nothing more than that. He tore at the earth with all of his might. His mouth, his throat, his eyes and ears, everything seemed to be filled with something that clogged and choked. He fought for breath but just gagged and spluttered.

Finally, there it was, just a pinhole of light, but it held the promise of an escape from this… tomb, he supposed. He scrabbled with everything he had and the light became larger. He choked, he gagged and retched and suddenly, it was light.

"Well done, Joshua" A female voice said, cheerily, "that's the tube out, you've done it!"

"Nice to have you back, Mr. Oakshott" A male voice added.

"Try to drink a little water, Joshua" The female voice suggested and he was aware of a white plastic cup being held near his mouth.

The sudden intense light and the booming sound overwhelmed him but he drank, or attempted to, as suggested. Much of the water seemed to go down his chin and his neck, but some trickled into his parched mouth and ran, in a rivulet, down his throat. In that moment, it might have been the finest champagne, he was so grateful for the relief and the sense that his body was starting to function normally.

"You weren't breathing all that well, when you came in, Mr. Oakshott" The male voice explained, cheerily, "So I'm afraid we had to give you a bit of a hand. Had to keep you in a medically induced coma, just for a bit, you understand?" The male voice asked.

Josiah attempted to nod, which prompted a resounding headache.

"Anyway, there's someone here to see you" The male voice went on, sounding pleased with itself.

There was a swishing noise as someone drew near to his bed.

"Hello, Josiah, good to have you back" Samantha said. She reached out and held his hand, tightly. He squeezed back and felt a tear making its way down his cheek.

"Samantha?" He croaked, desperately trying to focus.

"That's right, Josiah, I'm here"

"I can't…I can't seem to… focus on anything, I'm sorry" He whispered, hoarsely.

"You shouldn't be trying to do anything. You need to rest. You've had a bad time"

"And Archibald…where's…where's Archibald?"

"Right here, Mr. O." A cheerful, and very familiar, voice rang out from his right-hand side, "you can't get rid of me that easily"

"I can't see him" Josiah said, weakly.

"It's ok, Josiah, honestly it is. You've been unconscious for a while and your body will need to time to recover. Archibald is in the bed next to you. He has been all the time."

"They're keeping me in under reservation, Mr. O." Archibald commented.

"Observation! They're keeping you in under observation, Archie" Samantha corrected.

"Oh, right. Any road up, I'm alright but they don't know what she injected me with, so they're hanging on to me to see if owt happens"

"Injected? She?" Josiah looked perplexed as he sank back into the pillows.

"Yes, 'she' being Precious. Do you remember Precious, Josiah?" Samantha asked.

"Precious? No, I don't think so" Josiah tried to shake his head, but the pain stopped that activity in its tracks. He closed his eyes and began to doze.

"How is he, Mrs. Knight?" D.I. Wood was standing behind her.

"He's very weak. They've just brought him round, which is something, but he's not in a good way." Samantha looked up at the detective, with tears in her eyes.

"I'm sure he'll pull through, he's made of strong stuff" D.I. Wood in an effort to be comforting, went to pat her on the shoulder, and then thought better of it. "When he's in a better state, we'll need to ask him some questions"

Samantha darted a fierce glance in his direction.

"Not yet! Not yet!" D.I. Wood held his hands up in token surrender, "As I said, when he's more himself. We'll also need a few moments of your time, Sunny Jim" He said to Archibald, who was cheerfully devouring a pot of yoghurt.

"Oh yeah, whenever" Archibald nodded, scraping earnestly at the bottom of the pot.

"Is there any news on Jeannie, Inspector?" Samantha asked.

"Not sure, Mrs. Knight. D.S. Stone is with her now" D.I. Wood replied, then smiled as D.S. Stone walked onto the ward, "Well, speak of the devil...any news, Stoney?"

"She's conscious, sitting up and taking notice" D.S. Stone reported, "They seem to be happy with how the operation went but she lost a lot of blood along the way. Only time will tell, really, but we should be able to talk with her soon, except..."

"Except? What do you mean, 'except'?" D.I. Wood frowned.

"Well, you're not going to like it, sir"

"You seem to make it your life's work to tell me stuff I won't like, Sergeant, so what's new?"

"Ok, well, she'll talk to us. In fact, she wants to talk to us...but, there's one condition"

"CONDITION? What do you mean, there's a condition? She'll talk to us alright or I'll have her down the nick, pronto!" D.I. Wood fumed.

"Wha…What's happening? There was shouting. Who's shouting?" Josiah flung himself up in bed, panting and looking around, wildly.

"Inspector!" Samantha snapped, "He's meant to be getting some rest, do you mind?" She eased Josiah back down on to his pillows.

"Sorry, miss" D.S. Stone apologised, and indicated for his boss to follow him out of the ward.

D.I. Wood glared at Samantha and then followed his Sergeant.

"Bloody cheek!" He fumed, "Now, what's all this about a condition, eh?" He asked as they entered the bustling corridor, outside.

"She says she'll tell us everything but only…" D.S. Stone took a deep breath, "if Precious is there" He explained, in a rush, and flinched back, in anticipation of the storm to come.

"PRECIOUS?" D.I. Wood looked at his Sergeant with astonishment, "You've got to be joking! Not a chance!"

"She says that she deserves to know the truth"

"We all bloody deserve to know the truth! Particularly us. She's a serial killer, for God's sake! We've got her bang to rights on three murders and two 'attempteds' before we start. She doesn't 'deserve' anything, apart from a long stretch inside"

"Jeannie's adamant, sir, and you know what she's like"

Dead Reckoning

"I am not dragging that evil cow out of the cells and halfway across town just so that Jeannie can have a cosy, bloody, family reunion, it's not happening" He searched through his pockets for a reassuring cigarette.

"You can't smoke in here, sir, sorry. As for Jeannie, if she won't talk, I don't see how we can make her, particularly in her current state of health"

"This is a bloody nightmare, Stoney! God knows what the gaffer's going to say. I can't interview Oakshott because he's hammering on death's door, I can't interview Jeannie because she's not much better and wants a suspected serial killer present" D.I. Wood put his hand over his eyes and sighed deeply, "About the only one I can interview is Lurch and he's away with the fairies most of the time. What a bloody cock-up!"

"To be fair, sir, you could interview Ms. Knight. She'd be a valuable witness"

"Oh, be still my beating heart!" D.I. Wood groaned, "I shouldn't think that would be much fun for either of us"

"What do you want me to do, sir?"

"Oh, I don't bloody know!" D.I. Wood shook his head, sighed and frowned, "I've always thought that Jeannie knows more than she's been letting on." He paused and looked intently at his shoes. "Right, Stoney, we'll do it. Make arrangements for a full security detail to bring Precious DeVille here. Better make it tomorrow I suppose, then we might have a chance of getting old Oakshott involved as well, if he's up to it. I'll be glad to see the back of this lot, Stoney, and no mistake"

"Get back to the Caribbean brochures, eh sir?"

"Something like that, Stoney, something like that" D.I. Wood said with a faint smile and a faraway look in his eyes.

Chapter Forty-Nine
Family Affair

"Stoney, do you copy?"

"Yes, sir. I hear you, over" D.S. Stone replied into his two-way radio.

"What's the current sit-rep?"

"No, that's no good, sir. You have to say 'over'…over"

"Over?"

"No, you can't just say 'over', that doesn't mean anything at all. You have to say 'over' when you've finished what you're saying, sir, over" D.S. Stone explained.

"I know that, Stoney, give me a little credit…over"

"Right sir, did you want anything? Only, I'm only about 10 yards away, you could have shouted, over"

"That's hardly secure comms., is it? What's the current status…over"

"If you mean, is everything in place, then yes, it is, sir. We have a security detail at both ends of the corridor, officers on the stairs at both ends and on all of the exits. I shouldn't think there's a police officer to be found anywhere in Merkin-under-Heathwood, over"

"So, everything's covered?"

"Ahem"

"Bugger! Over. Erm, over"

"Yes, I think we have everything covered, sir, over"

"Roger that"

"Pardon, sir, over?"

"Fine, I've understood what you've told me"

"Sir?"

"What?"

"You didn't say, 'over', sir, over" D.S. Stone admonished.

"Oh, bugger this for a game of soldiers!" D.I. Wood seethed, he switched off his radio and yelled, "BRING THE PRISONER UP, STONEY!"

"YES, SIR...OVER" Came the shouted reply.

* * * *

In Jeannie DeVille's hospital room, a number of people had gathered awaiting the impending arrival of Precious, the prisoner.

Jeannie herself, was sitting up in bed, firmly propped up by a number of pillows. She was looking very pale, and frail, but was clearly ready for her performance. Otherwise assembled around the room were: Archibald Thurble, now out of bed and awaiting clearance to leave the hospital, fidgeting with his sleeves, as he always did when agitated. Next to him, and swapping gripes with him about their respective employers, stood Frank and Harry, from Cadwallader and Carruthers, no longer in custody but clearly less than happy to be dragged back into

Dead Reckoning

this. On the other side of the bed was Samantha Knight, torn between her concern for the clearly weakened Jeannie in the bed before her and Josiah Oakshott, in the wheelchair by her side, who had improved in the last 24 hours but was still very frail indeed.

The low murmur of inconsequential conversation stopped abruptly when the door to the room opened and D.I. Wood strode in, closely followed by Precious, handcuffed to D.S. Stone, who was bringing up the rear. Precious glared, icily, at the assembled throng.

"Right!" D.I. Wood commenced, looking around the room, "Thank you all for coming and apologies for the amateur dramatics but this Miss DeVille..." He nodded toward Jeannie, "insisted on it" He frowned at her.

"Ta for bringing 'er" Jeannie nodded and shifted slightly on her pile of pillows.

"I don't know why you've brought me here! There's nothing any of these can say that would be of any interest to me" Precious said, grimly, attempting to fold her arms but being foiled by the handcuffs. She glared around the room, focusing on Jeannie in particular.

"I'll have none of your nonsense, madam" D.I. Wood snapped, "and remember, you're still under caution, right?"

Precious groaned and looked down at her shoes.

"Go ahead, Miss DeVille, the floor's all yours" D.I. Wood said.

"Right!" Jeannie shuffled in her bed a little and cleared her throat, "ta for coming, all of yer. I'm sorry yer've all 'ad a bit of a bad time of it, just lately. Not that any of it's been my doin', as yer know."

Jeannie took a sip of water from the plastic cup by her bedside.

"Any road, this is 'ow it was. Nenette and me, as yer probably know, we was twins. Our parents, werl, they was killed in a car crash when we were quite young. The only relative we 'ad was our grandfather, Shepherd Mountjoy, 'im who lived at Evanley 'All. 'E took us in and brought us up. I think yer thought 'e were me dad, didn't yer, Josiah?"

She turned to look at the pale figure seated in the wheelchair to her left.

"Ah yes, indeed I did make that assumption, at the time" Josiah nodded, "I had no idea he was your grandfather"

"Werl, I don't suppose 'e were exactly how yer'd expect a grandfather to look. 'E were quite good fer 'is age, people useter say" Jeannie frowned, "Any road, there we were, two young girls and their grandfather, rattling 'round that bloody great 'all. It was a bit of a shock, coming from a loving family 'ome, as we 'ad done. Mind yer, it were quite the 'adventure, at first. We useter play 'ide and seek in all them rooms, an we 'ad races all round the grounds. It were fun...fer a while. Innocent days!"

"Huh, hardly innocent!" Precious snapped.

"Oh, we were innocent all right" Jeannie snapped back, "but I don't expect you to know owt about that! So, any road, we grew up an', though I say it meself, we were reckoned to be quite... attractive, yer might say, quite the catch, you know? We both 'ad our admirers, but I s'pose I did a bit better than Nenette, an' she 'ated that"

Jeannie took another sip of water.

Dead Reckoning

"I met Josiah 'ere, when 'e came to talk to Shepherd about 'is funeral arrangements. We 'it it off an' we started seein' each other, a bit, didn't we?"

Josiah nodded, and smiled fondly.

"Ha, not just 'seeing' was it? You never thought about the consequences, did you, either of you?" Precious yelled.

"As I have said before, Miss DeVille, it was not that sort of relationship!" Josiah managed to interject, somewhat weakly.

"'E's right" Jeannie confirmed, nodding, "it weren't like that. Shepherd, 'e would never 'ave stood fer it. We went out, a couple of times, an' I s'pose there was a kiss an' a cuddle, 'ere and there, style of thing, sorry Mrs." She said, looking at Samantha.

"It *was* a long time ago, Jeannie" Samantha smiled.

"Not 'alf it was!" Jeannie chuckled, ruefully, "When it came to, whatd'yercall it? Intimacy? Old Shepherd, 'e wouldn't 'ave 'ad none of that, not under 'is roof, which was a bit…how'dyercallit?…ironic, that's the one, given as 'ow things 'appened."

Jeannie sighed and took another sip of water. She pulled herself up on the pillows and winced with pain.

"Anyhow, Shepherd, 'e…werl, I dunner know 'ow to put it" She stopped, sipped some more water and looked down at her sheets, which she picked at, a little. "'E, erm … 'E took an interest in us, let's say. Werl… 'e took an interest in me, that's about the size of it."

"Oh no, Jeannie!" Samantha gasped.

"Yeah!" Jeannie nodded, "An'…let's put it this way, 'e liked to keep things in the family, if yer know what I mean?" She said, in a small voice, staring intently at the sheets with which she was fidgeting.

"What? What's that supposed to mean?" Precious snapped.

"Just be quiet, you!" D.I. Wood barked.

"Oh my God! I'm so sorry, Jeannie" Samantha put a hand to her mouth, leant forward and touched Jeannie on her arm.

"Ta" A tear rolled down Jeannie's cheek, "Any road, I fell pregnant. I didn't want none of it, but what can yer do? 'E were a big bloke, an' we was…just bits of girls. If 'e'd kicked us out, we'd 'ave 'ad nowt 'an we'd got no mam or dad to turn to. We were up a gum tree, if yer know worrImean" She sighed, deeply.

"So, anyhow, Shepherd, 'e took control, 'e organised all on it. That were bad enough, but the really bloody stupid thing was that Nenette, 'er who'd 'ated me 'avin' blokes callin', like Josiah 'ere, she was only bloody jealous about me an' Shepherd! Can yer credit it?" Jeannie shook her head, incredulously. "An' all the time, I thought I was protectin' 'er, huh!"

"Hang on! Are you…are you saying that… I'm…I'm the product of an incestuous affair?" Precious asked, hoarsely.

"'Ardly an affair, were it? It weren't like I 'ad any choice in the matter" Jeannie glared at Precious, "It's not summat I'm proud of and I'm sorry yer 'ad to find out, like this, but yer needs to know the truth"

"I think I'm going to be sick!" Precious choked and gagged. "I don't believe it! You're making this up! If what you're saying is true, then why does my birth certificate list my father as that man there?" Precious nodded toward Josiah, who was looking aghast.

"I didner know about that" Jeannie shook her head, "Like I said, Shepherd took over. When you were born, you were taken from me, straight away, I never even saw yer. "Eard yer, of course, ye 'ad a right set of lungs on yer." She smiled at the memory. "Any road, 'e made all the 'rrangments. 'E must 'ave sorted out the birth certificate, an' all. I s'pose 'e was bein' spiteful, puttin' Josiah's name down. It would be about 'is barrow, that"

"Rubbish!" Precious stamped her foot and scowled.

"It ain't. I wish it were" Jeannie said, quietly, "Shepherd, 'e went an' died not long after. Fell in the pond and drowned. Nenette, she cleared off with some bloke she'd met, so I shut the 'All up, moved inter the cottage, got a few cats, became Jeannie, the mad cat-woman, an' that was me" Jeannie shrugged.

"I had no idea, Jeanette" Josiah said, sadly.

"You're a liar! You've made up this cock and bull story because you just can't face the truth. That you and him abandoned me to the 'care system' and never gave me a second thought" Precious screamed.

"It's no lie" Jeannie said, quietly, "I often wondered what might 'ave 'appened to yer. 'Ow yer'd gone on. Thought about yer on yer birthday, an' all that. I never thought it would turn out like this, mind yer, but there yer are" She shrugged.

"I suppose a DNA test might put the matter to rest, eh sir?" D.S. Stone suggested.

"Good idea, Stoney! If Mr. Oakshott doesn't have any objections, of course?"

"No, none at all, Inspector" Josiah nodded, "If it would grant the young lady some form of closure, I would be happy to take part"

"Right, we'll get that sorted then" D.I. Wood, "that should settle your hash!" He glared at Precious, who stuck her tongue out at him.

"All them people what 'ave been 'urt and killed, it didner 'ave to be this way" Jeannie shook her head, sadly.

"Somebody had to pay!" Precious screamed.

"I reckon we all 'ave, over the years" Jeannie said, quietly, "Shepherd, Nenette, me...an' you. We've all paid a price, ain't we? So 'as some what never should 'ave, like Josiah 'ere, and 'im" She nodded toward Archibald, who blushed. "'Alf-drownded, and fer what?"

"Revenge!" Precious shrieked.

"Yer can't 'ave revenge on somebody who ain't done nowt to yer" Jeannie pointed out and shook her head, "Nah, let that be an end to it"

She sank back in her pillows, closed her eyes and let out a deep sigh.

Chapter Fifty
So The Story Goes

"Please, be careful, Jeannie" Samantha warned, in a worried voice.

"Ah, dunner fuss yerself, I'll be right" Jeannie stomped through her cottage door, clearing a path with her two arm crutches.

"Yes, I'm sure but this place is very cluttered and, what with that and the cats..." Samantha shook her head as she followed Jeannie into the cottage, step by painful step.

"I know me way 'round, dunner fret" Jeannie muttered, "Shift, yer little buggers!"

"It certainly is not 'wheelchair-friendly', if that is the correct terminology?" Josiah was struggling to get his conveyance through the narrow front door.

"Don't struggle to get through on your own, Josiah! I told you I would help"

"There's really no need, Samantha. I have to be able to manage on my own" Josiah said, grimly, as he reversed and swivelled.

"Hopefully it won't be too long before you're back on your feet" Samantha grabbed the arms of the wheelchair and tugged, dragging Josiah into the hall.

"I 'OPE 'E'S NOT SCRATCHIN' ME DOOR?" Jeannie shouted from the kitchen.

"She's really not great at gratitude, is she?" Samantha sighed.

"She has a somewhat, erm… robust attitude to interpersonal relations" Josiah agreed.

"Are your cats ok, Jeannie? I arranged for one of your neighbours to come in and feed them while you were in hospital" Samantha made her way into the kitchen.

"Ar, well, I ain't seen all on 'em, but them as is 'ere, they seems alright" Jeannie grudgingly agreed. "I s'pose yer'll want a cup a tea?"

"That would be nice but we won't stop long, will we Josiah?" Samantha looked pointedly at him, "We just wanted to make sure you were settled back in, after dropping you off"

"'Course, it'd 'elp if I knew where the bloody kettle was!" Jeannie said, opening cupboards, furiously.

"I did pop in and tidy up a bit" Samantha admitted.

"Knew some bugger 'ad been meddlin'" Jeannie chuntered.

"I think you might be a little grateful for Samantha's help, Jeanette" Josiah said, sharply, as he manoeuvred into the kitchen, "I know we would both still be stuck in hospital without her support"

"Ar, well, 'appen!" Jeannie conceded, reluctantly.

"Ahem, may we come in?" D.I. Wood tapped on the wide-open door.

"Detective Inspector? Fancy seeing you here!" Samantha said, with surprise.

Dead Reckoning

"We just wanted to make sure that Ms. DeVille here was ok, and also to bring her up to date with our investigation" D.I. Wood explained, seating himself at the kitchen table whilst D.S. Stone hovered near the doorway.

"Shouldna think there's much to investigate, is there?" Jeannie muttered, banging the kettle onto the stove.

"Well, the facts of the case are not under dispute, that's true" D.I. Wood agreed, reflexively reaching for a cigarette and then shoving the packet back into his pocket, grudgingly. "But certain new information has emerged"

"Tea?" Jeannie grunted, pouring water into the ancient teapot.

"Yes, please, that would hit the spot, it's a long drive here" D.I. Wood nodded.

"I know, *I* did all the driving!" D.S. Stone grumbled. D.I. Wood shot him a look.

Teas poured, Jeannie slumped into her usual seat, by the fire.

"So, what you gotta tell us then?" She asked, blowing furiously on her cup.

"Well, we've interviewed the woman known as Precious at some length, now" D.S. Stone explained, "We've been trying to discover the motivation for her actions"

"Apart from being barking, that is" D.I. Wood added, "Got any biscuits?" Jeannie nodded toward a tin on one of the shelves.

"I could just about understand her animosity toward me," Josiah said, reflectively, "but I fail to understand why she would want to harm Archibald or, for that matter, the others whom she's alleged to have murdered?"

"Yeah, that stumped us, too" D.I. Wood agreed, munching on a biscuit.

"From what she's told us…" D.S. Stone began.

"Thank you, Sergeant, I'll take it from here" D.I. Wood scowled at his colleague. "From what Precious has told us, Mr. Thurble was just collateral damage. She actually seemed to have a soft spot for him, believe it or not?" D.I. Wood shook his head, incredulously, "When Nenette and Hames tried to drown you both, she didn't feel able to intervene, but did what she could to help, or so she says?"

"She did make some efforts to bring us water to drink, that's true" Josiah nodded.

"Then, drugging Mr. Thurble later, to lure you, Mr. Oakshott, up to the Hall, she made sure he was unharmed. Which is more than she did for you!" D.S. Stone added.

"What was that business with Nenette and Hames about? And that other boy you said she had killed?" Josiah asked.

"Well, it seems…" D.S. Stone began.

"It *seems*…" D.I. Wood glared, "that she was trying to create some sort of a family for herself. She thought Nenette was you, Jeannie, as we know. Hames, she thought, could be some form of father figure and Jimmy, well, she had this notion that he could be a sort of footman or something in her Stately Home fantasy. When he wouldn't play ball, he had to go, of course"

"An' what about me sister, Nenette?" Jeannie asked.

"Apparently, her and Hames weren't into playing Happy Families much, either" D.I. Wood extracted another biscuit, "They were more interested in ripping off High Street Jewellers and similar scams. That wasn't what Precious wanted, so..."

"Yer kin understand, a bit, can't yer?" Jeannie mused, slurping her tea, "'Er wantin' a family, like?" She shrugged.

"She's still in denial about you and Mr. Oakshott" D.S. Stone commented, "and, of course, about the business with your grandfather. That's despite the DNA test we did proving conclusively that she's your daughter, Miss DeVille, and not yours, Mr. Oakshott"

"Yeah, werl, it's a lot to take in, I guess." Jeannie nodded, "I'd...I'd like to visit 'er, if that's allowed?" She added, quietly.

"What? She tried to kill you...and Mr. Oakshott!" D.I. Wood fumed.

"I know but...even so" Jeannie mumbled and shrugged "I'm all she's got"

"Well, she would have to agree" D.I. Wood scratched his head and looked astonished, "We'll have to see"

"What a mess!" Samantha shook her head.

"You can say that again, Mrs. Knight" D.I. Wood nodded.

"It's not"

"What's not?" D.I. Wood looked puzzled.

"It's not 'Mrs. Knight'"

"Oh, right, fair enough" D.I. Wood held his hands up in mock surrender, "*Ms*. Knight then!"

"No, it's not that, either" Samantha grinned, "In fact, it's not 'Knight' at all. It's 'Taylor'"

"Taylor?" D.I. Wood looked confused.

"Yes, I've reverted to my birth name, now that my divorce has come through"

"Divorce? I had no idea!" Josiah looked startled.

"The papers came in this morning's post, Josiah" Samanth patted his hand, "I didn't want to tell you, not until I was absolutely sure. You know how difficult Frankie can be."

"Oh...that's...wonderful, Samantha" Tears filled Josiah's eyes. "Actually, there's something I've been meaning to ask you, for some weeks now..."

"I know, Josiah, and the answer's yes, I would love to marry you" Samantha grinned broadly.

"How did you know?" Josiah asked, hoarsely.

"I just knew! I was hoping you wouldn't ask until I had finalised everything to do with the divorce. So, right now is perfect" She kissed Josiah lightly on the forehead.

"Oh, give me strength!" D.I. Wood rolled his eyes to the ceiling.

Dead Reckoning

"There is a condition, though" Samantha said.

"A condition?" Josiah looked surprised.

"Yep. You have to have Archie as your Best Man..."

"Oh, really?" Josiah looked concerned.

"That's right." Samantha said, emphatically, "And, given everything he's been through, not to mention what he's done for you, in the last few months, I think he deserves a promotion, don't you?"

"If you say so, my dear" Josiah nodded, "Actually, you're quite right. I have rather taken Archibald for granted"

"Nice to 'ear summat's goin' right fer some bugger" Jeannie nodded and smiled, "Should think all this malarkey's been a feather in yer cap, 'an all, 'annit, Inspector?"

"As a matter of fact, yes," D.I. Wood grinned, "given the number of murders and ancillary crimes solved in just one case, the powers-that-be, and my gaffer in particular, are very happy indeed. And I should say, I don't think it's any coincidence that my application for a secondment has been approved, as I had intended to tell my Sergeant on the way home"

"Secondment, sir?" D.S. Stone looked puzzled, "Not...surely not...to the Caribbean?"

"In a manner of speaking, Stoney!" D.I. Wood could not have grinned more broadly if he had tried, "I've got a 6 month research secondment in the Bahamas"

"You jammy…" D.S. Stone bit his lip.

"Now then, no jealousy, Sergeant. You know how it is, with rank comes certain privileges" D.I. Wood looked unbearably pleased with himself.

"Yes, but…who was it rescued them from drowning, eh?" D.S. Stone fumed, pointing at Josiah.

"Just the luck of the draw, Stoney" D.I. Wood leaned back and put his hands behind his head, "If anything goes wrong, it's me that gets the brickbats, so it's only right that I should get any rewards that are coming"

"And what is the subject of this 'research secondment'?" D.S. Stone asked, coolly.

"Ah, erm, well…it's mostly…logistical, in nature"

"Logistical?"

"Yes, to do with, erm…traffic mostly. You know, patterns and stuff" D.I.O Wood admitted, bashfully.

"Oh my god! You're going to be on traffic duty, aren't you?" D.S. Stone sniggered.

"No!" D.I. Wood snapped, "Well, not all of the time"

"Ha!" D.S. Stone snorted.

"Anyway, I think we've covered everything we need to here, for the time being" D.I. Wood sprang up, showering biscuit crumbs on the floor, "We'll be in touch, ma'am" He nodded to Jeannie and swept out of the room, with a sniggering D.S. Stone in tow.

Dead Reckoning

"We should be going too, Jeannie, if you're sure there's nothing else we can do for you?" Samantha stood up, smoothing her skirt.

"Nah, yer all right" Jeannie shook her head, "I'll manage"

Samantha wheeled Josiah to the cottage door.

"We'll come back soon, make sure you're managing ok" Samanth went to hug Jeannie, who backed away at first, then, with obvious awkwardness, deigned to be hugged.

"Ta" She said, with a catch in her voice, "it's good of yer. And mind, Josiah, yer've got a good 'un 'ere, dunna spoil it!"

"I know, Jeanette" Josiah smiled, "I don't intend to"

"Ah, well, mind yer don't, else yer'll 'ave me to reckon with"

"Bye then, Jeannie. I hope you get to visit Precious, if that's what you really want" Samantha waved as they made their way down the uneven garden path.

"Aye, it is" Jeannie nodded, thoughtfully, "They reckon it runs in families, don't they?"

"I'm sorry, what does?" Samantha turned and frowned.

"Twins!" Jeannie said and shut the cottage door with a thud.

THE END

More from Josiah and Archibald

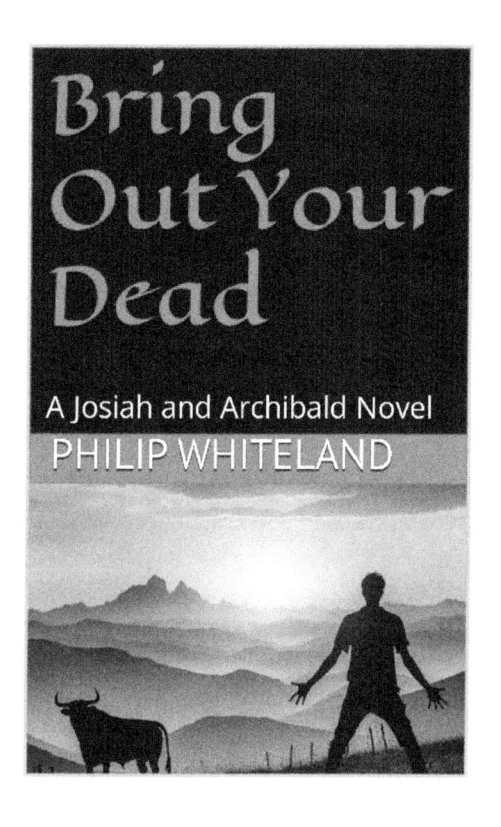

Bring Out Your Dead

A Josiah and Archibald Novel

PHILIP WHITELAND

The first full-length Josiah and Archibald novel

All Josiah and Archibald had to do was collect the late Sir Lewisham Carnock from his resting place in Alicante and escort him back to the U.K. Nothing could be simpler, could it? Well, yes, with Josiah and Archibald it could, particularly when an unfortunate turn of phrase leaves them marooned in Paris and forced to take the overland route to Alicante (complete with chickens in a basket). Even then, collecting the deceased Baronet proves trickier than anyone would imagine, as it would if you add in a nervous couple on their first overseas holiday (unless you count the Isle of Wight), a pair of detectives en-route to collect an escaped and very violent criminal, a femme fatale student with an unusual method of financing her studies and a 'corpse' that doesn't quite look like your typical English aristocrat. Put all those together and you have a recipe for the normal Oakshott and Underwood chaos, this time spread across Europe!

A Dubious Undertaking and other stories

The First Josiah and Archibald Collection

A selection of darkly humorous tales about two hapless undertakers, Josiah Oakshott and Archibald Thurble, and the troubles that befall them and their clients. Also, some stories about two precocious children you really wouldn't want to tangle with - Peregrine and Prudence. If you want to know who blew up the crematorium, why Mrs Anderby had an unfortunate encounter with some potting compost and how an Anti-Santa found himself in captivity, you could do a lot worse than read this book! If you like your humour slightly dark and rather silly, then this is the tome for you.

Grave Expectations

The Second Josiah and Archibald Collection

The second book featuring Josiah and Archibald and this time all the stories are about their misadventures, dealing with irate mourners, V.E. Day, social bubbles, unexpected musical tracks at cremations, the difficulties of 'staying alert', pub reopening, face masks, promotion, dismissal, pyres for Viking chieftains, the oedipus complex, feuding fiancees, personnel management and office romance. All this and the pandemic too!

A Subsequent Engagement

The Third Collection of Josiah and Archibald stories and

the Prequel to Bring Out Your Dead

Welcome, once more, to the rather odd world of Josiah Oakshott and Archibald Thurble, respectively owner and employee of Oakshott and Underwood, 'understanding and sympathy at your time of need'. If you're new to these two characters, where have you been? This, their third book of short stories, picks up from where we left them in Grave Expectations, very much in the throes of the oddities of the Covid restrictions and the heightened demand on their profession, and proceeds, through encounters with various eccentric clients, the bizarre leisure habits of Archibald's nan and their respective on/off romances, to an outcome that will challenge both of them.

Printed in Dunstable, United Kingdom